Aug. 6 - 2010

The Legend of Lieutenant Thompson

1st Lt. Denny Thompson
WWII - D-Day
Pilot - 8th AF
30 mission B-17
P

The Legend of Lieutenant Thompson

★ ★ ★

World War II

Neil Burckart

Library of Congress Control Number:		2016907833
ISBN:	Hardcover	978-1-5245-0000-9
	Softcover	978-1-5144-9377-9
	eBook	978-1-5144-9376-2

Print information available on the last page.

Rev. date: 06/10/2016

To order additional copies of this book, contact:
Xlibris
1-888-795-4274
www.Xlibris.com
Orders@Xlibris.com
736890

Lieutenant Dennis (Denny) Thomspson WWII Bomber Pilot 1944

Preface

Denny's adventures in the great outdoors started when he was twelve years old; this was the mid-1930s, and these were tough times. He took some of the money he had earned mowing grass and doing other chores around the neighborhood, and he bought a dozen traps. They lived on the edge of town, so Denny didn't have far to go; he walked out into the fields behind the house in Staples, Minnesota, and set traps in the drainage ditches and around a little lake. That started his career as a trapper and a hunter. He trapped all through high school, and a lot of the money that Denny made went to help the family.

In 1938, Denny bought his first car for a whopping $12, which allowed him to really expand his trapping operation; eventually, Denny had over five hundred traps that he looked at every day or two. He graduated from high school in 1940 and worked for the Northern Pacific Railroad and continued to trap until 1942, when he entered the service as an aviation cadet. He earned his wings and finally made it to England in a B-24, which he and a crew of nine flew across the Atlantic Ocean, from Hutchinson, Kansas, to Florida, then onto South America, then from Brazil onto Morocco. After a couple weeks' stay in Morocco, they were able to fly to England; from there, Denny flew thirty missions over Germany and France, including three on D-day in 1944. He was wounded twice.

Denny received thirteen medals: two Distinguished Flying Crosses, two Purple Hearts, four Air Medals, four Bronze Stars, and one French Freedom Medal. He was also recommended for the Silver Star for his mission to Cologne, Germany, where, after being hit in the face by a piece of shrapnel while on final approach of the bomb run, Denny picked himself up off the deck and completed the bomb run, hitting the target dead center, with blood dripping off his chin onto the instruments. When General Partridge received the request for the Silver Stars, he telegraphed back to the base: "We have a run on Silver Star. Give the lieutenant a Distinguished Flying Cross." Once he finished his thirty missions, he had an opportunity to be promoted to captain, but he had already been wounded twice. So he decided it would be more prudent to leave the European theater while he was still in one piece and come back to the United States.

During Denny's thirty-day leave, he got reacquainted with an old girlfriend, and they were married. Denny realized he actually missed the excitement of the trips to Germany. He was then shipped to Texas for fighter pilot training, then to California in early 1945; but before he saw action in the Pacific, the Japanese realized Denny was coming and surrendered (now I don't know that it happened quite that way, but I'd like to think it did). Denny was discharged in late 1945, after the surrender of Japan.

Denny with Red Fox, 1938. 16 years old Minnesota.

Denny returned to Staples, Minnesota, where he resumed his trapping career since no one had been trapping the area since he left and there were little critters all over the area. He would catch an average of fifty muskrats a day; and that first year, he caught 150 minks, with each of them at $30 to $50 a pelt. He did quite well that winter; as soon as the trapping season was over, Denny resumed working for the railroad.

Then in June 1947, he bought an army-surplus jeep, hooked a trailer to the back of the jeep, and, with his sister and brother-in-law, drove to Alaska. That was the beginning of an extraordinary adventure that took him all over the Alaskan territory, most of the United States, Africa, and Indonesia.

Denny bought his first airplane in 1949. Sixty years later and with more than a dozen different airplanes, Denny had clocked more than *twenty-five thousand hours as a bush pilot, just in Alaska*—the most of any other pilot in the history of aviation in Alaska. Denny estimated between thirty-five and forty thousand landings and takeoffs in some of the roughest, most hazardous conditions imaginable, yet not one fatal accident in all that flying.

In 1978, Denny and a group of friends and associates started a safari company in Central Africa after almost losing his life in 1980 in a revolution in the Central Africa Republic. Denny decided Alaska was much safer and friendlier. For over the sixty-plus years Denny has lived in Alaska, he has lived more action-packed adventures than most of us can dream about.

Starting out with a couple of polar bear hunts in the early 1950s, Denny would build his guiding service into the biggest exclusive hunting territory in Alaska. He had exclusive hunting rights in areas from the Alaska Peninsula to the Wrangell Mountains and north to the Brooks Range—more than any other guide in the Alaska territory. This was before the Super-Cub, the Maule, and all the other modern-day transportation we now use to get to and from our hunting areas. This was also before all the modern thermal coats, pants, socks, and shoes. Moreover, they were still wearing beaver-skin coats, native-made mukluks, and bulky big old mittens. There were no scopes on most of the rifles to start with and very few regulations. As Denny would say, "Those were the good old days." To this day, Denny enjoys hunting as much as ever and right now is preparing to go out to Naknek and make arrangements for another season of salmon fishing on Bristol Bay. I hope you enjoy reading about the best bush pilot to fly the tundra as I have enjoyed telling the story.

The first time I met Denny was in 1984. I was building houses in the mountains in California, and a friend of mine and his brother and a couple of friends had made arrangements to go moose hunting in Alaska. They had been talking about it for weeks, and as I remember,

I was very envious. As the time drew near for them to go, one of the friends decided he couldn't make the trip and had to drop out. Ken came to me and asked me if I would like to take his place. I said yes, but I would have to make sure I could afford it and ensure I had all my bases covered while I would be gone. I finally convinced myself (with lots of encouragement from my father, who had always wanted to hunt in Alaska but who by then was eighty-five years old and couldn't walk any longer). Ken's brother had hunted moose with Denny about fifteen years earlier and was telling all kinds of stories about Mr. Thompson.

We flew out of San Francisco, changed planes in Seattle, then again in Anchorage, where we caught a commuter plane to King Salmon. That's where I first met Mr. Thompson, who had a big cigar in his mouth, a Naknek baseball cap, and a jacket that obviously had many years of experience.

Denny is one of those people you don't have to get to know; five minutes and it seemed we had been friends for life—at least that's the way it was with me. We had a good hunt, and I got a big moose, two caribou, and a black bear; it was a very exciting and a successful hunt. If I don't run out of paper and ink, I may include that story somewhere in the book later on; but for now, this story is about Denny Thompson, the World War II hero and the best bush pilot to ever fly the wilds of Alaska. If you dispute that, bring me the evidence; no guide has had more game in the record books over a longer period of time or has clocked more hours than Mr. Thompson.

The stories you are about to read are not hearsay. They were told directly to me over the campfire with a cigar in one hand and a drink in the other. To me, those evenings were the best part of the hunt or eating at the dinner table. When I decided to take on this worthy cause, Denny and I sat for days with recorders running and my taking notes as fast as I could write. Even now, as I struggle to get the facts right, I have to call Denny frequently for more details. It's a magnificent story. I hope I can do it justice.

And I hope you enjoy reading it!

I think when Denny popped his head out of the womb, he looked around and said, "That wasn't so bad. What's next?"

Denny's Mother and Father; Carl & Rica Thompson 1916

The Thompson clan Denny, Bobby, Jean, Ron, Vern, between the four brother they collected five Purple hearts during WWII

Chapter One

Denny's life began at 2:45 a.m. on July 27, 1922, in a small farmhouse in Fargo, South Dakota. He was the fourth of five children of Carl and Ricka Thompson. Little did Ricka suspect that this little creature would encounter challenges beyond her wildest imagination: getting a pissed-off skunk out of his trap in the Minnesota drainpipe; nursing a flak-riddled B-17 bomber across the Strait of Dover after completing a successful bombing run over Berlin, Germany, in 1944; stopping a charging jaw-snapping polar bear with a rifle he wasn't sure would even fire in the sixty-below-zero weather; and flying out of the jungles of Africa in the middle of the night to keep from being caught up in a revolution that eventually took thousands of lives, including that of his friend Donnie McGinski one of his guides— and the exile of the president of Central Africa MR Bokassa.

Ricka Thompson had no way of knowing her son would meet these and hundreds of other challenges with honor and dignity. She also couldn't have known that *he would save many lives with his selfless deeds* and that he would affect hundreds of lives with his hunting experiences, which are still being written and talked about today many years after they occurred.

But we don't talk about Ricka's little bundle of joy in the past tense, not even now in the year 2016 I just finished a three-day visit with Mr. Thompson, where we talked about and relived many of his experiences that are to be included in this story. By the way, I'm very fortunate to have been on numerous hunts with Denny from Alaska to Africa and in the Lower 48. I know firsthand what a great person and good friend Mr. Thompson is.

Denny's young life met a series of moves as his father had to relocate several times to find work in the late 1920s and all through the 1930s. When Denny was old enough, he started doing chores for the neighbors and made a few dollars, which he deposited in the bank. They finally moved to his grandparents' farm in Iowa. "Then came the Great Depression," Denny said, telling me about his father taking him to the bank to withdraw his money, but the bank only paid seven cents on the dollar; his first banking experience was not good.

Denny's adventures started in the mid-1930s, when he was twelve years old. "Those were tough times." He took some of the money he had earned mowing grass and doing other chores around the neighborhood and bought a half-dozen traps. They lived on the edge of town, so Denny didn't have far to go. He walked out into the fields behind the house and set traps in the drainage ditches and around a little lake. That started his career as a trapper and a hunter. He trapped all through high school and caught mostly mink, muskrat, and fox; a lot of the money that Denny made went to help the family. But in 1938, Denny bought his first car for a whopping $12. It was a 1928 Chevy. That allowed Denny to really expand his trapping and taught him how to fix just about anything. He graduated from high school in 1940 and went to work for the Northern Pacific Railroad, but he continued to trap until 1942, when he turned twenty. At that time, he entered the service as an aviation cadet in the Army Air Corps, a dream of his ever since a friend of his father's had paid for him and his friend to take a ride with a barnstormer who was giving rides in his biplane at a county fair in 1934. Denny went to Texas for basic training; he was then shipped up to a training facility in Omaha, Nebraska, where he went through special training "and excelled in training." When they arrived in Omaha, it was estimated they would be there for approximately six months of training. This was to learn the crucial elements of navigation and how to drop bombs and hit your target. Denny had never had the opportunity to go to college, as many of the other young men did, three thousand in all.

In two months, the air force decided they had to have "the brightest of these young men, right now" so they could finish their flight training and head for Europe, where they were needed to fight the Nazis. Of the first one hundred cadets to graduate, Denny was the *number two* cadet to graduate out of the three thousand, a rather significant accomplishment and telling achievement for the young man from Minnesota. Denny always wanted to be the best he was capable of being; this allowed him to excel in just about everything he ever decided to do. Once that training was completed, he was sent to Salt Lake City for additional training and then onto Phoenix, Arizona, and eventually Alamogordo, New Mexico, where he finished training as a pilot and bombardier on a B-24 and B-17.

After their training, they were assigned to a B-24 to fly to Herington, Kansas, to get some additional instrumentation installed in the airplane. However, upon takeoff, something went wrong with the fuel system; it malfunctioned, and the plane crashed just off the end of the runway. Everyone survived the crash with just a few bumps and bruises. The crew was then flown to Hutchinson, Kansas, where they picked up a new airplane, another B-24.

Around March 1, 1944, as Denny remembered it, they (on one single plane) left Kansas and headed to Florida. Their destination is Morrison Field at West Palm Beach, Florida.

The next day, they left Florida at 5:20 a.m. and flew to Trinidad, where they arrived eleven hours later. Now keep in mind this is a *crew of kids*, some of them not old enough yet to vote. Denny's plane, yet to be named the Problem Child, was the only aircraft to make this trip by themselves; there would be fifty aircraft in this group that would fly from Marrakech, Morocco, to Scotland and then onto Lavenham, England. Other than the flight engineer who was forty-four years old, the oldest man in the squadron, the next oldest man was twenty-four years old; and Denny was twenty-one.

The plane was thoroughly checked out overnight. The next morning, Denny and the crew left Trinidad at 5:30 a.m. Their destination was Belém, Brazil, which was a seven-and-a-half-hour flight. That afternoon, Denny picked up a small monkey from a native boy selling everything from snakes to spiders and probably his sister if he had one. They left Belém the next morning at 7:20 a.m. on a four-and-a-half-hour flight to Fortaleza, Brazil, with the monkey and about one hundred pounds of bananas stuffed in the front gun turret. The plane was then thoroughly inspected and checked over; this took approximately twenty-four hours.

The next leg of the trip was all the way across the Atlantic from Brazil to North Africa. They took off at 8:30 p.m. and headed east across the Atlantic Ocean. They finished their run-up at the end of the runway and checked all the gauges. Denny turned to his friend and copilot George Balthazor from Wisconsin and asked, "Well, George, are we ready?"

"We're ready, Chief. Let's get this bird in the air," replied George.

With that, Denny moved the throttles forward the B-24 rolled down the runway slowly picking up speed, Denny pulled back on the controls they cleared the end of the runway and headed toward the dark continent of Africa. Everyone took one last look at the beautiful green landscape of Brazil, with the sun in their eyes; they were soon surrounded by the greatest expanse of water any of them had ever imagined.

After a couple hours of flying, Denny remembered turning to the flight engineer, Sergeant Walker, and saying, "Hey, Sergeant, you keep this son of a gun flying because I'm not a very good swimmer."

"About five hours into the flight, one of the crew carelessly laid his jacket over the little heater that was in the cockpit and started a fire. The monkey went wild. We didn't see him for a couple hours. I thought maybe he bailed out. I remember the only thing I could get my hands on quickly was a couple of cans of citrus juice. It did the job, and the rest of the trip was uneventful."

They next sighted land about two the next morning. As they were making their approach into Dakar, they spotted several wrecked airplanes just short of the runway. Unfortunately, among them was one of the planes that had left from Brazil the day before; it ran out of fuel just twelve miles short of the runway. At 9:10 a.m., Denny and his crew landed at Dakar, Africa, the most westerly point on the African continent.

As Denny and George were taxiing to the parking area, the number 4 engine started to spit and sputter. Denny looked at the fuel gauge. It was on empty. The flight across the South Atlantic took twelve hours and forty minutes. Denny commented that the place was weird, so totally different from anything these young man had ever encountered. They took off the next day from Dakar at 6:30 a.m. and landed at Marrakech, about 150 miles south of Casablanca. There, the crew had to wait two weeks for the rest of the squadron to show up. It wasn't safe for one or two planes to fly without escort off the coast of France to get to England. The Germans still owned the skies over France at that time.

Pulling liberty and going into town to have a drink and see the sights this part of the world was very different, and no one felt comfortable. This was an old French training base, but 90 percent of the people were Arabs, for a bunch of country boys this was a strange and mysterious place. They had another major inspection, and the plane was checked over thoroughly from front to back as well as top to bottom. Other than a few minor adjustments, the plane had survived the trip quite well.

The next two weeks were very boring as the crew waited for the rest of the squadron. Except for a couple of days, about a week after they had arrived, Denny remembered they were having lunch. They could hear this rumble way off in the distance, which kept getting louder; pretty soon, the coffee in their cups started to ripple. They all rushed outside to see what was causing the commotion. About five miles to their south, they could see a large number of planes. At first, they thought it was the rest of their squadron; but in just a couple of minutes, they could see that these planes were much bigger. It was a group of B-29s, fifty in all, and they were headed for the Pacific theater. Every one of those planes had two crews and an extra engine on board. At that time, they were the biggest aircraft that existed in the world; from Marrakech, they would fly to India, where most of them would operate out of India and bomb Japanese positions in China and Indochina until the Americans had secured an island large enough and close enough to Japan to be able to bomb Tokyo. When they went back into the little coffee shop, Denny had left the monkey tied to his chair. It crapped on the seat of one of the chairs while they were outside, and one of the guys sat in it. That was just about the end of the monkey.

They had an opportunity to tour the B-29 airplanes while they were at Marrakech; they were beautiful big aircraft, so they all were hopeful they would get transferred onto this new airplane. The next morning, they all took off successfully—except for one, who crash-landed just off the end of the runway. No one was badly hurt, if Denny remembered right, and the plane never caught on fire. The next week, they got a little braver and ventured off into some of the local hangouts, where some of the French soldiers, some of the mechanics, and a couple other flight crews like them who were waiting for the rest of their groups to show up hung out. Denny thought, man-to-man, almost every one of them felt very uncomfortable and never stayed around for very long; it kind of reminded him of when he was a freshman in high school. Even when they were walking down the street, he never felt completely safe. On March 31, the other crews finally showed up; their planes also had to go through the inspection routine. Denny said they were ready to go on March 3; however, the weather was bad in England, and it stayed that way until March 10.

The squadron, all fifty planes, left Marrakech at 5:30 a.m. on April 11 and arrived at St Mawgan, England, about ten hours later. St Mawgan is at the very southwest tip of England. The next morning, they took off for Scotland to stay overnight and then went onto Lavenham, England, where they were stationed for most of their tour of duty in Europe.

Lavenham was a small English town, some twenty-five miles from the North Sea and about seventy miles north of London, in Suffolk, England. The town was small, with probably 1,200 people, and had been there a thousand years, perhaps longer. It was situated on a ridge above the Britt River. Most of the surrounding area was in pasture and fields. As a point of interest, a couple of scenes of the Harry Potter movies were filmed in Lavenham in 2010. Denny said he wished they had a little of Harry's magic when he was there.

One thing Denny said he remembered was the sheep. When they would be returning from a mission, they could see hundreds of white spots all over the fields—that is, if they could even see the fields because of the fog and low clouds, which seemed to be almost a permanent fixture covering these beautiful green hills.

Chapter Two

Getting down to business, April 14 through the 20, we had school. On the twenty-first, we were scheduled to make our first bomb run, but the hydraulic pump went out.

We had an air raid warning that morning. The Germans dropped some bombs on another base not very far away. I was working on a painting for the nose of our B-24. We had decided to call the old girl the Problem Child because it seemed like we were always fixing something on that damn plane. One day, I chalked the outline of the sultry young lady that was to be the Problem Child with the intent of painting the next day. Well, wouldn't you know it! We got one of those rare rainy nights in England that seemed to occur quite frequently; at any rate, it washed all the chalk off the front of the airplane. I had to start all over the next day. I did get the outline of the young lady painted on the nose of the airplane, but it probably took me two weeks before I had her looking like she does in the picture.

For one reason or another, mostly because of bad weather, we didn't actually fly our first mission until May 7; but in the meantime, we all got very well acquainted with the Swan, the local pub in downtown Lavenham. The Swan was our home away from home and our refuge when things got really tough, the only place we could go to help us forget about the empty bunks back at the base.

On May 7, we were to bomb the rail yards in Liege, Belgium. Our commanding officer was Colonel Bernie Lay, an Ivy League man who would go on to later write several books about the air war in Europe.

Colonel Lay was the only person out of four hundred personnel on this bomb run who had ever crossed the English Channel. All the rest of us were as green as grass; probably half of that four hundred were not even twenty-one years old yet.

Because of the weather and lack of experience, we had to make two runs over the target to be able to get on target with our bombs; we were also nervous. I had no idea if we hit the target or not. The flak was bad, but when we got back to the base and described the mission, some of the guys who have flown ten to twenty missions said it was nothing. "Wait until you go visit the Germans in Happy Valley (Ruhr Valley)," they told us. "The sky gets so black from flak that you have to turn on your landing lights to see where you're going." Some of the guys had a tendency to exaggerate a little; several planes were shot up pretty bad, and Lieutenant Colonel Bernie Lay eventually wrote the book *Twelve O'Clock High*, which was about our unit. It was later made into a movie. His plane lost two engines, but he was able to make it back to the emergency field.

As we were making our turn, I remember looking up; part of the group we were flying with was crossing over our position with their bomb bay doors open. I could see the stacks of bombs in those planes, and that was a very unsettling moment for a young pilot on his very *first mission*. We had a few holes in the stabilizer, but nothing serious; we didn't get to bed until 1:30 a.m.—a long day.

On the tenth, the whole wing took off at 6:00 a.m. We flew north about eighty miles in a slow climb; there, we started a slow lazy circle. For two hours, we would slowly climb to a higher altitude; the planes were always loaded to the max, and we were required to get to an elevation of approximately sixteen thousand feet before we could start crossing the channel. Once we reached that altitude, we headed out over the North Sea. Our entry point was almost always the Netherlands or Belgium unless we were making a bomb run into France; then we flew south.

On this particular day, after two hours of flying in circles, we then headed out over the North Sea; the mission was to bomb a German airfield at Brussels. About halfway across the channel, the mission was called back. At the time, we didn't think too much about it. We felt perhaps it was bad weather over the target; but later, I believe it could've been the fact that the Germans had been tipped off and knew our exact destination and time of arrival. On a lot of our missions, they knew. At the base, we had a spy who was tipping off the Germans about our flights; as hard as they tried, I don't believe they ever caught the person who was tipping off the Germans. After we finished our thirty missions and left, I heard later that they found a radio and all the necessary gear to send the messages in a little stone pump house setting just off the base, well within a short walking distance. That information would give them a distinct advantage to intercept our bombers with the maximum amount of fighters, which they would have time to bring in from other bases. Further, they would have all men available and manning maximum antiaircraft units; the combination could be devastating, as it was on several occasions later on in the campaign.

On the eleventh, we were awakened at 5:30 a.m. We were briefed, and then we had some breakfast; then we took off at 10:30 a.m. The mission was a jet fuel refinery on the border of France and Switzerland. We were about halfway to our destination when the navigator on Bernie Lay's lead plane had gotten the whole squadron off course, and we flew right over a well-defended German airfield, which was well protected by some very accurate antiaircraft gunners. The first salvo shot down the first two lead planes, Colonel Lay's and one other. Several other planes were also badly damaged; eventually, one of them was lost. All the personnel on those three planes had to bail out. With the exception for the colonel and his copilot, all other personnel were captured by the Germans. We had been flying the number 3 position when the two lead planes went down, so we were now left in the number 1 position and with the responsibility to destroy that oil refinery.

I was the pilot and the bombardier. When we got close to the target, I would turn over the controls to the copilot, then climb into a very small compartment in the nose of the airplane, where the bombsight was located. From there, I would take over the control of the airplane; and for the next ten to fifteen minutes, it was my job to bring us over the target and release the bombs. Once we dropped the bombs, the co-pilot, took over control again, until I could get back to my seat.

Since this was only our third mission, I don't remember a lot of details about the bomb run. But I do remember that when we made the turn to start our bomb run, the black smoke was so thick I couldn't see the ground most of the time. I remember the copilot saying, "Hey, Thompson! You want me to turn the running lights on so you can see?" There were two other planes that were also shot down. I don't remember who they were. I do remember when we finished the bomb run and was climbing back up into the pilot seat. I remember looking up and seeing parts of airplanes floating toward the ground and, in one case, a parachute with nobody in it. We had numerous hits; one of our engines was smoking so bad that we had to shut it down. Without any bombs, we could keep up with the rest of the squadron with just three engines. Other than that, there was nothing that hurt the old girl enough that she couldn't fly. Lieutenant Duncan's plane was on fire but made it back to the English coast, where they all bailed out. Duncan broke his leg, if I remember right, but everybody survived. To date, that was the toughest mission.

Lieutenant Colonel Lay avoided getting captured by the Germans and just lay low, knowing that an invasion of France was going to happen in the near future. About two weeks after the invasion, Lieutenant Colonel Lay made it to the American line and was shipped back to England. We never saw much of him after that. I was congratulated by our commanding officer for making a good drop and was promoted to lead pilot and bombardier, to fly lead in most of our remaining missions. The reason I was promoted was because out of our first three missions, the one I led was the most effective and did the most damage.

Chapter Three

We were given a new airplane for our fifth mission. My new plane was another B-24: Chief Wapello, named by a young aviator from Nebraska. The next couple days, we had several missions scrubbed because the crew had diarrhea due probably to nerves because of the trip to Switzerland on the eleventh. That was a tough trip; most everybody lost a friend that day. (It does make you think.) After we landed, we were picked up by jeeps and trucks and were taken to the debriefing area; there was a little shack just outside the debriefing area, where they would give you a shot of whiskey, if you so desired, before you went into the debriefing room. On this day, I think even the nondrinkers took their shot of whiskey. In the debriefing room, everybody had to relive the day and describe what happened and what could be done to make it better, if anything, and what we would do differently if we had to do it again. This helped the brass try to figure out what they could do to make the flights more effective and with less loss of life; this was the routine after every flight. The next few days, we had training flights, and we worked on sharpening our skills in flying tight formations; the bombardiers definitely worked on becoming more efficient.

On May 18, they bussed in about forty young ladies from the surrounding countryside and small towns, and we had a dance in one of the big hangars. Everybody had a great time. I was told that some of the girls wore two coats and had an extra scarf stuck in their pockets. When it was time to go home, they gave the coat and the scarf to their boyfriend, and he put them on and joined the girls on the bus for the ride home. I'm not sure how they got back to the base the next day, and I never heard of anybody getting in trouble. A number of guys that were stationed there on a more permanent basis married some of these English girls. The next time we had a dance, I watched very closely when it was time for the girls to board the bus and go home; sure enough, this night, there were five more girls who got on the bus instead of getting off.

On the twentieth, we rolled out of bed at 2:00 a.m. We had our briefing at 3:30 a.m., which usually didn't take too long. They showed us a map, gave the navigator the information he needed, and tried to prepare us for what we should expect on our way to the target and what specifically we should be looking for once we arrived. We took off at 6:00 a.m., heading for a rail yard at Liege. We had to abort just a few miles from Dunkirk because our number 4 engine malfunctioned, and we had to turn back. That morning, one of the planes blew up right after takeoff, and six men were killed. The next couple of days, we had practice flights.

On the twenty-second and twenty-third, most of us went to Scotland on what they called flak leave, where the military had set up what they called flak houses. I heard once there were fifteen of them spread throughout northern England and into Scotland. There were Red Cross ladies who ran these houses with some back home luxuries that we really couldn't get anyplace else in England. Scotland was a nice country, which looked like it offered good hunting. It was very hilly and rocky—a pretty country, a lot different from the flat corn country of Iowa or Minnesota.

On May 25, we were back to work. They had us up at 12:30 a.m.; and we took off at 5:45 a.m., heading for Montagne, France. Colonel Taylor of the 486th was hit hard. He had his windshield shattered by flak, so he had to abort and return to the base, which he did safely. This was a relatively easy run, with light flak and good weather. We had good hits on all the targets, when you can see the target and are not being tossed about by exploding antiaircraft shells, it certainly makes it a lot easier to do your job. If the missions were all like this one, it would have been a lot more fun. But we had yet to make a trip to Germany; the old-timers told us that was usually a little rougher ride.

On May 28, there was a lot of talk about the upcoming invasion of France; we saw more high-ranking officers at the base in the last couple weeks than I had seen since I've been in the air force. That day, they had us up at 3:45 a.m. to have our briefing and breakfast, and takeoff time was 10:15 a.m. Why in the hell did we have to get up before 4:00 a.m. when we didn't take off until after 10:00 a.m.? I never could figure it out.

The target: the oil refineries at Leipzig, Germany. (The official records showed Lutzkendorf.) Wherever we were, there were lots of guns, and the flak was bad; at times, it sounded like we were in a hailstorm. When I was getting into position to start the bombing run, I saw a shell, probably an 88, pass not one hundred feet in front of the plane, going straight up; about three seconds later, there was a flash and a loud explosion. I often wonder what would've happened if that gunner had waited just about two seconds longer to fire the cannon. I don't remember if we lost any planes that day, but just about every plane was hit and had holes that had to be fixed. I was not looking forward to another trip like this. The total flight was eight and a half hours, but it seemed much longer.

On the twenty-ninth, we made another trip to Hannover, Germany. The official records show Politz. On this trip, we got our first look at the German jets. They were unbelievable! Our guys wouldn't have much of a chance unless we ganged up on them. There were also a couple dozen German fighters, mostly Messerschmitt Me 109s and the Focke-Wulf Fw 190s. Ducking in and out of the clouds, they'd make a pass at one or two of the planes and then disappear; finally, one of the gunners got lucky and caught one before he got back into the clouds. After that, the rest of them just disappeared.

We lost two planes and crews that day. I don't know if they bailed out or not because we couldn't see them from where we were. One thing I remember about this particular trip was the cold; it was always cold at twenty-five thousand feet, but this day, it seemed unbearable. While I was making the bomb run, I was shaking so hard that it was difficult for me to make the necessary adjustments and concentrate on the target. And if I breathed on the bombsight, the glass would freeze over, and then I'd have to scratch the frost off the glass before I could see again.

The next day, May 30, was an interesting day because we headed for Münster, Germany. The target was the airfield; it looked to us like they were trying to cripple the Germans' ability to put planes in the air during the upcoming invasion. We had no idea when or where that would be, but it was for sure it would happen sometime that summer. We arrived at the target on time; the plane was nice and level, with very little turbulence. It made a good run, and the bombsight was dead on the target. The bomb bay doors were opened, and with the push of a button, bombs away. But nothing happened; the damn bombs wouldn't release. We were in heavy flak over and around the target, which was always a major concern, especially when you have a plane full of bombs; it would take only one hit in the right spot to set off that whole load of bombs. We finally had to give up and head home with the rest of the formation; we spent the next hour kicking the bombs out of the plane one by one as we crossed Germany heading home. Two planes were crippled and had to be ditched in the North Sea. All aboard were rescued except for one man, who was lost. I thought about that scenario every time I flew over the channel or the North Sea.

The next couple days, we had practice flights. I caught up on rest and wrote the long-overdue letter to my girlfriend back in Minnesota. I played a couple of crap games. I made a couple hundred dollars in one game and lost part of it the next night but still did okay. Then of course, we had our usual trip to the Swan, as the Englishmen would say, "to have a bit of ale." But I don't like warm beer, so my choice was usually whiskey or gin. Sometimes we had more than just a bit.

We tested several planes that were being repaired. The weather had been stormy, and when it was not raining, the clouds were only one hundred feet off the ground.

June 6, 1944, was D-day. We woke at 12:30 a.m. for our briefing at 1:30 a.m.; we are supposed to depart as soon as the weather broke. The mission was France, just across the channel; we were told this was the day of the invasion. It was still stormy, but the barometer was rising; at

3:30 a.m., we were told to saddle up and fill the sky with aircraft. The report was that the channel was full of ships, with more boats than the world has ever seen in one place at one time. The reports were that tens of thousands of young men would lose their lives on that day even if the invasion were successful and perhaps a hundred thousand if not. There were planes in the air when we woke up; we were informed we were to make three trips that day. It was not a good day for bombing; the clouds were broken at best, and we could see the target only once in a while. Our first run was the German headquarters at Lesue, France. The day before, planes had dropped leaflets warning the people in town to evacuate because we would be bombing the town the next day. Even with the miserable bombing conditions, we still managed to do adequate damage to disrupt the Germans' communications. It was very difficult to be as accurate as I would've liked to have been, especially on that historical day.

We were on our third mission over the channel when we were called back because of bad weather; some of the planes disregarded the orders and went on to the targets. Our fighters did a great job the entire day; there was hardly a German plane to be found, and when he was sighted, he was probably shot down. We were told the Allies had *two thousand bombers* in the air, and I never heard how many fighters flew that day. But altogether, the Eighth Air Force flew eleven thousand sorties in just that one day. I believe; everywhere you looked, you could see airplanes. The second trip across the channel that morning gave me the first good look I had at the ships in the channel. Unbelievably, it looked like you could walk from one ship to another, and I heard later that there were about seven thousand ships and boats, but it seemed like more than that.

The next day, we were up bright and early. We were made to understand that the invasion was considered a success; beachheads were established, and supplies were pouring in. There were no reports on casualties yet. That day, we did not have a very good day since our mission was the marshaling fields at Charleaubryant (our records indicate Montjean). We made the drop, and that went well. But on our way back, we were flying over Rennes, France, when Schwab's plane, which was flying on our left wing, took a *direct hit*. Three chutes were seen, but that was all. Another plane that got hit caught on fire and blew up; there were no chutes.

On June 8, some of the group went to an area north of Paris, We didn't fly this mission since we had to test-fly several of the planes that were being worked on. Several of the planes didn't return that day, and we had very bad weather and no word on the missing planes.

On June 11, we got word that the missing planes had crashed in the channel with no survivors. Weather has been very unsettling. They scheduled flights, but then they got scrubbed.

On the fourteenth, we took off at 4:00 a.m. (no sleep). Our destination was Lille, France, and the mission was to bomb the airfield. When we got there, the target wasn't as we had been briefed, so we didn't drop our bombs. A mission like this, where we didn't encounter any fighters or have any flak, was not counted as a mission, which meant it didn't count as one of the thirty we had to fly. We headed back to the base, landing at about 10:00 a.m.; by 11:00 a.m., we were rebriefed for another mission at 2:30 p.m., but it was scrubbed just minutes before we were to take off.

On June 15, we were briefed for a drop on an airfield across the river from Paris; none of us forgot our last mission in the Paris area. It was rough, and we made a run on the field but didn't drop on the primary target because the clouds were too thick. We then went to our secondary target, another airfield. This one we could see very well; we knocked the hell out of that one, especially the hangars. There were a few fighters on the ground when we attacked. I didn't hit any of them, but some of the other guys did. There was a lot of flak, but it was very inaccurate, especially for the Paris area. It had now been ten days since D-day. The invasion was definitely a success even though there were many casualties; the numbers were not nearly as bad as they had expected. On every trip we made over France, we could tell things were not going well for the Germans; the front lines were steadily advancing. The flak seemed to be less intense, and there were far fewer fighter planes than before the invasion.

On June 16, 1944, we had school; everybody had a tough time staying awake.

On the seventeenth, we rolled out of our racks at 12:00 a.m. and were briefed at 1:00 a.m. for takeoff at 4:30 a.m., which was scrubbed at 3:30 a.m. So we all went back and hit the sack. We were alerted for an afternoon flight at 2:00 p.m. to bomb an airfield at Alenton, France, which was only about fifty miles east of the beachhead. We made three runs on the target, but it was so well camouflaged we couldn't be certain of the target, so we didn't drop. We then made a run on a secondary target but weren't able to drop on that one either. So we went looking for targets of opportunity, and we were following the river Seine; we were cruising along at twenty-seven thousand feet, quite content. The weather was good for a change, and we were enjoying the scenery, if that's possible at twenty-seven thousand feet. All of a sudden, the navigator—who, I guess, was looking out the front of the airplane—yelled in the intercom that we had flak dead ahead. There were lots of flak, for we had stumbled onto a major antiaircraft emplacement; it was dead ahead, and we hardly had to change course. So we bombed the hell out of the gun emplacements and then headed for home. We didn't lose any planes, but several were hit and badly damaged, but they were able to make it home; the entire squadron throttled back just a little so the two crippled planes could keep up. Once we crossed the French coastline in the north of France, we started our descent to a warmer elevation. On our trip home, we were flying over the beachhead at Le Havre when we saw a plane from another bomber wing that was headed south into France. One of their planes took a direct hit by flak and blew up right over the beachhead at Le Havre. Seeing something like that makes you realize how lucky you are every time the tires hit the ground and you're still in one piece.

On June 18, we started a forty-eight-hour pass, caught up on some sleep during the day, and then hit the pub in Lavenham that night. I decided to drop my mother a note in the morning. I was sure she was hearing about all the deaths during the invasion. The next day, we went to Colchester to wander around and have a couple drinks and then headed back to the base. We got back to the base just in time to go visit the friendly folks at the Swan. After a few drinks, I headed back to the barracks to catch up on some sleep. However, if I remember right, when

I got back to the barracks, there was a rip-snorting crap game in progress just a couple of bunks from mine. With all the yelling and commotion taking place, I knew there was no way I was going to get any sleep. Plus I could just envision all that money lying there on the floor somehow winding up in my pocket. Not only did I not win all that money, but I also didn't get any sleep. The next morning, reveille was way earlier than I was ready for.

On the twentieth, we rolled out early, and it was one of those unusual days on the Emerald Island when the skies were blue with just a few scattered clouds. Usually, the North Sea looked like the meringue on top of your mother's favorite pie; but that day, there was only an occasional whitecap. It actually gave me an uneasy feeling; you couldn't tell where the water ended and the sky began, and there was no horizon.

We did our normal two-hour climb out to reach sixteen thousand feet before we headed southeast and over the Belgian coast. With only a slight breeze, it was a very smooth flight almost all the way to the target; we had an occasional disruption of peace and tranquility as we flew over some of the German "happy gunners." The target that day was the oil refineries at Hannover. We arrived at the target at 11:15 a.m., and we were at twenty-seven thousand feet. It felt like about 150 below zero, but the flak brigade was doing everything they could to warm it up for us; there was flak everywhere: above us, below us, and right in our midst. Lieutenant Irwin just off my left wing took a direct hit with a full load of bombs and blew up. There were no survivors. They never knew what hit them, and M. R. Brown, a friend of mine who was a navigator on another plane, was hit with scrap metal and killed. This was all happening as we approached the target. I got the plane lined up as best I could before I turned it over to George; then I headed downstairs and up front to my bombardier station. There was so much black smoke and so many exploding shells that I could only see an occasional glimpse of our target. We were the lead plane in the squadron, so I had to be as accurate as possible because everybody in the wing would be bombing using my lead. I think every plane on that mission was hit, some pretty bad. When I finished the bomb run, George banked the old bird to the left, being very careful not to collide with one of the other ships in the area. The sky was full of planes; it was an unbelievable sight. For ten miles in all directions, I could see planes: *our planes.* As soon as we cleared the flak area, we got the squadron back in formation just in time to meet the Jerries in their Me 109s. They came like a swarm of bees out of our starboard. Lo and behold, no sooner had they started their attack than the "Lone Ranger and Tonto"—our beautiful P-51 Mustangs—came. The 109s had to fight it out that day because there weren't any clouds to duck into, and they paid the price. The estimate was that the Germans lost forty fighters and pilots in that one battle. We lost one fighter, but eight bombers and crews, a total of eighty men, almost exclusively to flak. There were lots of empty bunks that night. (By then, the monkey had the run of the barracks, and of course, he had his favorite crew members who always brought him treats and played with him. Unfortunately, one of those favorites was one of the eighty that didn't return that day. The poor little guy just sat and watched the front door to the barracks for a week. Sad!)

We had lots of holes in our airplanes, but nothing serious; there were several holes amidships that you could've stuck your head through with no problem. But in spite of the flak, we had a good drop, with oil tanks exploding and burning everywhere—one of our best missions to date. After all the excitement was over, I decided to check on the crew and see if we had any serious problems. Shackle Gruber, one of our waist gunners, was standing there counting the holes in his brand-new suit. "Hey, Lieutenant Thompson, would you look at this? Those bastards shot four holes in my brand-new flight suit," he said.

I couldn't help but smile, but still, I had to ask, "Are you okay? Did any of those bullets draw any blood?"

"I don't think so Lieutenant,"

I replied, "Don't worry, Gruber. I'll see if I can get you a new suit." I continued on back to check on the tail gunner. Half of the Plexiglas in his little cubicle was missing, and he was about to freeze to death. So I helped him get up and out of that turret and to a place where it wasn't so drafty.

That afternoon, some from our group tried to bomb Pas-de-Calais, one of the locations where the Germans launched their rockets that rained down on London almost every night, causing death and destruction. Not a good mission because that was probably the best-defended target in our itinerary. I hadn't been there yet, but I was sure I would have the pleasure sooner or later.

On June 21, 1944, we were briefed for the run to Calais; we took off at 6:30 a.m. We were just over the channel, but Lieutenant Balthazar became sick, so we had to abort. There was not a tear to be found on that plane. Nobody wanted to make that mission.

We were awake at 1:15 a.m. on the twenty-fourth. We took off at 4:15 a.m., flying the number 2 position; it seemed they kept moving us from number 1 and back to number 2, then back to the front of the pack every couple missions. Our mission that day was the Châteaudun airfield. We made our approach at twenty-five thousand feet. I took my position at the bombardier station. George handed over to me the control of the plane as I got set up for the bomb run. There was quite a bit of wind, but everything checked out right. I double-checked because something didn't look right to me, yet everything confirmed we were on target. So we opened the doors, and bombs away. We dropped too soon (miscalculated the wind, I guess); it was a poor job. It wasn't because of the flak, which was very light. There were lots of bombers in the area; we had to be very careful, but that wasn't the reason for the missed target.

Also, this was the first time we saw some rockets fired at other planes. We also saw a jet fighter. That afternoon, when we returned to the base, we calibrated the instruments. I was not at all happy with that day's run, and I suspect we might have instrument problems. With all the bouncing around that plane had to endure, it's surprising more things didn't go wrong.

On June 25, we got to sleep in that morning; nobody whispered in my ear to get my ass out of the rack until 7:00 a.m. We even had a leisurely briefing and breakfast, like normal people do. I read some mail from home. I got a letter from Jean that day and took care of a few odds and ends.

We took off at 1:50 p.m., and we started the day as deputy lead number 2. Trinary was in the lead; two hours into the mission, his number 4 engine went out, so he had to turn around and return to the base. We then slid into his position and took the lead. We bombed a bridge over the Marne River (records indicate the river Seine). I think calibrating the instruments was a good idea because I got very good hits on the bridge. We estimated that 85 percent of our bombs hit the target; at twenty-five thousand feet, that isn't bad. I believe the poor job we did on the last mission was mostly because of the instruments. That day was helped by the fact we were not being knocked around by flak.

June 26 was stormy and windy; we all got a break that day. I slept almost all day. At about 4:00 p.m., I commandeered a bicycle and headed for the Swan. Now the Swan, mind you, was about a mile and a half away in downtown Lavenham. It was an old community pub that had been there for at least five hundred years. They served some good Irish whiskey, some excellent Scotch, gin, and some not-so-excellent warm beer, which I tried once—and once was enough. The trail into town from the base was not on the road that was about half as far again. So being good Americans, we found a shorter route to the pub—across country through a field and some woods, and there we were. Now if it was raining, which it was most of the time, and the trail got a little muddy, it could be quite an exciting ride from the base to the pub. But two to three hours later, the ride from the pub to the base could be downright hazardous to your health.

I remember returning to the base one evening in an absolute downpour. This time, I was on foot—no bike. I was about halfway through the woods when I heard somebody groaning down over the bank. I decided I had better check it out since it may be one of my crew. Luckily, it was not one of my men, but one of the pilots on one of the other ships. He and his bike had strayed from the path and ended up in the brush and briars about twenty feet from the path. Once I got him back up on the path, we were both covered in mud, and he was shit-faced. He was so drunk he never would have made it back to the base by himself. However, he felt that the prudent thing to do would be to return to the Swan, strictly for medicinal purposes to cleanse his wounds with some of that good Scotch whiskey. I finally convinced him that one of the Red Cross girls at the officers' club could probably do a much more efficient job, so he sat in the mud, contemplating his options. He finally decided I was wise, well beyond my years; then he asked me, "Do you think the little Irish redhead is on duty tonight?"

On the twenty-seventh, we had school in the morning, and flights were scrubbed for the afternoon.

On June 28, we took off at 4:30 a.m. to bomb the airfield near Marne River. Contrails were very bad, and we were number 2 in the low squadron. A group of B-17s crossed over us and caused the high squadron to break up in the contrails at the French coast. Captain Peck was command pilot and ordered the mission to return to base; all this work, and it didn't even count as a mission.

On the twenty-ninth, there was more bad weather, really bad. It was raining so hard—at times, we couldn't even see the planes parked on the other side of the runway. The wind was blowing so hard it blew some of the tin off a couple of the buildings.

One of the guys in the control tower swore he saw three sheep, an old doe, and a couple of lambs go sailing by his window in the control tower. Now that's windy. That day, they switched us over to B-17s; we took a vote and decided to name her Sweet 17, Now it was my job to get her painted.

Chapter Four

On August 1, 1944, we had our first real mission in the B-17. I liked this plane much better than the B-24. It just seemed to handle better, and we could haul a bigger load. I was hoping they would locate the bombardier's sight somewhere other than right up in the nose. Whenever I was sitting there and we were making our bomb run, for some reason, I felt like there was a great big bull's-eye painted right on the nose of that aircraft. The target this day was the airfield at Tours. Last night, we shot some craps and then played a little poker. I had just hit the sack, and they called us for briefing at 4:45 a.m. We took off at 10:10 a.m., and we were the lead for the low squadron, with clear blue skies and contrails for as far as you could see. The P-51s caught up to us over the channel and just sat back and took it easy; they spotted a German column on the road below. Four of them dropped out of formation and decided to have some fun. But we were so high we couldn't really see for sure, except it looked like they destroyed every vehicle on the road, which didn't take but a couple minutes.

We were making our approach from the northwest; the weather was clear, with not a cloud in sight, when all hell broke loose: flak everywhere—high, low, right, and left. There were about fifteen minutes before I had to take the controls and start the bomb run, so I decided to check on the crew; in addition, there was a lot of chatter on the radio. I knew we were getting hit pretty badly. Everybody was hanging in there because there wasn't any place to hide, nothing you could get behind or into that would give you any protection. The outside skin of the ship was about the thickness of a can of Spam; they were all a little nervous, but otherwise intact. When I got to the tail gunner, he was in bad shape since the Plexiglas had been shattered, and he had some cuts on his face and hands and had been hit in the arm by a chunk of flak. He had successfully stopped the bleeding but looked a little pale. I tried to talk him into getting out of the turret, but he said he would ride it out until we finished the bomb run. I got back to my bombardier station and got everything set up. By then, I could see the target; we were getting bounced all over because of the explosions from the flak. But I was still able to keep the sight on the target, and for some reason, there was just a little pause in the flak when I pushed the button and released the bombs. Once I knew all bombs were away, I closed the doors and made a beeline back to my normal seat upstairs. Even though there wasn't much to protect you, it just seemed much safer than being down there in that Plexiglas bubble.

We made a good run, a very good run; we hit the runways and airstrips. The 486th High Squadron hit the hangars and fuel depot. I was convinced there wouldn't be any planes flying out of that field for quite some time. As soon as we were clear of the flak, I went back and grabbed a couple of the other guys, and we helped pull the tail gunner up on deck; his wound was not very serious, though he looked like hell because of all the scratches and nicks on his face. It did earn him a Purple Heart and, of course, a couple days' recovery in the hospital. We all accused him of goldbricking just to get some time off, but later, I would learn to appreciate what it meant to get nailed by some of that flak. We got everybody back to the base safely, and he spent a couple weeks in the hospital recuperating and was back flying with us before we knew it.

For some miraculous reason, we didn't lose any planes on that mission, but we were really shot up. We had holes everywhere! I counted over two hundred holes just in the stabilizer, not counting the main body of the airplane. We got back to the base at 4:45 p.m.; the mechanics worked all night fixing the critical areas. They had us ready to go the next morning. Those men were some of the hardest-working people I had ever seen. I know there were days and nights that they didn't get any sleep.

On August 2, I was supposed to have the day off, but I heard they were going to fly a mission over one of the buzz bomb sites at Caen, France. Supposedly, there was very light antiaircraft cover in that area, so

I volunteered. What the heck! It was another mission, and if it was an easy one, so be it. The site was a little west of Caen, France. We flew number 2 lead; the area was extremely well camouflaged. We each had our own targets. I was able to find my target, and we made a good drop, but some were not able to find their targets and had to abort (no drop). Very little flak and no fighters and that's what I call a good day on the Western front.

On August 3, I took my day off and went to Colchester, England. There was a buzz bomb hit near Milford; other than scaring the heck out of a bunch of sheep, there was no damage. They said it was fired from the site at Caen, France, where we had just bombed the day before. I guess that was to show us that we weren't the hotshot bombers that we thought we were. A lot of those rockets that the Germans were firing into England were mounted on trucks and were very mobile; they could hide them in gullies and in the woods, covering them up with some camouflage, and they'd be impossible to see.

On the fourth and fifth, the group went to Hapsburg, Germany (the records indicate Nordholz), and Magdeburg, both of which are near Berlin. Lots of flak! We had German fighters come up to greet us. I was just getting into position for the bomb run up in the nose in my Plexiglas bubble when I heard George yell over the intercom, "Look out, Thompson! Dead ahead!" I looked up, and coming straight at us was an Me 109. I could see the constant flash of his guns from both wings as he closed the distance very rapidly; he was probably traveling at four hundred miles an hour, and we were traveling at about two hundred. I could see his tracers going right under the belly of our plane. If he had just raised the nose of his plane a couple degrees, that would've been the end of Sweet 17. I thought for sure he was going to plow right into our airplane, but at the very last instant, he dove straight down. I don't think the tail of his airplane was more than thirty or forty feet from where I was sitting; he was so close that I could see the rivets on the tail of his airplane.

After that first pass, the P-51s kept them busy and shot down four of the Germans. Lieutenant Squire's radio operator was killed when a piece of flak hit him in the head. These were both very rough missions. We flew lead both days. On the way home, we flew over some canals. Germany had rivers and canals that seemed to go everywhere, making for a unique transportation system where they could move just about anything on barges in that part of Germany. I had seen this area before and admired their ingenuity, but that day, it seemed the British had poked a little hole in the levee with one of their big sixteen-thousand-pound bombs. Some of those canals are elevated to cross little valleys or low areas. The Brits had placed one of those big bombs right in the middle of one of those elevated canals and completely destroyed it; there was about two hundred miles of that part of Germany that looked like it was under about a foot or two of water, but the real interesting thing was there were hundreds of barges sitting high and dry in those canals—*quite a sight.*

August 6 was spent sightseeing Europe, where we got to visit Berlin again. We had nice clear skies; they could see us coming for a hundred miles as there were contrails everywhere. For as far as I could see in all directions, there were groups of bombers spread out all over northern Germany. I wondered to myself, "When the Germans look up into these bright blue skies, they see sometimes as many as two thousand of these bomb-belching demons spreading death and destruction throughout their country. What in the hell is wrong with them? Can't they see there's only one way this war is going to end?" Every day they had fewer bridges to cross, fewer airfields to take off from, less fuel and ammunition dumps to get supplies from, and very few railroads left that are operable. Of course, we were going to lose more men, more planes, more of just about everything; but it wouldn't compare to what they were going to lose.

We went in at Heligoland Bight and flew straight over the middle of Berlin; then we cut back and bombed an industrial area, machine shops, etc. We had very good hits. We saw German jets before we reached the target, and on our way out, we saw four Me 109s under us and close as we made our turn and started our bomb run. We had very heavy flak, and Lieutenant Hatfield's plane took a direct hit on his number 3 engine; it blew the engine right off the wing, but somehow the wing stayed intact, so he continued to fly. One of his crew panicked and bailed out right over the target. No telling what happened to him. On our way out, we were flying north along the Elbe River; when we flew over Hamburg, the oil refineries were ablaze. Some of our boys had done a very good job.

It was obvious the Germans were very good at repairing what we tore up, but there was a limit to their manpower and their resources, and it was obvious we were rapidly depleting both. Some of our planes were very heavily damaged, but everybody in our group made it home. There were a few wounded warriors, but we were all able to walk away. I didn't realize it until I touched down on the runway at Lavenham that two of my tires had taken hits and were flat, so I had to fight to keep the plane out of the mud and get it off the runway before somebody ran into the back of us. Usually, the planes landed just a minute or two apart, which meant we didn't have much time to clear the runway. We heard one man bailed out and that his parachute got caught on the tailwheel of another aircraft at thirty thousand feet; one can only imagine what the outcome was.

August 7 was an easy day. It involved training for lead crews, and I made $100 shooting craps. The sergeant and I decided to check out the hydraulic system on Sweet 17. It seemed a bit sluggish on our last trip. While we were making our way across the runway, in between the landing aircraft coming back from a mission, a B-24 hit the ground pretty hard; and it was obvious she had lost her brakes, for she went by us at about eighty miles an hour.

I'll never forget this: there was a preacher on his bicycle crossing the end of the runway when this B-24 came rumbling down the strip, heading right for him. He didn't see it until the very last few seconds. He jumped off his bike and lay flat on the ground while the bike continued to wobble across the runway; the plane went right over the top of him, the nose wheel just missed him on the left, and the right landing gear cleared him by no more than a couple feet on the right. That same landing gear hit the bike dead center and flattened it like a pancake. After the plane rolled on by and out into the pasture with the sheep, the preacher sat up and looked at his bike, picked up his hat (which had been blown fifty to sixty feet away), gathered up the pieces of his smashed bike, and continued on his way. All we could surmise from that experience was that "it's good to be close to the Lord in times of peril."

On August 8, we had a tricky mission: we had to bomb just behind the Canadian lines just west of Caen, France. The Germans were holed up in the hedgerows, and the Canadians were taking big losses, trying to get them dislodged. We were to come in at a very low elevation for us to try to bomb those hedgerows without hitting Allied lines. There were a lot of planes in the area, which always makes one a little nervous. The Canadians had laid out flares, indicating the perimeter of the Canadian lines and the German lines. There was a lot of flak off to our right, but not much where we were flying. Right as we were turning to make our bomb run, we saw a plane off to our right take a direct hit; we counted four parachutes, but no more. We went in at about twelve thousand feet. As a rule, we were way too high to be able to see the guns that produced all the flak, but that day was an exception; we were looking right down their gun barrels. We had to be right on target, with no room for error, because we were dropping less than a half mile from the Canadians lines—*no room for mistakes.*

That day, we had a very special observer, General Doolittle, who was in a P-47 just watching the show. I believe we had good hits, and once we were done, the P-51s strafed the area several times. Very good mission! We heard later that the Canadians were able to dislodge what was left of the Germans in the next couple days and continued their advance toward Paris.

On August 9, after the run of the day before, we were ready for a big day. We took off at 6:15 a.m., crossed the channel, and went in below Rotterdam in the Netherlands. We were supposed to bomb a ball bearing factory in Austria. We were able to climb to thirty thousand feet and pick up a little help from the jet stream; the only problem with the jet stream was it usually wasn't a direct tailwind. As a rule, it usually tried to blow you off course to the east. So we had to be very careful and maintain contact with known landmarks, such as cities, rivers, and mountains, if there were any. However, on this day, the clouds were quite thick when we got into Germany. The farther south we went, the worse it got. I was looking ahead, trying to pick up any landmarks that we might recognize.

"George, do you remember any mountains in this part of Germany?"

George slid his glasses down his nose and peered over the top of his glasses at what I was looking at. "Lieutenant, as I remember, this area is pretty flat. My guess is those are thunderheads, big thunderheads."

"Captain, you want to try to go around them? Let me look at the chart. You know we picked this route because we didn't have to go over the heavy flak areas. I'm afraid if we change course, we will run into more flak. George, while I check out the chart, you start to climb. I'll check with Magellan and see what our options are."

Magellan was our navigator. The prognoses were not good—fifty miles either side and we were in heavy flak areas. George looked to me like we had better try to get over the tops of those storms. So we continued to climb; and as we got closer, the thunderheads were much higher. We leveled off at thirty-one thousand feet, tightened our seat belts, and advised the crew to do the same. We were above some of the storms, but there were others that went well above forty thousand feet—very typical of a Midwest storm you might see in Nebraska or Iowa in August at about three or four o'clock in the afternoon.

As we entered the storm front, the updrafts and high winds created turbulence much more dramatic than the flak. The turbulence from flak, I would say, was bumpy; this turbulence tossed us around like a rag doll. One minute, we would rapidly rise a couple thousand feet; the next minute, we would drop three to four thousand feet, like a roller coaster. The whole squadron had to spread out to keep from being thrown into another plane. We were able to avoid most of the big thunderheads, but the view was something I remember to this day. The clouds below us and all around us had constant cloud-to-cloud lightning, with flashes that looked like spiderwebs across the sky; then there were streaks of lightning that shot past the plane and into another cloud. When we couldn't avoid the big ones and had to fly through the big thunderheads, that was a show words can't describe. One second, it was pitch-black; the next moment, it was lit up like the inside of a lightbulb. Some of the thunder shook the plan; there were all sorts of weird shadows. Once in a while, we could see another plane; they didn't look real—they looked like ghosts. This front was only about twenty-five miles wide, and we were through it in about ten minutes, but it seemed like an hour.

We continued on for another fifty miles perhaps, and then we ran into more thunderstorms just before we reached the Austrian border; we had to turn back. By then, we were not sure where we are. Without any land references and because of the increased cloud cover and the wind and stormy weather, we got blown off course and were lost. We had to drop down to about twenty-five thousand feet to get out of the jet stream. So we turned back north and had to fly over the happy gunners in Germany. We knew one thing for sure: we hadn't crossed over Allied lines. As we tried to find our way home, we kept running into the boys that delivered the flak. In a normal situation when we knew where we were at, we had all the nasty areas where the flak was bad, outlined in red on our map. But on this day, we hadn't a clue other than the fact we knew damn well we were still in Germany!

By the time we were nearly out of Germany, it began to clear, and I could see this railroad track running right in the same direction we were flying. So I decided to follow it, and bingo! We hadn't flown more than fifteen to twenty minutes when I spotted a rail yard with lots of equipment and railcars; we decided this was a great place to get rid of our bombs. I quickly made my way to the bombardier station and got into position as quick as I could. It was one of those days when everything worked just like a clock. I found the target and made the necessary adjustments, and we dropped our bombs on a small-town rail yard, St. Vith in Belgium. We thought we were still in Germany but later found out that we were not.

Most of the bombs were fragmentation and incendiaries that made good hits on the rail yard and car barns. Still off course, we were flying in overcast and flew right over Liege, someplace you really don't want to be. We were hit hard by flak. Despite not being over the flak area for very long, several of the planes sustained very heavy damage, with several men wounded. But we didn't lose any planes. The weather finally cleared, and we got back on course and flew home with the high squadron. When we realized where we had bombed—a town in the occupied country of Belgium, which was off-limits for indiscriminate bombing—we thought for sure we were going to be in big trouble. But when the intelligent reports came back from the undercover people in

Belgium, it was learned that there were over three thousand German troops at that railroad yard, waiting to be shipped to the front lines; most of them were killed or wounded because of our attack on the rail yard, and no more trains would run from that station to any place for the duration of the war.

Denny's B-17G over Berlin Bomb-Bay door open

Part of Denny's crew Lavenham England 1944, it's too bad we don't have more good WWII pictures but Denny lost all his flight suits pictures souvenirs in the 1964 earthquake.

On August 13, we were having breakfast when one of the Jerries' buzz bombs hit near the base, causing a big hole in the ground, but no other damage. Some of the guys were kidding us about not doing a very good job the last time we visited Caen, France.

We took off at 9:30 a.m. We were sent to bomb a German installation west of Cherbourg. We flew down the peninsula, west to about even with Paris, and cut back at an angle to go between Paris and our front lines. As we were making the cut, we had lots of flak that it sounded like a hailstorm on a tin roof, and a B-17 took a direct hit off to our right. I didn't have much time to look, but I never saw any parachutes. We picked up a few more holes, but nothing serious. After you saw something like that happen, you sometimes wondered when it was going to be your turn. It was times like that, even though you may not be a very religious person, I guarantee that you catch yourself asking God to watch over you and help you get home safely.

We split up into three plane elements, and each element picked their target. The first and third divisions were in the same area. We hit roads and bridges near Dreux. I zeroed in on a crossroad full of German tanks and trucks; we hit them head-on, and we could see vehicles and tanks flying in all directions, which felt good. We turned home and went out past Roivenand and Dieppe. A few more holes in our plan, but nothing disabling. All things considered, basically a good mission. Maybe by taking out those tanks and troops, we might have saved a few American and British lives.

On August 16, our crew drove to Bury St Edmunds for radar training. But the field was full, with planes parked everywhere, so we had to return to base and go the next day. We made a little trip to the Swan and had a couple drinks; then we got in an argument with one of the limeys about who was the best general: Patton or Montgomery. They really were a hardheaded bunch.

On August 21, I started my furlough. I went to London for the night and had the privilege of listening to the buzz bombs all night. It really was a lot of fun to go to London. There was the Piccadilly Circus, where your imagination was the only limit to what you could do. Then there was the Red Cross Rainbow corner which was built on the order of a juke joint and a soda fountain just like back in the States. They had rooms where you could get paper to write folks back home; and one room had a jukebox where you could sit, drink soda, and listen to all the latest music from back in the States. It was a very well-designed and well-run facility, where hundreds of thousands of GIs spent some very valuable time in between missions. During the day, it was a pretty peaceful place, with lots of people cleaning up debris and making repairs to the streets; otherwise, it was pretty much business as normal. At night, you spent a lot of your time in a bomb shelter listening to mothers and babies crying and praying that this situation would someday end and life would get back to normal. At this point, I doubt anyone could remember what normal was and it's a wonder any of those people were still reasonably sane. They had been going through this same routine for over five years now; and from what I understand, it was much worse during the early days when the Germans were actually bombing the city virtually every night.

On this trip, George and I met these two very attractive young ladies. They told us when they got off work that afternoon, if we would like, they would show us things about London the average pilot never gets to see. That, of course, sounded very intriguing to George and me. That afternoon, we rented a suite in one of the nicer old hotels in downtown London; we just felt that you shouldn't be underprepared. Like any good Chamber of Commerce personnel, the young ladies showed up promptly at 6:00 p.m. We could tell they were very impressed with the accommodations. After we got to know one another and had exchanged valuable information about our ancestors, we all felt a little hungry and decided a nice meal was the next order of business, and the girls knew just the place. They decided to freshen up a bit. So being gentlemen, we let them use the powder room first. George and I talked about how informative the first part of the tour was and thought it would be a nice place to revisit. The girls finished and looked beautiful. George and I felt honored to be escorted by two such classy English ladies. It was my turn and George's in the bathroom. I was just about to turn on the water when I heard the front door close, and I thought for a minute about who would be coming in our room. So I stuck my head out the bathroom door, and the young ladies were gone—and so were our wallets.

George and I were stark-ass naked, and we tore out of the room and down the hall, negotiated the twentysome steps down to the lobby in about three big steps. When we reached the lobby, we spotted the girls just going out the front door; we shouted for them to stop. Seeing what was going on, the guard grabbed the two would-be thieves. We retrieved our wallets and made a hasty retreat to our room. We decided we were still hungry, so we made our way to a nice pub and had an excellent meal and a few drinks. While we were there, we met two more of London's finest. When they heard we had a room at this classy old hotel, they said they had always admired the exterior and had often wondered what it was like inside. Well, George and I being such civic-minded young men agreed to give them a tour. They truly admired the décor, especially the ceiling. We had a very enjoyable evening.

The next day, we took the train to Liverpool along the western coast of England and saw some very pretty country. We fell asleep on the train; we didn't get a lot of sleep the night before, so we slept right through Liverpool. But we woke up in time for Southport, which was a great, beautiful old town with a lot of structures that were five hundred to a thousand years old. If you were to just look at this old town, you could hardly detect that there was a war going on anyplace in the universe; we didn't see many young men, but there was an abundance of young ladies. The people were going about their business, I suspect, just like they had been for the last thousand years.

On August 29, we returned to base and found out that Lieutenant Duncan had been shot down over the Berlin airfield on the twenty-seventh. Dolan and Brown were also on the crew. The right wing was hit and threw the plane on its back; five parachutes were seen to open. It would be months or years before we knew if any of them survived. Hannahan and Everett, friends of ours, were also on the plane.

On August 31, we went to radar training School to learn all about radar at Snetterton Heath near Norwich with the ninety-sixth group and the 413th squadron. We were located right on the edge of Sherwood Forest. We found out Robin Hood had been drafted and sent to France.

little John, they said, was living in Dublin with his auntie, and the Merry Men. They were having a merry good time while all the men were off to war. I didn't blame them.

Therefore, we were back to the base on the ninth with lots of new information tucked away in our brains before we moved to Sudbury on the tenth. Sudbury was approximately ten miles northeast of Lavenham; We were going to Sudbury because they were short of leaders since they had lost the majority of their experienced pilots to lead the missions; we filled in several different times over the next couple weeks.

On September 11, we made a mission to the Magdeburg oil refinery. We had the honor of having Major Hammett ride with us on this mission; we took off at 6:15 a.m. with two squadrons from the 487th and one from the 486th. We went in at Heligoland island, and we came out through Belgium over Leigh. There were lots of small flak on the way in we thought maybe we were going to luck out, but the flak got much heavier over the target and near the rally point. They had smoked pots going full force, almost totally concealing the targets, so we had to bomb by checkpoints. The flak was low at first, but they improved their accuracy considerably by the time we got to the target. Our number 3 plane was hit in the number 1 engine, with lots of oil and smoke. Two other planes from the 486 didn't make it back; one landed in Brussels, and the other crew had to parachute, but they were fortunate enough to get into friendly territory. Lieutenant Houston had to drop out of our formation and joined another on the way home. They were hit by fighters; one of our gunners got one of the Me 109 German fighters. I was sick for the next two days.

Bright and early on the morning of September 13, we were alerted for a mission to Berlin. We received our briefing, had some breakfast, and then were on hold for four hours before the mission was finally scrubbed. I hated that—once I was ready to go, I wanted to go. There was definitely a change in our attitude in the last few weeks; at the beginning and for maybe the first dozen missions, it seemed to be exciting, and everybody was enthusiastic, and I actually hated to miss a mission. But recently, I noticed there was not near the laughter and joking around that went on a month ago. We tried not to think back about the planes, crews, and friends that we've lost; nobody would talk about it. I tried not to even think about it; when a new crew came in, nobody tended to want to get to know them. We just kind of kept to ourselves. Even the crap games weren't nearly as exciting as they used to be just thirty days ago.

We all seemed to be superstitious; we did certain things before or after every flight. When I returned from my third flight, one of the Red Cross ladies gave me a cup of coffee and a donut and said, "Good luck, Lieut!" Now I had a cup of coffee and a donut after every flight, and I added a donut for every mission. I was now up to fifteen donuts, one for every mission completed. That may seem a little strange, but I swear I was afraid to stop eating donuts. I couldn't wait till I had my thirtieth one. I also dressed exactly the same every day we flew a mission. I had a white scarf that some lady knitted for me. I've had it ever since. If someone took it away from me, I think I'd refuse to fly. There were other things too, like how you got in the airplane or what you did when you were in the airplane—just little things that seemed important in your mind. No one wanted to break that routine.

On September 17, we did a lot of test-hopping. We saw hundreds of gliders and C-47s. Evidently, there was a big push to run the Germans out of Holland, so they were sending in the paratroopers and the gliders behind enemy lines. I was hoping they would do a better job than they did on D-day. We were still trying to bomb the buzz bomb sites, but they were tough; we went over and bombed during the day, and they sent buzz bombs back to London every night. I didn't think the brass even know where some of the sites were located. As I said before, some of them were on trucks; and they just moved them from town to town or one patch of woods to another, we probably won't get them all until the boys on the ground totally occupied those areas.

On the nineteenth, our mission was to hit the refineries at Salisbury, just north of the Ruhr Valley, near the north coast of the Netherlands. We started to hit bad weather; we were just about sixty miles ahead of the front. We could see lightning and black clouds right on our tail. We went into Belgium past Liege, near Frankfurt. We hit a large storm front at IP and had to turn back. Major Avery was the command pilot, and Lieutenant Murphy was deputy lead. The whole Eighth Airborne was on the same course; there was lots of traffic at the turn.

Our formations got pretty well mixed up, but we were able to get reassembled again; our plans were to hit the marshaling yard at Limburg. But another group had already bombed it to smithereens; everything was burning, and it appeared there was nothing left to destroy, so Lieutenant Lindberg spotted a big cement bridge over the Rhine. Our bombs hit it square in the middle; and we could see chunks of concrete flying, big holes opening up on the bridge, and bombs being scattered all over the river and the edge of town. Some of our group hit Coblenz; the entire area saw lots of fire and smoke, and we also spotted some smoke at Frankfurt. We saw scattered flak too, but not bad.

They were firing rockets that day when we were over the target; so far, it didn't seem that they were very accurate. I hoped it stayed that way. When we were flying home over the Netherlands, we saw lots of gliders and C-47s headed toward enemy lines near Brussels. It seemed every day that we flew these missions into the middle of Germany, the Allied lines were steadily moving to the east.

The three-day pass started on September 20. I thought about going to Colchester. Colchester is an interesting old town; it is claimed to be the oldest settlement in England, once being the capital of the Roman Empire in England. It's also thought to be Camelot during King Arthur's time, with lots of old Roman buildings. It's a good place to go to get away from the war for a couple days.

On September 23, I got back from my three-day pass. While I was gone, Lieutenant Ross got hit over Frankfurt; with his plane on fire, two men jumped. Lieutenant Ross sideslipped the plane and was able to put out the fire; he was then able to land in Belgium in friendly territory. Three men were hurt, but not seriously. Lots of gliders went over the base that afternoon, all headed for the Netherlands, I suspected.

Chapter Five

On September 26, we were rousted out of bed bright and early in the morning. We were briefed, had some breakfast, and prepared for another sightseeing tour over Germany. That day, our mission was to hit the marshaling yards in Ludwigshafen; we bombed with Mickey (radar), which made a good run; there was plenty of flak about the time of bombs away. We made a sharp left turn directly across the heart of the city; we picked up a very strong tailwind as we made the turn, so we were not over the target or in the flak very long.

It was estimated that there were over two hundred guns in that area, and it seemed that every one of them was firing at us. With our tailwind, we estimated our ground speed to be over three hundred miles per hour. We were lucky that day. I don't believe we picked up any extra holes. We were flying over low clouds almost all the way back to the Netherlands, just a little ways from the coast. Four Me 410s came up through the overcast, went under our right wing, and made a pass at the low squadron. We had a whole covey of P-51s keeping an eye on us; as soon as those Me 410s saw the P-51s, they ducked back into the clouds, and that's the last we saw of them. We exited the area at Crux Haven. Heavenly Body was hit hard over the target; two engines were smoking, but they kept her in the air. The pilot probably thought he could limp back to England, but he had to ditch in the North Sea; all crew members were lost. It was a long day, with far too much excitement.

On September 27, we thought for sure, after that trip yesterday, that they'd give us a day or two off; but no such luck—we were going to be on the hot seat again that day.

They had us up at 1:45 a.m. We had our briefing at 3:00 a.m. and took off at 5:45 a.m. We were headed back to Ludwigshafen.

That day, we were supposed to hit a chemical plant on the Rhine River. Lieutenant Murphy was in the lead, with Todt as their leader. We were flying deputy lead with Captain Fuller as command pilot. We went into Belgium at Ostend and just north of Brussels; the overcast was 70 percent to 80 percent. We had to bomb with instruments; the overcast was just too heavy to see our target. Lieutenant Goldberg thought we dropped a little early; we had no way of knowing for sure. As we went in, the flak was well below us; at bombs away, we turned right and saw heavy flak at the altitude we had just been. That was a lucky break for us.

We got out pretty lucky. A couple other groups were ahead of us, and they got hit hard with heavy flak. A couple of wings were to bomb the marshaling yards again. The third division hit in that area, with lots of P-51 support. It was a very uneventful mission for us outside of the fact that we were very tired. The monkey turned up missing; everybody was looking for him, but no luck. The poor little guy lost his last best friend last week, maybe he decided to look for them?

The second division hit Kassel; just as they were approaching the target, they were hit by *150 fighters*. By the time the battle was over, *we lost 28 bombers*. I didn't hear the tally on how many men, but you know it had to be at least *250*. Hopefully, some would make it to the underground and get out. Once in a while, an airman would show up at the base, which was shot down several months before; he would look up some of his old friends, maybe hung around the officers' club for a few days, and give a couple of talks to the pilots about what it was like to work with the underground in Belgium and France; then they would send him back to the States for thirty days before he was reassigned to a new duty—it wouldn't be flying bombers into Germany.

On one such talk, I remember, the pilot was shot down over eastern France, not too far from the German border; it was late in the afternoon, which he felt worked to his advantage. It was dark before they could get a search party organized. As he was floating to the ground, he counted six other chutes scattered over about a square mile; and on the ground, there appeared to be German soldiers in all directions. He picked several areas he definitely didn't want to go, then kind of put a plan together—*if he survived the landing.* He said he dropped right in the middle of a barnyard with ten to fifteen dead cows; they were so bloated he felt for sure that if you touched one, it would explode. He decided not to even try to hide his chute and leave it right out in the open where they could find it; then he made tracks through the mud, going west toward the American front. Once he got into the trees, he changed direction completely and headed north; according to his map, there were several small towns eight to ten miles to his north. Hopefully, they were not occupied by the Germans, and perhaps he could find someone that would help him get back to the American lines.

After walking about two miles, he ran into a German column of perhaps one hundred soldiers; he could hear dogs, so he assumed they were searching for the rest of the downed airmen and himself. He knew that by daylight, the search would get very intense; the countryside was strewn with little farms fifteen to forty acres, a little barn, a few hogs and chickens, and a half a dozen head of cattle. He could sleep in the barn, but he was sure that would be the first place they would look for him; he was careful to stay out of the mud, where he would leave tracks. He eventually spotted a manure pile. With an old fork with a broken handle, he carefully made a small a hole in the back side next to the briar bushes he felt he could get into; he then pitched a little manure in the area where he had walked, hoping the odor from that would cover up his scent. He carefully rubbed cow dung on the handle of the fork for the same reason; he then crawled in the hole and commenced to completely cover himself up. Other than the odor, it was relatively comfortable. That night, it rained; the next day, he could hear tanks and trucks as well as talking and yelling until sometime in the middle of the afternoon. During that time they had visited the barn, he could hear the dogs and the handlers encouraging the dogs to try and find something; the dogs evidently didn't pick up any trace of his whereabouts, so they moved on. He chose to stay in the manure pile until after dark and actually got a little bit of sleep.

He waited until about ten o'clock, then slowly eased his way out of the barnyard onto an old country road that was headed northwest. By then, he was starving; several hours later, he arrived at one of the little villages. Now that he was there, he had no idea how to make contact with someone that could help him; there were no lights other than a few candles. The little town consisted of primarily one street, with shops and homes on either side; he was about halfway down the street when he heard a motorcycle approaching. He felt that it could only be a German, so he ducked in between two houses and hid behind an old barrel; he got a glimpse of the rider. He looked like a German messenger who was in a hurry to get somewhere; he moved back out into the street, still perplexed as to what he should do. Finally, that question was answered. Standing in the shadow was a middle-aged man who asked him in broken English if he was a pilot; they hid him in a little basement and never told anyone else in town that he was there. Two weeks later, on a rainy night, he was delivered to the American front. I've heard a half a dozen different stories about how pilots escaped, but I just thought this one was a little unique.

On September 28, Colonel Taylor ordered us to stand down for two days. With buzz bombs going over every night, we must be in buzz bomb alley. The 839th, our group, was the only squadron to fly that day; they went to Meersburg. They said it was the worst flak they had hit since Châteaudun. Lordi was shot down, as was Lawson. I had no idea if there were any survivors; we learned that day that we definitely had to fly thirty missions. We were in hopes that we would fall under the old regulations, where you only had to fly twenty-five missions; they changed that just about the time we got here. There were even rumors now that they were considering extending that to thirty-five missions, but we were assured that day that we didn't have to worry about that. Thirty missions was going to be our number. Shaklett and Kuhlmann signed for thirty to finish with us.

On September 30, Pendleton and Hall flew the mission. I stayed at the base. They reported no flak; but two planes ran together over the target, crashed, and burned.

There was definitely a spy, or spies, there on the base. Axis Sally, very much like Tokyo Rose in the Pacific, was on the airways every morning, talking about different things that happened here on the base that she would have absolutely no way of knowing if someone wasn't calling her virtually every day or two. This meant there had to be a radio transmitter somewhere close to the base. A couple days before, she said she was thankful that we had found the monkey, which we had! Just the day before, he was in one of the old wrecked bombers, sitting out in the field, four or five hundred yards from the barracks. How could she have known that?

On October 1, they had been working on our plane for the last couple days; we had to take it for a couple of test runs. This old plane had more patches than original metal. We got paid that day and went to Lavenham for the evening; there was talk that we should finish our thirtieth mission within about thirty days. We just hoped and prayed that we would get to finish that thirtieth mission.

On October 2, 1944, the mission was Kassel; we were to bomb the marshaling yards by PFF. There were five Ju 88s on the airfield. We were supposed to bomb the airfield in the clear while we made a run on PFF. Flak started just before bombs away a little below and behind us and to the right. They were getting our range just as we dropped our bombs; we turned left and made our exit. The formation wasn't in the flak for very long, which didn't hurt my feelings. We flew lead with Major Avery as their leader and with Lieutenant Hoell in deputy lead with Captain Harmon. We were first wing over the target, with the 486 in the lead, all third division, and part of the first hit Kassel. Ten wings in all bombed the city. A plane from the 486 blew up at the rendezvous point. Two planes ran together that morning; they crashed near Sudberry, and the bombs went off. There was not much left of either plane; they were from Rattlestone.

On October 7, our mission was the Luxendorf oil refineries; they were about four miles from Meersburg. We went in at Zierikzee which was to the right of Hannover, then southeast to the target. We were just approaching the target when one of the waist gunners yelled over the intercom, "Hey, Lieutenant! Look off to your left, ten o'clock!" Lo and behold, there were thirty or forty Me 109s and Focke-Wulf 190s mixing it up with a bunch of P-51s and P-47s, which was a rare treat; there was an intense dogfight to our left. As we were approaching the target, we saw several fighters going down in smoke; we couldn't tell if they were ours or the Germans. They were just a little too far away. We were just on the edge of the heavy flak, and some of the guys had to fly right through the middle of it; we had some, but not nearly as bad as it could've been. The sky was so black it reminded me of the pilot that told us, "Sometimes it gets so dark you have to turn on the landing lights." I think this was one of those days.

That day, Capt, Price led the flight with Major Eberhdart. There was lots of smoke over the target, not only from the flak, but the smoke pots. We left the area the same way we came in past Hannover and Zierikzee.(refered to as Zider-zee) I believe this was the flight. I had just returned to my seat when something almost lifted me out of the chair; a piece of flak hit the ceiling and landed right at my feet. I picked it up, and it burned a hole in my glove—it was so hot. I knew it had hit the back of my jacket someplace, but I wasn't going to take it off to check just now; it was about twenty below zero at twenty-seven thousand feet.

When I got back to the base, I found that piece of scrap metal had gone up inside my jacket and tore a hole in most of the lining and the collar and exited. It hit the roof and then bounced back by my feet; if that piece of flak had been six inches farther forward, we wouldn't be writing this story today. It was one of those moments you're not sure why you were spared, but you just thank the good Lord that he was watching over you.

On October 8, we all got prepared to fly the same mission; but at the last minute, it was scrubbed. There were lots of new guys on the base, some of them replacing crew that would have finished their thirtieth mission and some replacing crew that didn't get to finish their thirty missions.

A couple of the guys and myself decided to go check out the Swan; it had been a couple days since we were there. We just wanted to make sure everything was still intact; we had a couple of drinks. There was nothing important going on. I decided to write my name on the wall along with a lot of other guys that had done the same. I put my name next to another flyer named Chuck Yeager. Turns out, I chose some very exclusive company. At that time, Chuck was a fighter pilot, just another flyboy trying to live through his final mission.

On the ninth, they had us up early in the morning; we got our briefing out of the way and then grabbed some breakfast, and I picked up enough extra to make myself a sandwich.

Our mission that day was the Mainz rail yards; we had to bomb that day by PFF. We flew deputy lead to Lieutenant Hall, with Captain Schilling as command pilot. There were lots of planes in assembly line that day, the most I've seen since D-day. The second and third divisions went in at Flushing island past Antwerp while the first division went in at Ostend. The second division hit Koblenz, and the first hit Mannheim. Our target was the southwest side of town. The second was bombing on our left, and the first was bombing on our right. We had to bomb with Mickey (radar) through 100 percent overcast. I couldn't have told you if we were over the town or a river or a mountain as I couldn't see a thing. Lieutenant Goldberg thought we had good hits. We turned left and got out of the area as fast as we could.

The flak was very inaccurate while we were there; the groups behind us got lots of flak. It was reported that there were 190 guns at this town. I think they underestimated that there was flak for at least fifty miles before we even got to the target; there had to be more than 190 guns. The groups that went in ahead of us reported fighters on the way in; we didn't see any of them. We had lots of P-51s and P-47s protecting us—very easy mission.

October 10–12 saw bad weather, with lots of wind and zero visibility. I didn't even see any ducks flying those days. If I had known we were going to have this crappy weather, I would've taken a trip to London, visited the Rainbow Center, and maybe even ventured over into Piccadilly.

I remember the first time I ventured into a pub in that area; we were standing at the bar. I had just finished ordering our drink when a couple of girls came up to see how we were doing. One of them stuck her hand down the inside front of my uniform; that about scared me to death. But I was soon able to conquer my fears. I thought we had a couple of pretty aggressive girls back in Staples, Minnesota, in high school; but they were pussycats compared with these girls. Somebody said they were French. I wouldn't have a clue. I finished my drink, left that place, and headed for the Red Cross Rainbow Center. I guess this country boy wasn't quite ready for the prime time yet! But on my next trip to London, guess where we went. George and I made many trips to London, and these little English maidens were usually on our list.

On October 13, we were briefed for a mission to Cologne. I haven't been there yet, but I've heard the reception committee goes all out for you. I was really looking forward to this mission, but son of a gun if they didn't scrub it! Too bad.

Chapter Six

On October 14, well, I guess I was celebrating a little too early. It seemed like the brass had all at once decided Cologne would definitely be our next tour stop. I woke up at 4:00 a.m. The rain was beating down on the old tin roof like hail. I just knew the mission would be scrubbed, so I rolled over and decided I could use another couple hours of sleep. But before I could even get my eyes shut, this jackass came in the front door and informed us that we may be getting some fall showers here in England, but that all of Germany was basking in bright sunshine.

And the Germans were making ready for our arrival; we would probably be welcomed with an honorary twenty-one-gun salute. I thought you bet if we could get by with a 210-gun salute, we would probably be lucky. We hadn't been told yet; for sure, it was Cologne. I just had this gut feeling. If it was Cologne, it was going to be a rough ride; the 487th had already been there a couple of times, and we had lost a number of ships and men. But it didn't really matter much; there were very few easy targets. If it was worth bombing, it was worth defending.

We got to the briefing room at 5:00 a.m. sharp; the mission was delayed for one hour. It seemed we were going to have the benefit of one-hundred-plus-mile per hour jet stream at about thirty thousand feet, which meant we could get there a couple hours early and maybe catch them by surprise—fat chance of that happening.

We took off at 10:30 a.m.; our target was the ordinance depot, and if we had to go to radar, we were to hit the marshaling yards. Our primary mission target, the ordinance depot, was on the western edge of town; our secondary target, the marshaling yards, was near the center of town. We were leading the third division. Lieutenant Hall was in the lead, and our plane was deputy lead (second position). First division was over the target first, we were next, and the second division last. We went in at Ostend, then south to Achen, where we made our turn to the left and headed straight through the flak area to Cologne. A very strong jet stream tailwind took us through the flak area and over the target at about three hundred miles an hour. That helped a little, kind of like shooting mallards, which fly fifty miles per hour, compared with shooting teal, which can fly close to a hundred miles per hour. The sky reminded me of an August afternoon in western Minnesota—only it wasn't the buildup of thunderclouds. It was a thick black smoke from the exploding flak that surrounded the squadron; one of the planes on the outside of the formation had taken a hit and had to abort and head for home.

We were still a half an hour from the drop area; we had a shell that exploded so close that it just shook the whole plane. I thought for sure we were goners, but by some miraculous reason, we only picked up a few more holes and nothing serious. It was probably the most intense flak I had ever been in. I was not looking forward to getting up in that Plexiglas bubble in the front of the plane to make my bomb run, but that's what I was going to have to do in just a few minutes. I checked with the crew. So far, everybody was present and accounted for.

I sat down and reached for my half-eaten Spam sandwich. The next thing I knew, I was sprawled out on the deck, with excruciating pain on the left side of my face. My oxygen mask was kittywampus on the side of my face. I jerked off my mitten and put my hand up to the side of my face; the silk liner that we wore under our mittens was covered with blood. When I touched my cheek, I could feel something sharp; when I looked at my hand, it was covered with blood. Then my tongue found the piece of metal that was sticking through my cheek on the inside of my mouth; then I had this terrible metallic taste in my mouth. By then, I was spitting a considerable amount of blood.

Then I heard Lieutenant Balthazor ask, "Thompson! Thompson! Are you okay?"

I mumbled, "I think so," as I pulled my bloody hand away from my face. I couldn't feel anything; my face was numb. Then I turned to look at George, asking, "How bad does it look?"

"Shit, man! You have a chunk of steel sticking out the side of your face! Did it go all the way through your cheek?"

"Yes, I can feel it with my tongue."

"Did it get any of your teeth?"

"I don't think so."

"Can you fly this boat into the target?"

"Yes, sir, I think so. I know so. This pisses me off. Somebody is going to pay for this."

"Okay, Thompson, she's all yours. This is one of our last trips. Let's make it a good one."

With blood dripping off my chin, I made my way to the bombardier station, took the controls, brought the plane directly over the target, and pushed the button for bombs away. Blood was everywhere; it was dripping off my chin. I had to keep dumping the blood out of my oxygen mask; the whole front of my flight suit was bloody. The piece of flak that hit me had come through the fuselage from up front; luckily, it had spent the majority of its energy before it found me. After the drop, I made my way back to the controls, but I felt George was in better condition than I was to take the ship home. One of the problems I had on the way home was that piece of metal got very cold and was causing severe pain in the side of my face; one of the guys got me an old hand towel that I could put against the side of my face to ward off some of the cold.

As I remember it, we had a relatively easy run, all things considered for a Happy Valley mission. But it was not as easy a mission for some others, though; two planes ran together during their bomb run just ahead of us and crashed, and the group that came in behind us hit very heavy flak and got shot up pretty bad.

After fifteen or twenty minutes, the bleeding almost totally stopped; on our way home, the crew, of course, had to come forward and see how I was doing. Once they realized I was in no imminent danger, they all commented on how funny I looked and that I really should be a little more careful when I was shaving. But I got the last laugh on them because I got to spend a couple weeks in sick bay, and I got all kinds of attention. I didn't realize it at the time, but this would be my last flight with this crew. By the time I would get out of the sick bay, they would have finished their last mission and be on their way back to the States. It is something you just don't think about, but it is emotionally unsettling. Once we landed, the doctor and his group picked up myself and three other wounded personnel and took us to the hospital about ten miles north of the base.

I remember there was this tall blonde nurse. I think she must've been from Sweden; she said, "Ahu, Mr. Thompson, that's a good Swedish name." She assured me that if there was anything I needed, just ask her; later, when I thought about it, I wondered if that possibly meant something more than a glass of water. When I saw some of the other people that were there, I realized again that I had been very lucky. This was our twenty-seventh mission. While they were waiting to fill my position on the Sweet 17, they loaned the airplane out to another crew while their plane was being worked on, and they were shot down over Berlin. It was the end of the Sweet 17—a sad end for such a faithful old plane.

My crew got another airplane to finish their last three missions, which they did while I was in the hospital; no one was killed or hurt, which I was very thankful for.

Once I returned to duty, I was given a new airplane and flew with another crew like myself who had only a few more missions to complete to get the thirtieth.

On October 25, 1944, they released me from the hospital; for the next couple days, I just hung around the base while the captain tried to find me a crew to fly with so I could finish my last three missions. My crew from the Sweet 17 had finished their other three missions and had already been shipped out. I remember it was a very lonesome feeling. I really didn't know any of the new people and, honestly, didn't care to. It took the captain a couple of days to find me another plane; he eventually put me with a crew that, like myself, only had three more missions to fly. The skipper of that plane had been wounded four days earlier.

On October 27, we took several practice flights and went through some specific maneuvers just to get to know one another; the crew seemed to be just about like me, counting the days and missions until we could go home. I understand that while I was in the hospital, one of the planes from the 486 clipped the top of one of the farmhouses before daylight on an early-morning flight; all were killed, and there was a little boy sleeping upstairs in the farmhouse. I guess he was hurt but was expected to survive.

On October 28, we rolled out of bed at 4:20 a.m. I realize the one thing I enjoyed the most other than the big blonde nurse at the hospital was the fact that I didn't have to get out of bed at four o'clock in the morning; we had our briefing. Our target that day was the oil refineries at Hamm, Germany. We had already been there about a month ago, but they decided there were some parts of the refinery that were still in production. We were given all necessary information and told to get some breakfast; we would probably be rolling down the runway at about 9:00 a.m.

We did our slow easy circles in the sky for the next two and a half hours, then headed east to the coast of Belgium. The sky was clear, with slight winds—just about ideal conditions; we approached the target. I crawled into the plastic bubble up front, got positioned over the bombsight, and took control of the plane; we had a little different load that day. We had a half a dozen two-hundred-pound bombs and four big bundles of printed propaganda. These were what we would be dropping that day. There was quite a bit of flak, but inaccurate; most of it was below us. I zeroed in on the target, made minor adjustments, and bombs away.

As soon as the bundles of propaganda left the plane, they came apart in the strong winds; all those leaflets were floating all over the sky at thirty thousand feet. God only knows where they wound up; at that height and with a good strong wind, they could've made it all the way to Russia. We made our turn in the direction where there wasn't any flak, made a hasty retreat, and headed toward home. This had been one of the smoothest and easiest missions that I could remember. I just hoped the next two would be as uneventful. When we got back to the base, we were informed that we had hit a bull's-eye, and the bombers that had followed our lead did likewise. It appeared we almost totally annihilated that refinery; hopefully, they could put a big X over it and never have to go back there again. The brass upstairs evidently felt this was an exceptionally accurate drop, and I was awarded my first Distinguished Flying Cross.

On November 2 was mission number 29, whose destination was Meersburg. It was not a nice place, at least from our perspective. It was one of those places where we had to fly over flak for about a hundred miles just to get there and another hundred miles to get out. We were as high as we could get, about thirty thousand feet, but they could still reach us; they were just not nearly as accurate at that elevation, but they were still able to do considerable damage. Our target was the marshaling yards on the edge of town; again, we were pretty lucky that the weather wasn't bad. A few scattered clouds at the target, but the target was in the clear most of the time. I had lots of time to set up, find the target, and get all the knobs dialed in. We made a nice smooth run and dropped our bombs, but we still knew we were going to have a bumpy ride going home. We made our turn and headed back to England, but we still had a hundred miles of flak to fly over before we were in the clear. I really had a bad feeling about this mission. When I woke up that morning, I was in a cold sweat—something I wasn't used to. As a rule, I just get up, thinking, "One more day, one more mission." I think as you get closer to the final mission and after losing so many friends, you just can't believe you're going to be allowed to come out of this alive. But all my worrying was for nothing; we made it home in pretty good shape.

On November 6 was mission number 30—the one I've been waiting for! We rolled out of bed at 2:30 a.m. The briefing room was a strange place that morning. I didn't recognize one person other than our commanding officer and the ten guys I had flown with on the last two missions. The copilot and I decided when we got back that afternoon, we would go to London to celebrate the completion of our thirtieth mission. I never liked to make plans for after the mission until the mission was over, but we did. I always felt it was bad luck; we took off at 6:45 a.m. We spent the next couple of hours circling the northern part of the island, gaining altitude. By 9:00 a.m., we turned southeast and continued to climb as we headed for the Belgian coast.

I was messing with my new electric flight suit, trying to get it adjusted just right so I could be as comfortable as possible; we leveled off at twenty-seven thousand feet. Our destination that day was Ludvigharvin, Germany. We had been warned that the Nazis had moved more guns in around the target area; the target was the IG Farben chemical plant; this was one of Hitlers blue ribbon projects, this company was very involved in the rise to power of Hitler. We had not destroyed yet, and they intended to defend it with everything they could muster.

We were making our approach, with lots of aircraft everywhere. Lieutenant Mitchell had the controls as I made my way toward the bombsight; we had flak everywhere. It was ripping into the plane constantly. I glanced toward the back of the planes; as I got out of the pilot seat and made my way to the front of the plane and the bombardier station, I couldn't believe the amount of holes I saw in the airplane and their size—some were as big as my head. You could smell the burned powder and the hot metal; every time there was a close flash of an exploding shell, you instinctively ducked.

Hey Lieutenant, when I drop these bombs, you get us the hell out of here as fast as you can. But for God's sake, be careful of the other aircraft." Denny yelled! As he made his way to the bomb sit.

I had never seen anything like this in all my thirty missions; this was the worst by far. As I started toward the front of the plane, there was a flash and explosion just off to our right; the concussion knocked me to my knees as the plane rocked violently. I glanced to the back of the plane, afraid of what I would see. There were lots of holes, but I could see everyone was still standing. The flight engineer was working on some cables that had been severed; those cables were going to the rear stabilizer. He was splicing them like you would fix up the fence back on the farm, but it did the job; then I turned to go to the bombardier station up in the nose of the plane.

The flight engineer said, “Hey, Lieut, the inboard engine on the starboard side is smoking badly. I think we should shut it down before it catches fire.”

“Okay, Sergeant, I agree,” I replied.

I made my way to the nose and sat down. I had just started to look for the target when there was another ear-shattering explosion; black smoke enveloped the plane somewhere above us. Suddenly, my right arm bounced about a foot off the armrest, and I had pain—pain like I had never had before. My arm felt like there were a thousand sharp knives stabbing it. My first thought was, “My arm had been shot off!” I knew I had been hit. I could see several pieces of steel sticking out of my flight suit, and I could see the blood starting to ooze out of the suit. But I could still move my fingers; that was a relief.

“Thompson! You okay?” asked the sergeant.

“I think so. Damn this hurts!”

“You going to be able to run that contraption and drop the bombs?” he asked.

“I'm going to try, Sergeant. You make sure you keep this plane flying. We don't want to lose her on this last trip.”

The Swan Levenham England.

Denny At the Swan 2009

I got myself situated. I knew I was probably one of the best bombardiers in the Eighth Air Force; and by God, that day, I was determined to make them pay for my throbbing arm. At that point, something came over me. I wasn't worried about getting home. I guess I was tired, and I don't think I really cared. I got lined up on the chemical plant (a monstrous complex) and bombs away; and we banked to our left, made our turn, and leveled off. Every time I moved my arm or even just my fingers, the pain shot up through my shoulder and right up the back of my neck—it really hurt. I was just making my way back to the captain's seat when an 88 mm shell came up through the bottom of the plane about six feet in front of me, just behind the fuselage, and went out through the top of the plane. Thank God it never detonated!

The flight engineer was cussing; he had just spliced these cables, and the shell had just torn them apart again. I looked at the navigator; he was sitting at his little desk with his head in his hands, in total shock. The shell had missed him by only two feet. I checked to see if he was okay; he shook his head yes, but I could see he was just terrified. I grabbed him by the arm and told him he had to get us back home and to be careful that he didn't fall through that hole in the floor, which was only about three feet from where he was sitting. He looked at the blood dripping from my fingers and asked, "Lieutenant, are you hurt bad?"

"I don't know how bad I'm hurt, but I know that it hurts very bad."

After seeing my wounded arm, I guess he realized there were other people in the plane worse off than he was; he seemed to pull himself together and got back to work, charting our course back to England. The sergeant had commandeered one of the waist gunners to give him a hand repairing the broken cables; there was another horrific explosion just off to our left. The flash was blinding, and the smoke in the plane from the exploding shell was so thick that we could hardly see for a couple minutes. I thought for sure that was going to be the end of us. I checked in the back. There were more holes, but everybody seemed to be okay. The sergeant and the gunner were working as hard as they could to get those cables fixed so we could control the plane. I looked out the port side, and our outboard engine was spewing oil and starting to smoke like crazy.

"Hey, Lieutenant, feather that engine!" I yelled.

We were now on just two engines; we would start losing altitude and falling behind the rest of the squadron. There was another explosion just under us, and a couple more pieces of hot metal went ripping through the plane but somehow missed anything vital. I sat down but didn't mess with the controls; the lieutenant had everything under control. I just needed to think.

"Thompson, what do you think? Did we hit the target?"

"I think we creamed it. I think we creamed it George

I had good visibility and was dead on at bombs away, so if everybody else in the squadron followed my lead, there shouldn't be anything left.

"Hey, Sergeant, as soon as you guys get those cables fixed, I want you guys to jettison everything in this plane that we don't absolutely have to have."

There were a couple Mustangs just off our starboard; they could see we were in big trouble. One of them got as close as he could and gave us a thumbs-up, as if to say, Good job guys "You keep that baby flying, and we will keep Jerry from adding to your grief."

I told the engineer, "We have a couple Mustangs watching over us, so let's throw all the guns and ammunition out. Then let's take an ax to that gun turret in the belly and see if we can chop it out."

The crew went through the plane from one end to the other. The guns and ammo, of course, were the heaviest that we were able to get rid of; but there were other stuff, such as a few boxes of miscellaneous equipment and a few cases of parts. For the next two and a half hours, we fell farther behind until we eventually lost sight of the squadron, and we were losing altitude more rapidly than I had hoped.

We crossed the Belgian shoreline at about 1,200 feet. I was thinking perhaps we could make it to the English coastline, which was another eighty miles before we had to bail out. I looked down at all that water. I hated the thought of bailing out over the channel; that probably frightened me more than anything. Down at this elevation, the air was heavier, the plane flew better, and thank the good Lord we didn't have a headwind. My arm was throbbing, but at the moment, that was the least of my worries. A half hour later, we crossed the English coastline at about six hundred feet; we still had about sixty miles to go. We made a quick calculation and dumped a couple hundred pounds of fuel; we were down to four hundred feet. We would now have to try to land or crash-land if we couldn't make the runway; there was no bailing out at this elevation.

The lieutenant said, "Thompson, is that the little hill about two miles in front of the airport I see?

"Hell George I don't know we have never come in this low before" a minute later George yelled Thompson I see the airport-were going to make it.

For a moment, my arm didn't even hurt; those nine words were, without a doubt, the best news I had heard all day. One of the crew fired a flare.

I got myself strapped in so I could help with the landing. My arm hurt like hell, but I could still use it; we got the gear down. Thank God that worked; we just skimmed the grass at the end of the runway, but we were on the runway. What we didn't plan on was that one of our tires had been shot up and became flat. So as soon as the plane settled onto the ground, it pulled us right off the runway into the mud, but it stayed upright; we shut everything down. I looked around to make sure everyone was accounted for, and then we climbed out of the plane.

Lieutenant Thompson 1944, ready to leave for England

Visit to Normandy 2009

We had fired a rocket on our approach to indicate we had a wounded man aboard—*me*. The ambulance and the flight surgeon were there almost as soon as we were able to exit the plane. I could remember looking at that plane. I quickly counted over two hundred holes, and I hadn't even started; there had to be in excess of five or six hundred holes in that airplane. All I knew was they never tried to fix it up; they just scrapped it. And gave the crew a different plane.

The doctor said, "Not you again, Thompson," and handed me a bottle of whiskey. "Well, Thompson, I understand this was your thirtieth mission. And from the chatter I heard on the radio, it was a damn good one." Nothing left but burning rubble.

"That's right, Doc, and my last—and I'm damn glad of that."

The hospital was about ten miles away; it served about ten different bases in that area. It also had a bunch of army personnel who had been wounded in France and Germany during and after the invasion. I remember there was a bunch of guys who liked to call themselves tank jockeys; a lot of them were there for frostbite and frozen fingers and toes.

Ceremony at the Coleville cemetery Ohama Beach Denny the only WWII vet in the line up 6-6-1999

Denny and an actor from the Movie 12 o'clock High on the old Control tower at the Lavenham Base the movie was about the 487th bomber group, (Denny's group)

Denny Pete Kerns a friend and Pat also an actor in 12 o'clock high

I could feel every bump in that road my arm was killing me. By the time we reached the hospital, I had consumed a considerable amount of my bottle of whiskey, with just a little help from the doctor. When we got to the hospital, the doctor asked me, "Can you walk in, or would you like to be wheeled in?"

"Doc, you'd better wheel me in." This was not because of my wound, but I think I drank too much of that whiskey. I hadn't had anything to eat since very early that morning, and that alcohol was having a more-than-normal affect. My arm wasn't hurting as badly, but my head and stomach were rapidly deteriorating.

"Doc, you think I could have something to eat?"

"Not just yet, Thompson. When we start taking that scrap metal out of your arm, it's liable to make you sick to your stomach. I'll make sure you get a first-class meal, reserved only for our special guests here at the Prima Donna Hilton."

As the doctor left, a couple of nurses started to get me ready for the operation; they were preparing to take their scissors and cut the sleeve of my flight suit so they could remove it off my arm without irritating the wounds. A couple of the pieces of metal were still protruding through the uniform.

I protested adamantly. "This is my brand-new electrically heated flying suit, and you're not going to cut it all up!"

Just about that time, a familiar voice said, "Ah, Mr. Thompson, do you remember me? This is Olga."

"Yes, ma'am, I sure do. Are you going to operate on me?" I asked. by now I'm completely shit face, totally numb.

"Not really, but I will help." Then she handed me a handful of crackers. "You better eat these before the doctor gets back, or he'll take them away from you."

Lieutenant Thompson 1944 Lavenham England ready for take off.

Lieutenant Thompson 2009 Normandy France

They then started to work the sleeve off my arm; by the time that little process was completed, I was seriously wondering what it really would have hurt to just let them cut it off, but they had done a good job preserving my suit.

The doctor returned; and for the next three hours, they dug and probed at my arm, eventually removing ten pieces of shrapnel. By this time, the alcohol had worn off, and my arm was throbbing and hurting so badly. I couldn't even appreciate all the attention I was getting from Olga and the rest of the crew. I did manage to eat something after the operation was complete. I had no idea what it was; they then gave me something that knocked me out for about twenty-four hours. It took me a couple of days before that arm quit throbbing, and I even felt like talking, and anybody who knew me knew that was unusual.

When I started to feel better, I got up and moved around. I realized there were still a lot of men in the hospital who had been there during my first stay, a lot of them guys whom I had gotten to know on my last visit. Some of them were missing arms and legs, with the majority of them in much worse shape than I was; almost all of them to a man complained about the inadequate clothing they had for fighting in winter conditions, and real winter had not yet set in. My recovery went well; the third or fourth day I was in the hospital, the captain came by to inform me that I had been awarded my *second* Distinguished Flying Cross for what they considered an exceptional mission under very difficult conditions.

I didn't know it at the time, but the crew and the squadron commander had recommended me for the Silver Star. But Major Partridge in Doolittle's office turned it down, claiming they had given out more Silver Stars than normal recently and he had to be a little more conservative. My recovery went well without complications; one serious setback was when the doctor informed me that Olga was married to one of the base MPs. Other than that, I found out later they had missed one piece of shrapnel in my wrist. I still have it there today, but it doesn't bother me. *I just consider it a souvenir from a time in my life that I'm very proud of.*

It took about eleven days before they turned me loose. During my first evening back at the base, my commanding officer invited me over to the officers' club; he wanted to talk with me.

We sat down at the table and had a couple of drinks; he asked me about some of the missions and how I felt about things in general: the planes, the equipment, etc. I gave him my opinion; then he offered to promote me to captain if I would stay on for several more months instead of being sent home and reassigned. He told me that we were the most efficient and accurate bomber group in the entire Eighth Air Force to date. I was told later that we remained the most accurate and efficient through the duration of the war, something I'm very proud of since I led most of those missions.

I asked the commander if I would have to fly any more missions; he felt most of my time would be spent training, but I would still have to fly an occasional mission. It was tempting, but I really didn't want to ever get in another one of those bombers and make a trip over enemy territory; the risk was just way too high. The Eighth Air Force had a higher percentage of casualties than any other branch of the service during the Second World War, be it the army, navy, or marines. I felt I was one of the lucky ones and that I should get out while I was still in one piece. So I turned it down.

I made up my mind; one of my first missions was to try to commandeer some warm clothes for some of these tank jockeys. I knew we had dozens of the old sheepskin flying suits we had traded in for our new heated flying suits; they were just sitting in a warehouse on the base. I talked to the base commander and eventually got close to one hundred of the sheepskin suits turned over to the guys going back to duty in their tanks; with those suits, there was also a number of wool-lined boots, which they seemed to appreciate as much as they did the suits.

I hung around the base for about two weeks, gave several talks to some of the new crews, went to the Swan for one last visit or two, then was shipped up to Prestwick, Scotland, to wait for a ship to take us home.

I remember we were at a barracks in the middle of a hot crap game with about a dozen other guys, all waiting to be shipped home, when a young captain came in and announced that if there was anyone there with two Purple Hearts, they would get to fly home in an air transport instead of having to go by boat. I grabbed my money and my bag, and I followed the captain.

The plane was a C-54, and it took about sixteen hours before we reached New York City. There were no seats, just benches along the side of the airplane; they were made of wood, but it was still much better than taking a boat, which would've taken us about ten days.

We flew right by the Statue of Liberty and past the Empire State Building, and we landed in Washington DC; there was a brass band to greet us, and there were a couple dozen fighter pilot heroes on our flight. Like myself, some of them were wounded and had casts on their arms or legs. We were all treated like royalty. I stayed in the Washington area for a couple of days and then was put on a train to travel back to Minnesota; the accommodations on the train were first class. I had a sleeper and a ticket to the diner car.

I arrived at Staples, where I was greeted by my parents and Jean Lee, the young lady who had been kind enough to write me a number of much-appreciated letters during the last couple years.

After about two weeks, I was sent to California to a rest camp, where I spent the next couple of months; then I was shipped back to Texas. Once I got to Texas, I was given thirty days' leave. I caught the train and went back to Staples, Minnesota, where Jean and I were married. I bought a 1939 Plymouth, which we used to drive back to Texas.

I was a flight instructor for the duration of the war. The war finally ended; the whole country, I believe, celebrated for at least two to three days before the country got back to some kind of normality.

All at once, the war was over; what had been such a major part of our lives for the few previous years all at once no longer existed. One day, I received notice that I was being discharged; within three days, I was gone—no celebration, no fanfare. It was just over with, and it was time to move on.

Jean and I settled in Staples, and I went back to trapping and working for the railroad.

A couple years later, I tried to reenlist in the air force, but there were so many young men like myself that couldn't find work and were trying to reenlist. The waiting list was six to eight months long, and there was no guarantee. New plans for a new time.

After a number of years, I learned that a number of the old Eighth Air Force groups were getting together for reunions. I attended my first reunion at Boeing Field in Seattle, Washington, in 1980 and have attended numerous gatherings since then.

I started attending D-day celebrations on its fiftieth anniversary in France in 1994 and have attended one every five years since that time, the last one being in 2014.

Footnote: I'm enclosing several pictures and articles relative to this portion of the story. Denny Thompson has been recognized as one of the most highly decorated pilots in the Eighth Air Force, with *thirteen medals*. Further, it's been claimed by more than one individual that because of Denny's ability as a pilot and bombardier, he probably killed and wounded more enemy combatants than any other single person in the war. But like Denny says, it wasn't just him—it took nine other men to get to and from the target and, more than once, a little help from the man upstairs!

There is also a website you might like to look at: <penwa69@yahoo.com>.

Denny, and Jean, Denny jr. and Jerry Martin,
Denny's brother in law Jerry's birthday

Jean & Jerry Martin (Denny's sister) and Denny Thompson in Minnesota just before they left for Alaska ten days later they pulled into Anchorage, tired and dirty but full of enthusiasm. Denny bought the jeep for $400.00 army surplus brand new.

Chapter Sevens

The war had ended. Denny and Jean had returned to Staples. Denny was restless, but he didn't let it bother him. However, he just felt there was something missing, which is quite understandable when you consider that for the last four years, he has been in the most intense drama to ever engulf the world.

Most of us can't even imagine what it had to be like to live on the brink of death and destruction for months on end. And now here he was with a beautiful new wife in a sleepy little Midwest town, where the most exciting thing to be talked about over coffee in the little local restaurant at the corner was the rumor about the basketball coach possibly having an affair with one of the cheerleaders.

Denny was well aware of his obligations and never for a moment thought about neglecting them, but his flair for adventure and challenges was always present; sleeping just under the surface. Denny felt there was something missing but didn't spend a lot of time worrying about it.

That fall, Denny and his father took a trip to South Dakota to do some pheasant hunting; in those days, the daily limit per person was twenty roosters each, with the possession limit of sixty birds per person. In three days, he and his father returned home with a total of 120 pheasants; to this day, when Denny talks about that hunt, you can tell it rates right up there at the top.

Denny thought a lot about what he wanted to do; of course, the first option was to go back to work for the railroad at $160 a month.

In the service, Denny had been making $400 a month; to Denny, that definitely appeared to be a step backward.

Denny checked out the fur prices and found them to be quite favorable as fall and early winter set in. Denny retrieved his traps from his father's garage and decided to see what he could catch. Within several days, it was obvious no one had trapped his old area since he had left about four years ago, and there was an abundance of game; the first week, he caught 14 minks, 250 muskrats, 6 foxes, etc. The minks alone were bringing on an average $40 a pelt. Denny made more money that first week than he could make in six months working on the railroad. That winter, Denny went on to catch over 150 minks, 1,000 muskrats, some 60 foxes; beaver, bobcat, and even a skunk hide brought a couple of dollars. Denny made more money in four months of trapping than the president of the bank made the entire year.

Denny and Jean enjoyed their summer of 1946. Denny spent some time looking for new trapping areas for the coming fall and did quite a bit of fishing on some of Minnesota's many lakes. When the trapping season 1946–1947 was over with, Denny had done very well; but unlike the first year, there were more people trapping than before, partly because word had gotten out of Denny's success the previous year. Denny could see it was not going to be as good in the future.

Jean was due to have a baby in early spring, and that was one more responsibility that Denny had to think about.

The desire for adventure was still gnawing at his subconscious; the trapping had been a good antidote, but now that seemed to be less of an adventure and just plain old hard work.

Denny decided to reenlist in the air force. However, when he made the attempt to do that, he was told it would be at least six months before they could consider him because there were so many ex-military that were trying to reenlist.

Denny decided whatever future he had wasn't there in Staples, Minnesota; there was no doubt in his mind that he could find work.

But the age-old desire to climb the hill just to see what was on the other side was starting to stir within Denny's subconscious again.

In the 1930s, several families from Staples had moved to Seward, Alaska. Since then, approximately sixty people in total had resettled in the Seward, Alaska area. Friends and relatives left behind in Staples kept getting these reports of deer, moose, bear, and fish that wouldn't fit in the boat; to Denny, that sounded like a place he would like to go. Plus the reports also mentioned that there were good-paying jobs.

He talked it over with his brother-in-law Jim who had been a sergeant in the army and was having the same problem of trying to find a good-paying job. After conferring with their young wives, they decided to make the trip and check it out in person.

Chapter Eight

Denny bought an army-surplus jeep and a trailer. Denny, his sister, Jean and brother-in-law Jim put their worldly possessions in that trailer and struck out for the Alaskan territory, over four thousand miles to the northwest. Jean Denny's wife could not make the trip at this time because of the new baby, so she stayed behind with the promise that Denny would either come back to get her or would come back to Staples and find something else to do.

The trip across the civilized part of southern Canada was tough enough, and the Alcan Highway across British Columbia and Alaska was an adventure all of its own; the highway was brand-new and had been built by the U.S. Army during the war—no asphalt, just gravel and mud and an abundance of chuckholes.

For lack of facilities and to save money, they primarily camped at night along the road, usually got four to six hours of sleep, and were on the road again before the sun came up; by the way, the Alcan Highway stayed pretty much the same until the 1980s, when it was finally paved.

The old trailer had wooden spokes, and due to the constant beating from the chuckholes and the dry weather, the spokes started to give out; a couple hundred miles west of Big Delta, Alaska, Denny and his brother-in-law took the spare tire off the jeep and drilled new holes in the rim so it would fit the trailer and limped on into Anchorage ten days after they left Staples. The trip that day would be hard to imagine, especially if you've ever ridden in the early 1940s army jeep. One can't even imagine what four thousand miles would've been like. But Denny said it really wasn't that bad; just about every night, they stopped along a lake or river. He said in half an hour, they could catch more trout and grayling than they could possibly eat; there were moose, bear, caribou, mountain goats, wolves—just about any type of wild creature you could imagine. They saw them every day on the Alcan Highway.

The weather was very cooperative from Minnesota all the way to Fairbanks; there was very little rain, which meant the gravel roads were very dusty. The dust at times boiled up through the floorboards in the jeep, coating everyone aboard with a thin film of lime dust. This meant everyone aboard usually took a dip in the creek or the lake that night when they stopped. As young people during that period of time, they seemed to be capable of making the best out of whatever the situation presented, and that's exactly what these three young travelers did.

In 1947, Fairbanks was a very small town. Denny said they reached Fairbanks about lunchtime; they spotted a restaurant along the road and decided to treat themselves to moose burger and a fresh cup of coffee. He said when they got the bill, they about fainted—their first lesson in the cost of living in Alaska.

Shortly after they left Fairbanks, it started to rain, and it rained all the way to Anchorage, a couple hundred miles. Denny said by the time they reached Anchorage, there had to be six to eight inches of mud on the tarp of the trailer. Jim and Jean decided to stay in Anchorage with some friends for a week or two. So Denny left the trailer with them, loaded a few of his things in the jeep, and headed for Seward.

Now, mind you, this does not sound like a big endeavor; but in 1947, there was no road between Seward and Anchorage. He had to drive to the pier and hire a scow to take him to the other side of the bay, where there was an old dirt road that led to Seward. The scow couldn't get all the way to the shoreline; when he drove off the ramp of the boat, he still had about fifty feet of mud before he was in the clear. Believe me, it was nip and tuck, but he finally churned his way through the mud to dry land.

The road to Seward was little more than a trail through the woods, about eighty miles; through beautiful timber, every turn in the road presented the opportunity to see another moose or bear. Denny said he had traveled about halfway. He came bouncing around the corner and slammed on the brakes; his first thought was somebody had parked a locomotive across the road. He blinked his eyes a couple times to get everything in focus and discovered it was not a locomotive at all, but the biggest animal he had ever seen, other than an elephant at the county fair. Standing in front of him was a full-grown bull moose, probably somewhere between 1,400 and 1,600 pounds. They sat there for quite some time, just staring at each other; the moose did not seem the least bit concerned and eventually just disappeared into the woods.

Denny was convinced this was his kind of country. He arrived at Seward about midafternoon; he had the names of a couple of people from Staples who had moved to Seward sometime during the war; what was once a busy, bustling military town was now about a quarter the size it was during the war. The army had basically just walked off and abandoned everything. There was a set of military barracks and living quarters in the middle of town.

Chapter Nine

Denny wasted no time; the next day, he rented a unit for $50 a month. By that afternoon, he was hired as a winch operator on the docks. Every place Denny looked, he could see opportunity; there were old military buildings that could be purchased for next to nothing. He had arrived just in time for the salmon run; when he wasn't working at the dock, he would get a day job working on one of the fishing boats. It only took a couple of trips, and Denny realized he would have his own boat the next year. He said he believed there were about six bars and taverns for every church in town. He couldn't ever remember going to the bar to have a couple of drinks and that there wasn't a brawl; most of the time, it was settled by the loser being dragged out in the middle of the street and abandoned while the rest of the crowd laughed about what a poor fighter he was.

It took Denny almost the entire summer to get used to all the daylight. In June and July, the sun never set until about eleven o'clock at night. He seemed to always find plenty to do as long as there was daylight. Denny could see all kinds of opportunities and things he could do to make money, but as the summer wore on and the Aspen traded in their emerald green leaves for their beautiful golden capes, Denny decided it was time to bring his beautiful young wife and son to the Alaskan territory. Jim and Jean Martin had stayed in Anchorage for only a couple weeks, and then they made their way to Seward; like Denny, they rented one of the old military barracks and were next-door neighbors to Mr. and Mrs. Thompson.

Denny didn't spend his entire summer working; the long days and short nights gave him ample opportunity to explore the Kenai Peninsula. There were few logging roads and some roads the military had put in, but the majority of the peninsula hadn't seen much change in the last thousand years. Moose and bear were abundant, and fishing around the peninsula was beyond comparison; at that time, you could catch two-hundred-pound halibut right off the pier. And every summer, when the salmon spawned, they were so thick in the inlets and streams; the water just boiled.

He had his old .30-30 he had brought with him from Minnesota; when the middle of September came and moose season opened, he was ready.

Denny had done enough exploring and had seen a number of bull moose in different areas; he had studied the animals enough to know he wanted to shoot his moose very close to one of the old roads where he could skin it, cut it up, and load in the jeep without having to lug the meat through two miles of timber. Denny had received an abundant amount of advice on where to go and what to do. He was getting pretty good at sorting out good information and advice from just plain old bullshit. And it became apparent that the latter of the two was much more abundant, leading him to the conclusion that his intuition and common sense in most cases would serve him well.

The season had been open for a couple of days; before Denny got a day where he could get off early enough in the afternoon to go hunting, several people had already shot their moose and were telling the gruesome stories about packing it out of the woods to a point where they could pick it up with a truck. Denny was hoping Jim could go with him, but he had to work another shift. Denny picked up his .30-30 and a box of shells, had the wherewithal to throw in a couple lengths of rope, and headed up the mountain out of Seward to the west; there was a little valley about six to eight miles out of town where Denny had seen several nice moose and lots of tracks. He parked the jeep about a half a mile from where he intended to hunt; he stuck a half a dozen shells in his rifle and a couple more in his pocket and walked slowly down the old road.

Denny hadn't traveled more than a couple hundred yards when he thought he heard something in the brush, not very far off the road; he froze in his tracks, anticipating the appearance of a magnificent monarch, strolling into the road maybe a hundred feet in front of him. Bang! There would be his moose; all he had to do was back the jeep up to it, skin it, cut it up, and throw it in the back of the vehicle. All at once, the noise stopped; there was not a sound. Denny never moved, but his heart was thumping. He was sure whatever it was could probably hear it; after a couple of minutes, he decided to take a couple steps; the ground was damp, covered with pine needles. He very quietly walked, not moving more than thirty feet. Then he heard a racket in the brush not more than fifty feet to his left, as they would say in the military, at about ten o'clock.

All at once, busting out of the brush were two half-grown black bear cubs and their mama; she spotted Denny immediately, stood up on her back feet, and let out a big growl the cubs disappeared into the brush on the other side of the road so fast he never even saw them go. The mama stood there on guard till she was sure they were out of harm's way; then she dropped to all fours and took a couple leisurely steps toward the other side of the road, as if to say, "Don't screw with me, buster, or I'll have you for lunch," never for an instant taking her eyes off Denny. Once she reached the cover of the trees and brush, she made haste; and he could hear her and the cubs crashing down the hill, putting as much distance as possible between her family and Denny. A nice black bear was on his list of animals to hunt, but he didn't want to shoot an old sow with a couple cubs.

Denny stayed put for ten to fifteen minutes to kind of let things quiet down, then slowly continued down the trail to where he hoped he would find a big old bull moose standing right in the middle of the road; as he neared the bottom of the hill, he could hear something off to his right. It sounded like somebody splashing in the water; after the bear incident, he was just a little bit more cautious. Denny moved forward another hundred feet; whatever was making the noise was not very far off the road. There was a little creek that crossed the road, and the noise was coming from an area no more than fifty to seventy-five feet below the road; curiosity finally prevailed, and Denny decided to try to get close enough to see what was making the noise. As quietly as he could, Denny moved through the trees and brush; very slowly and quietly, he worked his way around a little cluster of fir trees.

Not seventy-five feet in front of him, he could see the antlers and the upper body of a big bull moose. Denny moved a couple of different ways but could not get a good clear heart shot. He decided he was close enough to take a head shot; the explosion of the .30-30 echoed across the mountain. Several grouse were startled and took flight; the next sound he heard was a gigantic splash, which wasn't at all what he wanted to hear. After fighting his way through the brush and fir trees, there lay his first bull moose in about two feet of water—not at all like he had planned it.

Denny concluded the first order of business was to remove this rather large member of the deer species from this oversized mud puddle. He felt the best solution would be to get the jeep and pull the moose out of the mud so he could at least gut the animal; that would make him manageable. He was almost to the jeep when he realized he had left his rifle leaning against a tree. Denny just hoped if there was a papa bear in the area, he would keep his distance. Denny had an ax with him; he hacked a little trail down to the moose, tied the rope around the antlers, and hooked the rope to the rear bumper, which took a strain on the rope. The tires spun, but Mr. Moose never moved; this was getting to be a bigger challenge than Denny had planned; one of the guys at the dock had given Denny a White Owl cigar. He decided this was as good a time as any to light up and review his options. He walked back down to the moose and stood there for a moment, looking at this large animal. All at once, the light went on. He didn't need this whole beast—only the quarters, back straps, head, and horn.

Two and a half hours later, Denny was headed back to town with about seven hundred to eight hundred pounds of choice Alaska moose meat. Over the next couple months, he would get another nice big moose and a respectable black bear.

Chapter Ten

Denny left Seward right after Thanksgiving; his destination was Staples, Minnesota, to pick up his wife and baby. He caught an Alaskan airline to Minneapolis and spent several days visiting friends and relatives, and they were on their way to the wild and woolly Alaskan territory. Denny said he remembered quite distinctly the trip back to Alaska: "The first leg of our trip was from Minneapolis to Chicago, where we transferred to an Alaskan airline, which wasn't much more than a cargo plane, a DC-4. It didn't have seats as we know them today. We just sat along either side of the airplane side by side. The plane wasn't pressurized, so they could only fly at about twelve thousand feet. I remember it was bitterly cold in the airplane and extremely rough flying through the mountains." They made one stop in Canada to refuel and then continued on to Anchorage, the entire trip taking almost twenty hours.

From Anchorage, they caught a train to Seward. The trip was normally quite scenic;, but this particular day was your typical midwinter. It was foggy, cold, and gloomy—not a sightseeing kind of day.

A good portion of Seward was the old Fort Raymond military base, which had been constructed during the early stages of the war; in 1945, after the war, the military just picked up all their guns and ammo and left everything intact just the way it was.

Denny, Jean, and the baby spent the rest of that winter in the old military barracks. Denny said there were nights when he thought for sure they would freeze to death; he had no idea how many cords of wood he must've burned that winter.

He worked every minute he could; he had already decided he wanted a fishing boat for next year's salmon run, and he had also decided he wanted to buy an airplane. But the first thing on his agenda was to build a house where the three of them could live in reasonable comfort.

Denny bought a lot not too far from the barracks and was able to scavenger enough lumber to build a nice little two-bedroom home. Along with building the home and his job on the docks, he felt with the long days and lots of daylight, he still had plenty of time to pursue his desire to become a commercial fisherman. He found a surplus military boat, which he was able to buy at quite a reasonable price. At that time, it was not legal to have a motor on your fishing boat; you had to either use sails or row.

Denny and Jim fished every spare minute that first year in 1948 and did quite well for beginners. Other than a lot of hard work, 1948 became quite routine for Denny; he learned how to juggle three or four projects and had them all going on at one time, and that became a way of life for Mr. Thompson. I have to say, even today at ninety-two years old, if he doesn't have two or three different things going on, he becomes very bored.

Denny did remember one particular halibut they caught that summer that turned out to be quite an adventure; he said they were fishing about a mile east of Seward. They were fishing around a little rock island that stuck out of the water thirty to fifty feet and was covered with bird droppings and seals; they were fishing in about 150 feet of water when one of the poles started to bend. They were riding an incoming tide, and he thought they had just snagged a rock. Denny grabbed the pole and released the brake so they wouldn't break the line. It was when he jerked on the line to see if he could break it loose that he realized it was not a snag; there was definitely something on the other end of that line, which had other ideas than to come to the surface, be bashed in the head, and be eaten for dinner.

The fish headed for deeper water, towing the boat and two unwilling passengers; the fish ran at least a half a mile before it tired and had to stop and catch its breath. At that point, I was able to take in some line; but the fish resisted and took off on another run, this one much shorter. Each time the fish made one of these runs, he was pulling them farther and farther away from the docks and the little town of Seward; this routine lasted for over three hours before they got their first glimpse of what they had at the other end of the line. As they suspected, it was a giant halibut, which easily outweighed either one of the men in the boat.

Before Jim could get a gaff in the fish, it decided to escape once more. The fish dove and made a couple more short runs before it finally surrendered and allowed itself to be pulled over to the edge of the boat. That's when the real fun started; it took every ounce of strength the two men could muster to hoist this fish into the boat. Once the fish was in the boat, it started to flop violently, trying desperately to get back into the water; the sides of the boat were way too high for the fish to accomplish that feat, but during the process, the fish broke a couple of the seats in the boat and knocked two more of them over the side into the water. Denny and Jim had to be careful that they didn't get hit with its lethal tail, and they somehow had to kill this fish before it knocked a hole in the bottom of the boat; by the time they were able render this beast unconscious, they were both exhausted. By this time, it was nearly ten o'clock at night, and they had approximately a mile and a half to row back to town. It was after midnight before they got this monster hoisted up on the pier. When they picked up their check the next day for their two-hundred-pound-plus halibut, the hard work associated with getting that fish back to town didn't seem quite as bad.

Chapter Eleven

The year 1949 was kind of a turning point for Denny; the military had decided to sell one of their outposts that was part of the Fort Raymond complex, but it was on a small island about seven miles northeast of Seward. Denny put in a bid for $1,600 and won the contract; this included thousands of feet of buildings: some of them three stories tall, oil storage tanks, barracks, and numerous other types of buildings. His idea was to dismantle and sell the lumber to a rapidly growing market in that area. The new highway between Seward and Anchorage was just being finished in 1949, which would open this entire area up by allowing much easier access to Anchorage than before.

Denny said he remembers this was the hardest work he thinks he'd ever done in his entire life; they salvaged hundreds of doors and windows, and he bought a small tugboat and a barge and would hire some guys from Seward to help dismantle the structures. They would load the material on the barge, and Denny towed them back to Seward; some of that he used himself to build several buildings, including an apartment building, but most of it he sold. All of this was going on while he was still holding a job at the docks running winches.

Denny said when they started dismantling the buildings, it was extremely hard to pull the nails so they could salvage the lumber. So he came up with the idea of setting off a small explosion inside the building, which he felt would loosen up the nails. Sure enough, he was right; a couple of sticks of dynamite hanging from the rafter in the middle of the room would create enough concussion to loosen the nails adequately to allow the men to get a hammer or a bar behind the head of the nail and pull it out without ruining the lumber. He said they would light the fuse and then run for cover.

One time, he remembers, they decided that if a couple sticks would do a pretty good job, why not use four sticks and that might even work better; he said that when the smoke cleared from that explosion, the whole end of the building was lying on the ground. The roof had collapsed, and they were afraid to go inside the building. Denny said he decided double was too much, and they stuck with their original plan.

Denny said he sold a lot of the lumber to different areas in the inlet and even some over in the Anchorage area—definitely a lucrative business, but with an extraordinary amount of hard work.

He continued to work on this project into the summer of 1950, but other adventures were tugging at his subconscious. Denny said when he finally discontinued any activities at the old fort, he had perhaps dismantled only 10 percent of the overall complex, and what he left is basically still there today.

In 1950, Denny bought his first airplane: a Taylorcraft. It was a little two-passenger airplane, with not much power and didn't handle very well. But it did allow Denny to explore many areas on the peninsula and the surrounding areas there was no other way to get to other than by air.

Chapter Twelve

In 1951, Denny bought a Piper PA-11 Cub; at that time, it was the prerunner to the Super Cub, which later became so popular all over Alaska. The PA-11 was a 90 hp plane; eventually, there would be the PA-18 Super Cub, which had 150 hp.

In 1951, Denny got his first real taste of big-game hunting; he and three buddies of his from Seward, with two planes, flew down the Alaskan Peninsula, about two hundred miles southwest of Kodiak Island, and hunted brown bear.

J. Hammon, a friend of Denny's who was a former game warden and who later in his career served eight years as governor of Alaska, told Denny about an area about two hundred miles south of Kodiak that had lots of brown bear and some real monsters—if you were lucky enough to find one. That was good enough for Denny, so that was the destination of the first brown bear hunt he ever participated in.

The four men were ready to leave shortly after daylight, but it was foggy, and they couldn't see more than a couple hundred feet; they checked and double-checked their gear and had a couple more cups of coffee. Finally, at 9:00 a.m., they could see a couple patches of blue sky and decided that it was a good time to go. They climbed out to three thousand feet and headed southwest; by then, the sky was bright blue with scattered clouds. Their first stop was Kodiak; they topped off the fuel tanks, then continued down the peninsula. Their location was just north of the Pavlof Volcano at Bear Lake; this was a good-sized lake they could land on and, from there, hunt in just about any direction they chose.

When they left Kodiak, they flew due west across the Shelikof Strait; once they hit the mainland, they turned almost due south. They hadn't traveled more than ten miles when they started seeing moose and a few bears; they dropped down to about five hundred feet in elevation so they could get a better look. They basically flew around the hills and mountains and down the valleys, and before they knew it, they spotted a couple of landmarks that Mr. Hammon had told Denny to watch for.

The bear population was definitely increasing the farther south they went; once they located Bear Lake, Denny felt it only prudent to scout the area out thoroughly before they set the planes down. After about fifteen minutes, they had spotted at least twenty brown bears; at that point in Denny's career, he really didn't have any way of judging the size of a bear from the air. Later on in his career, he could tell you within about one hundred pounds, but that was a lesson yet to be learned.

Denny spotted one that he wanted about a mile downstream from the lake along a little creek; it appeared the old boy was feasting on last year's salmon run, and he was bigger than anything Denny had ever seen. You could spot dead salmon on every little sandbar and all along the shoreline; everyone in the group had basically decided the area they wanted to hunt. Even though there was a stiff crosswind, the landings were uneventful; there was a nice sandy beach they could taxi up to, with some good strong shrubs for tying down the airplanes.

The first order of business was to get a camp and a shelter set up. In this part of Alaska, the question isn't if it is going to rain, but when. It may do that three to four times a day, and the wind may blow eighty miles an hour—very unpredictable weather.

They chose a spot about fifty feet from the shoreline of the lake, a little flat area where the ground was sandy. The spot was surrounded on three sides by some alder brush, which made a pretty good windbreak. Denny and one of the other guys started setting up camp while the other two guys collected a bunch of firewood; they found a little spring and collected a couple buckets of water. Within a couple hours, everything was taken care of, and they still had five to six hours of daylight left.

Mr. Hammon had advised Denny to take some fishing tackle with them because the fish in this area had never seen a hook. They dug a few bugs out from under some rocks and decided that would be at least a start. Denny's buddy Frank was the first one to cast his bug in the lake; it didn't lie there for more than two seconds, and the battle was on. A six-pound rainbow trout took the bait and ran for cover; everyone else in the group hastily baited their line before Frank was able to coax his fish to the beach. Everyone else in the group had hooked a similar trout; they fished for about an hour, quit counting after about twenty fish, but only kept a half a dozen—enough for that night and the next morning. It was obvious it wasn't going to be difficult to have fish anytime they wanted.

They all decided they wanted to look the area over to see if they could spot a bear or two and determine just how difficult it was going to be to get close enough for a good shot. They headed northwest toward an area that seemed to have the highest concentration of bears they had seen when they were flying over the area. Denny's bear was to the northeast of camp and far enough away that any shooting in this area shouldn't bother him at all.

Not one of the four men had ever shot a brown bear before, so camp was a little like four adolescents getting prepared for their first date; they all checked their weapons about four or five times and made sure they each had a pocketful of ammunition. They were quite sure that most of the stories they had heard had been greatly exaggerated—in fact, in some cases, just plain and simple lies. But of all the stories they had heard, they were convinced there had to be some merit and some truth. Whatever was fact or fiction didn't really matter at that point. They were quite sure when this hunting trip was complete, if they were successful, they would then be the experts.

One thing they had been told by enough different people they trusted was that you didn't ever get between an old sow and her cubs; and this could happen very innocently, especially when you're moving through this kind of terrain, with tall grass and brush. In some places, the men couldn't see more than ten feet in any direction; they had walked perhaps a half a mile, trying to keep the wind in their face.

Among several facts Mr. Hammon had told Denny, brown bears don't have the best eyesight in the world, but they probably do have the best sense of smell; they can smell things for miles, and they also have excellent hearing. So the essence of the story is to stay downwind and be quiet.

As they moved through the alder brush and tallgrass, they could hear some type of dispute taking place between several of the large beasts; they estimated the fracas was perhaps yet a hundred yards away. But at the rate they were going, they would have to be about ten feet away before they could see anything. The first order of business was to try and find a high spot: a pile of rocks, a little knoll—anything that would give them an advantage and an opportunity to see what lay ahead. They spotted what appeared to be a little knoll about fifty feet up the hill.

Denny volunteered to work his way up the hill in hopes of getting a better view of the surrounding area; the rest of the guys would stay put for the moment as he worked his way around a couple of boulders. Just short of his destination, a racket of gigantic proportions erupted right under his feet; he had apparently been so quiet that he completely surprised a flock of ptarmigan. It was probably debatable as to who was the most surprised. Denny sat down for just a moment to allow his heart to quit trying to beat a hole in his chest as he turned to look back down the hill; the decision to make the climb was well rewarded. He had ascended to several feet above most of the surrounding brush and grass and now had a clear view of the surrounding countryside, including four different bears that were arguing about who was to have access to the next rotten salmon.

From Denny's vantage point, he was able to see several other bear farther downstream in what appeared to be an area that was more open, with less brush and tallgrass. As Denny looked at the four bears, he couldn't really see how you could approach them safely; the grass in the brush was right up to the edge of the creek. Two steps into the brush and the bears were out of sight. Denny felt that was way too dangerous, especially when it appeared there would be many opportunities; some of them would have to provide a safer opportunity for the hunter. As he looked around, he picked several areas; he felt could provide those opportunities, but that would have to wait until tomorrow; as he looked off to the west, the sky was a slate gray–black and an almost-certain indication there was an approaching storm.

Denny made his way down the hill, where the rest of the guys were patiently waiting to find out what the verdict was. He informed them what he had seen and what his opinion was; he felt they should abandon any idea of doing any hunting this evening and get back to camp, cook some of the trout, and make sure the tent was well secured, with a drainage ditch dug around it to keep the water out. He was quite confident they were in for a lot of wind and substantial rain. They also decided the planes should be moved about a hundred yards up the lake to where there was a little more of a hill, which would give them added protection from the wind. Further, there was some larger shrub and a couple of big boulders; they horsed the planes up on the beach as far as they could get them and then tied them down.

They were just finishing a delicious trout dinner when, lo and behold, about a quarter mile away, on the other side of a little inlet, an old sow with three small cubs walked out of the brush and found something to eat at the edge of the water; she eventually spotted the campfire down the lake, stood up on her back feet, decided that was not to her liking, and disappeared back into the brush. Everybody was thinking the same thing; they hoped that was the last time they would see her.

The sun had now disappeared behind that ominous black cloud bank, which was rapidly approaching from the west; the wind was picking up down here at the lake level, but several hundred feet farther up the hill, it was violently whipping the brush and the grass. The wind was so loud they could hardly hear one another talk. Denny put out the fire; he certainly didn't want anything blowing into the tent. The rain started with just a few drops; the men picked up their drinks and squeezed into the little tent, with just barely enough room for the four sleeping bags. The rain came in sheets. Denny peeked out the flap in the tent before he tied it shut; it was raining so hard he couldn't even see the lake. The men finished off their drinks, sat around, and listened to the storm rage on for about a half an hour; when it started to let up, they decided they might as well get some sleep.

The next morning was cloudy with a pretty stiff wind out of the south; this would be favorable for the areas they intended to hunt. The first thing Denny checked was the planes, to make sure they had weathered the storm adequately; they were in good shape. One of the ropes had slipped off the rock, but the other one had held firm, no problem. The guys cooked up a couple more of the trout and had breakfast fit for a king.

"Hey, guys, I'm going to cook up a couple of pieces of Spam and make a sandwich to take with me because I don't intend to come back to camp for lunch. Is anyone else interested?"

"Well, I guess I'd better take one then," said Frank.

Denny and Frank had decided to hunt together. Jack and Spence were old buddies, so they had chosen to team up. When they were making there approach to land they had spotted a little valley just over the hill, about a mile from camp, when they were flying in. There, they had spotted several nice bears and had decided that would be a good place to start.

Denny wanted to check out that big bear he had seen when he was making his approach yesterday. "Frank, I would like to go downstream and check out a bear I saw yesterday."

"Sounds good to me, Denny. I'll shoot a bear if the opportunity presents itself. But it's not that important to me if I get one or not, so let's see if we can get you one first. Then I'll see how I feel about the situation."

"Okay, Frank. My plan is to climb up to that ridge and follow it west. I think it will take us in the general area of where I saw the bear. At least we should be fairly close. Hopefully, from up on that ridge, we will be able to see down into the creek. If we can't find that big guy, maybe another one will suit my liking."

Denny and Frank fought their way through the heavy brush and grass at the upper end of the lake, then started their climb up the hill; the ridge wasn't more than 150 to 200 feet high, but in places, it was almost straight up and down. There were huge patches of brush that were so thick you couldn't even crawl through them on your hands and knees, and in some areas, they actually had to go back downhill a short distance just to get around the brush. About two-thirds of the way up the hill and about a half a mile down the ridge, the boys came to a large outcropping of rock; it appeared this was a favorite spot for a number of different animals; there were signs of foxes, wolves, and, of course, bears. The boys had a panoramic view of the countryside. They sat there for almost an hour; everything to their south and west was downhill from where they sat. With their binoculars, they could see for several miles; within approximately a mile, they counted six different bears, and they could not see down into the creeks in many of the areas because the creek banks were too steep. They could look down on the lake where the planes were tied so Denny could calculate the route he had flown on his approach to land in the lake; if he was correct, the area where he had seen the old bear was just about dead ahead, a half mile to three quarters of a mile.

As they sat there enjoying the scenery, they realized the skies were mostly clear. It was a beautiful dark blue, with a few pillow-like clouds just lazily floating about—what Denny would later learn to classify as a Chamber of Commerce type of day. The ridge was much better walking than the side hills; there was some brush and grass, but nothing that you couldn't walk through and, in most cases, maintain your view of the surrounding countryside—a comforting feeling in bear country. It only took about twenty minutes for the two men to reach the edge of the hill, where the ridge dropped off sharply into a small canyon or perhaps what you'd call a very deep ravine; they each found a comfortable spot to sit, and once again, they started to scan the surrounding countryside with their binoculars. It was only a matter of a few minutes when they had located most of the bears they had seen from their vantage point back up the hill, where they had last stopped. Plus, it appeared they had picked up two new candidates that they hadn't seen before; one of those appeared to be quite large, but he was at least another mile away up on the side of the mountain.

Denny thought to himself, "I hope that's not my big bear because he would be almost impossible to hunt." He was surrounded by brush and tallgrass as far as you could see. There virtually was no safe way to get close enough for a fatal shot.

From this point, Denny still could not see down into the creek where the old bear was gorging himself on salmon the day before. The men decided it might be advisable for Frank to stay there and keep an eye on the surrounding area; there was no telling where the old bear may have wandered off to if he left the creek. Denny slowly picked his way through the rocks and brush as he worked his way down the hill toward the creek; after a couple hundred yards, he could now faintly hear the sound of the water. But as of yet, he was unable to see the creek; it appeared over to his right, in about fifty yards. There was a ledge of rock that jotted out of the hillside. Denny was hoping it would give him a better opportunity to see what was between him and the bottom of the ravine; he moved to the new vantage point. It was everything he hoped for; he could see at least a quarter of a mile of the creek, except for a couple of spots where the brush was so thick along the creek bank that he couldn't see the water.

As he sat on his perch, overlooking the very steep ravine below, he estimated the creek to be over two hundred yards from where he was situated. Denny could see quite some distance downstream, and there was nothing in sight in that direction; he estimated the distance by the creek would be maybe two miles back to the lake where they were camped.

Denny decided to have Frank move down to this location before he started the next leg of his quest to locate a bear; as Denny stood up to motion for Frank to come down, he heard a shot way off in the distance. A couple seconds later, he heard another one, and then there were five shots in rapid succession; then everything was quiet for about a minute. Then there was one more shot. Denny had to figure that Spence and jack just killed their first bear. While Frank was making his way down the hill, Denny was plotting his next move; he decided to move to his left and downhill another hundred or so yards to another rocky ledge in hopes that it would give him a better view of the creek.

"Denny, sounds like the boys got some shooting."

"I counted eight or nine shots. Is that what you heard?" Denny asked.

"I didn't count, but that sounds about right. What's the plan??

"Well, I'm going to get down a little closer to the creek but still try to stay up on the hillside far enough to where I have a commanding view of the area. If I run into that bear, I do not want to be down in that creek. I just don't want to get in that creek bottom. A bear could come out of that brush on either side and be on you before you could even get a shot."

"If you see anything, whistle."

Denny climbed down the rock outcropping and disappeared into the tallgrass. Frank could watch his movements by watching the movement of the grass even though he couldn't see Denny. Fifteen minutes later, Denny emerged from the grass and climbed onto the next pile of rock; he quickly glassed the entire area with his binoculars; seeing nothing close of interest, Denny concentrated on the area along the creek. After about ten minutes, he excitedly turned and motioned Frank to come down. Denny continued to watch the area that had drawn his interest until Frank arrived.

As Frank climbed up on the rocks, he asked, "What do you see, Lieut? Do you have the enemy in sight?"

"I'm not sure, but I think there's a bear in the brush on the opposite side of the creek, about four hundred yards down the creek and just up the hill from those rocks sitting in the edge of the water. All you can see right now is kind of a dark area in the brush. But I was watching it a minute ago, and I'm quite sure I saw it move. Why don't you keep an eye on it while I go look this hillside over on this side of the creek to see how difficult it's going to be to get closer."

Frank kept an eye on the dark spot in the brush while Denny tried to find a spot closer to the bear that would be open enough to be able to get a shot.

"Do you suppose it could be a moose?" Frank asked.

"I guess it could be, but I rather doubt it. I don't think a moose would bed down in that area."

"I suspect the old boy got a belly full of salmon and is just having a siesta."

"Frank, it looks like there's another outcropping of rock almost directly across the creek from where we think the bear is. I'm going to try to work my way down there while he's still napping. Hopefully, I get there before he starts moving around. The wind's in my favor, so I won't worry about that. But I won't be able to see a thing while I'm in that brush and grass. So if he moves, whistle. And if he moves across the creek to my side, whistle a lot."

It took Denny almost a half an hour to work his way through the brush along the steep hillside before he reached his destination. Frank had whistled twice, but Denny couldn't see a thing through the grass; he assumed Frank had just seen the bear move and nothing more.

He was right; the new location positioned him directly across the creek from what they assumed to be a bear. Once Denny climbed up on the rocks, he could see what Frank was excited about; the old bear had decided to get up and do a little grooming, rubbing some of last year's hair off his back. He was wallowing around in the brush, first on one side and then the other. He motioned for Frank to work his way down to the new position. Denny estimated they were about 150 yards at most from the bear, and he was twenty to thirty yards from the creek. So if he came out of the brush and down to the creek, he would be an easy shot for the .270—not the ideal caliber everyone recommends for hunting brown bear, but Denny loved that gun, and it was comfortable to shoot. Frank climbed up on the rock pile and aimed his binoculars on the bear. He still couldn't see the details of the bear, but he could definitely see the outline.

"Hey, Thompson, I've seen Indian huts that aren't as big as that bear. You think that little peashooter you have can penetrate that hide? I think those bullets will just bounce off his side, and you'll probably really piss him off. Then what do you propose we do?"

"You keep that old .30-06 loaded and ready, but don't shoot unless I ask you to."

"Okay, Lieut. I'll wait until he chews off at least one of your legs."

"Not quite that long," replied Denny. "Start shooting once he gets my foot in his mouth."

They were situated about thirty feet above the creek, about fifty yards back from the edge of creek; the creek bottom was perhaps fifty feet wide, but only about half of that was water. Now the waiting game was on; the bear was up and moving around and very alert, so they had to be very careful not to move when he was looking in their direction. There was some grass they could hide behind, but there wasn't much cover; any communications had to be a low whisper or hand signals. The old monster finally decided he was ready for some more of that delicious rotten salmon and slowly started to make his way down the hill toward the creek.

Denny watched as the old bear moved through the brush toward the creek. He thought he would try a spine shot as soon as the bear was clear of the brush; both men were so engrossed in what the bear was doing. They had failed to see another bear working his way down the creek; he was on their side of the creek, hidden by the brush and grass most of the time. Without warning, the big bear exploded out of the brush,

Denny's first thought was, "He's coming after us." Then the reason for all the commotion became obvious: The smaller younger bear took off up the creek like a racehorse. After several warning growers and about a thirty-yard sprint, the old behemoth was convinced he had adequately disposed of the youngster and would be able to enjoy his lunch in peace.

"Hey, Thompson, did you see how fast that old bastard moved? You sure you want to shoot him with that popgun you have?"

"Would you shut up? You'll see. I'll get a good heart shot, and he will drop like a rock."

The old bear was on their side of the creek now, but still not very visible. But he was working his way back down the creek closer to Denny; eventually, he moved out into the creek in full view. Denny picked his spot. The rifle spit out its rather insignificant little hunk of lead. The old bear's head came to attention, but other than that, nothing much changed; he definitely didn't drop like a rock. The bear tried to determine what the noise was when Denny shot again at the same area;

this time, the bear saw where the noise was coming from and spotted the two hunters. He got off a third shot before the bear disappeared into the brush on their side of the creek.

Denny only had one more shell in the rifle. He fumbled around in his pocket and retrieved three more shells, quickly putting them in the rifle, all the time listening to the bear climbing the bank, getting closer; the brush was cracking. He could see the brush and grass move, but not the bear. The rocks were rolling down the hillside; and the bear was making ominous sounds, which were, to say the least, unsettling. Denny glanced at Frank; he was white as a sheet. He moved about ten feet to the left of Denny so he would have a clear shot if Denny failed to stop this angry old monster.

In just seconds, the bear was close enough; they could see the brush whipping violently from side to side. Denny was not one to get panicky about anything, but he was seriously wondering if he had even hit this beast and if so, where? As the bear got closer, he could finally see the bear's head—it was enormous, had to be at least two feet wide.

Denny took a head shot. The old bear let out a roar and paused for a moment, shaking his head violently. Denny felt that with just a couple more steps, he would have a clear chest shot. All at once, the bear disappeared from their view; there was a racket, with brush and rocks being dislodged and crushed as the old monster collapsed and slid down the hill into the creek.

"What do you think, Thompson? Is he dead?"

"I sure as hell hope so. Did you see the head on that bear? I didn't know bears could get that big."

"Denny, I think that bear's head is four feet wide, and his body is wider yet than that."

"I doubt it's four feet, but it's wide." The body of the bear looked to be at least a foot wider than the head on each side. "Well, should we go down and check him out? Denny asked.

He had been told several times that one doesn't walk up to what one considers to be a dead brown bear until it hasn't moved for at least ten to fifteen minutes; after, that one can consider he's dead. The men made their way down the hill, making sure they came out into the creek bottom at least a hundred feet downstream from the bear; they had no intention of getting very close until they were absolutely certain the bear was dead. Once they were clear of the brush, they stepped out into the creek.

They both stood there in complete awe of what they saw; this bear was so big he was damming up the little creek. They didn't have a tape but estimated the paws to be about fourteen inches wide and the claws on the front feet about seven to eight inches long.

This was a trophy of monumental proportion. However, the sad part of this story is nobody knew it; they just assumed that all brown bears got this big that they didn't even take the entire hide and just caped the bear back to its shoulders, not even taking the feet or the head.

Denny came back a couple years later and found the skull, which was still in the creek where they had left it; he took it back to Seward to have a couple people look at it. They felt it rated very near the top, but part of the lower jaw and cheekbone were missing, therefore making it impossible to get an accurate measurement.

Denny now feels that it probably would've squared off at about fourteen feet—truly a monster.

At that point, not one of the four men had ever heard of Boone and Crockett records; it wasn't until Denny started guiding that he realized what a fine specimen his first brown bear was. To this day, he estimates that bear would no doubt be among the top three or four ever killed in Alaska.

Denny had shot the bear in the heart at least once and probably twice. The last shot, the head shot, tore off most of the lower jaw and part of the cheekbone; and the bullet lodged in the front shoulder, painful but not fatal. All of the fatal damage had been done in the first three shots; it just took all that time before the bear succumbed to his fatal injuries.

Denny never again underestimated the tenacity of these creatures; big or small, they just don't die easy. With the cape over their shoulder and their mission accomplished for the day, Denny and Frank headed back to camp. By the time they arrived at camp, Spence and Fred had returned; they had also shot a big bear, but not close to Denny's. It was a barren old sow with no cubs and about as mean as they get. She came off the hill behind them as they were walking down a trail and started down the trail toward the two hunters, growling and snapping her teeth; they basically had to shoot her in self-defense. It took nine shots, and she dropped about thirty feet from the two hunters, who were frantically reloading their rifles.

That night, after a couple of drinks, the stories got even better; the next day, the weather was bad, so they fished a little and just hung around camp. But the third day was sunny, and two more nice bears were taken to conclude Denny's very first brown bear–hunting experience—bear number 1 of over a thousand brown bears that Denny and his hunters would take over the next fortysome years. Close to a hundred of them would come from this same general area. It was a big bear, but not the biggest. Denny had several over the years that he was quite sure were bigger than his first bear, but he will never know, and those others are still in the record book.

Denny on the left Bill Sims on the right with two hunters from South Dakota with 78 inch record book moose taken 50 miles south of King Salmon Alaska 1970.

Denny and Bill Sims record 79" moose

Another record book moose 1970

Chapter Thirteen

The next morning, they caught another couple big trout, had a good breakfast, loaded up all their gear and bear hides, and took off for Port Moller, just a short hop. There, they fueled the planes and departed; next stop was Egegik, which was about two hundred miles from there, then onto King Salmon.

While they were in King Salmon, a friend of Frank's told them about a little lake on their way back to Seward that he had discovered last summer. It was just loaded with big rainbow trout; the boys decided to take one more day and get in a little bit of fishing. The weather was picture-perfect; they found the lake with no difficulty, and within an hour and a half, they were having the time of their lives. They never kept a trout that was under ten pounds; they decided to stay the rest of the day and camp out that night and head home the next morning. They made a little holding pond along the edge of the lake, where they could keep the trout that they wanted to take home alive; the next morning, they put as many of the trout in the plane as they felt safe to carry and headed back to Seward—the conclusion of a trip most of us only get to dream of.

Once Denny got a taste of bear hunting, there was no turning back; he knew he had to pursue that endeavor. At this time, he didn't know much about the professional hunting industry, but he never for a moment doubted he could do it as well as anyone else and probably better than most. He realized he could pick up a lot of valuable information by talking to other hunters, but what he really needed was experience—that would come with time and patience.

After the bear hunt in 1952, Denny realized that everything he wanted to do was going to take money, so he worked even harder and started to take people on short trips in the airplane, over the glaciers and over to McKinley once in a while; these people would come in on cruise ships, and some were not satisfied to just sit on the boat for a couple of days; while they were in Seward, they could see the snow-covered mountains and some of the glaciers, and they wanted to see more.

It started out innocently enough. Denny was at the restaurant one day, and he overheard an older gentleman asking the waitress if there was anyone around that he could hire to fly him over the glaciers and around the bay and the Kenai Peninsula. They struck up a conversation; he also was an ex-military man, First World War vintage. They came to an agreement on the price, and Denny had his first customer. He had more and more requests as the year went on; it became evident that if he had a bigger plane, he would get a lot more customers.

This was also the year he took his first Boone and Crockett trophy.

It was mid-September; one of the local guys, a young fellow still in high school, asked Denny if he would help him. He wanted to get a moose for his mother and asked Denny if he would take him hunting. Eventually, Denny got an afternoon that wasn't jammed up with other hunters or other things that he needed to do. So he decided to fly thirty to forty miles south of Seward; there was an area down there where he had taken several nice moose, and it appeared they were quite abundant in that area.

Once they reached the area, they spotted a couple nice bulls at the edge of a small lake, so they knew right where to go once they secured the plane. Denny landed on the opposite side of the lake from where they had seen the moose; now, mind you, the lake might have been two football fields long and half that wide—not a big body of water by any means. The lake had a couple little coves that went into the trees maybe a hundred feet. Denny taxied into one of those, and they tied up to a small spruce tree a couple feet above the water; the area around the lake was dense cedar and fir trees, almost like a rain forest. The moose they had seen was about halfway around the lake, and right near the edge of the water; it would be perfect if they could get him close to the edge of the water so Denny could taxi the plane right up to the moose, load the meat in the plane, and be on their way. Although hunting moose was a challenge, it was not like hunting deer or elk; they are not the brightest creatures in the universe. One had to stay downwind and just be reasonably quiet, and they should be successful; the biggest challenge was getting them out of the woods once they've been shot.

As they worked their way around the edge of the lake, it was so thick in places that they couldn't see ten feet; once they got close to the area where they had seen the moose from the air, they finally had to get on their hands and knees because they could see a little better. They would go a few feet and then listen. They finally heard him splashing along the shoreline; it sounded like he was coming right toward us. Then there was silence, not a sound. Denny knew he was close, but he couldn't see a thing; he finally stood up very slowly. He could hear the water splashing against the rocks on the shore. Denny estimated they were no more than perhaps fifteen feet from the edge of the lake.

Denny could now see a little better; he kept moving his head from side to side, trying to pick something up that resembled a moose. Finally, he spotted a patch of dark brown through a hole in the branches, but he couldn't tell if it was front or back; he kept looking and finally saw an ear move. The moose moved a couple more steps. Denny knew then where the head was. He looked back at the kid; he was still on his knees and could see nothing. He motioned for Denny to shoot the moose if he had a chance; he basically just wanted the meat. Denny moved a branch just a little, knowing that if he made a sound, the moose would be gone into the thick brush, never to be seen again—not by them anyway. He could now see his ears and a part of his neck; the moose wasn't more than twelve to fifteen feet away; he decided it was now or never. The .270 delivered again; the old monster collapsed in a heap right at the edge of the water. Denny and the kid eased out of the trees to survey their quarry; he was a very respectable animal with a very nice rack of horns. The kid suggested that Denny should go get the airplane while he started to cut him up; that sounded like a good plan to Denny.

They had so much meat Denny had to make two trips to get it all. He cut the horns off and pulled them out of the water, but there was no way he could get those horns and the meat, so they left the horns. The meat was all they were really after. Denny kept one of the back straps, and the kid took the rest over to his mom.

About a week later, Denny was at the airstrip when a couple of hunters came in with a nice set of moose horns; everybody was talking about having it measured for the record books. As he was looking it over, he was thinking to himself, "I believe that rack of horns I left in the woods a couple weeks ago is bigger." The more he thought about it, the more he realized it would always haunt him if he didn't go get those horns and have them checked.

The weather turned bad for about a week, and Denny thought about those damn horns every day; eventually, they got a break, and the weather cleared. He asked the kid if he would like to give him a hand, that they were going to go pick up those horns from the moose they shot a couple weeks ago. The kid was ready and willing; they had a very uneventful flight. They landed and taxied up to the carcass. The bears and ravens had done a pretty good job of cleaning up the carcass—nothing left but some bones; at first, Denny couldn't find the horns. He wasn't quite sure where he had left them, but they finally found them a little farther into the woods than he had remembered dragging them. When they started tying the horns to the strut of the airplane, that's when Denny realized they were much bigger than the average.

A couple weeks later, he took the horns over to Anchorage, where a Boone and Crockett official lived; at first, he wasn't impressed and didn't really believe they were worth measuring. But the more he looked at them, the more interested he became. He started taking his measurements and making notes; he became a little more excited. After he checked his notes a couple of times, he then decided he was going to measure the horns one more time, just to make sure he didn't make a mistake. This time, he was very careful and precise. When he finally finished checking all his numbers, he said, "You know, Thompson, I believe you have the world record set of moose horns here. It will have to be checked by at least one more official, but I do believe it's number 1."

And it was number 1 for many years, and to this day, it's still in the top 10.

After it was confirmed that Denny definitely had the number 1 moose in the world, he was notified by Boone and Crockett that if he could attend their meeting in New York City, he would be awarded a certificate and a medallion in person. When the time came, Denny loaded the horns in his car and drove to Minneapolis with the family. He left them there to visit their relatives and flew the rest of the way to New York with the horns.

It was a grandiose event, with more dignitaries and big-time hunters than Denny had ever seen or heard of, let alone all congregated in one place. When he was presented with his certificate, he was given a standing ovation—one of those moments in your life that gives you a nice warm feeling every time you think of it.

Chapter Fourteen

In 1953, I bought a Grumman Widgeon amphibian and started Seward Air Service. I could then fly six passengers at a time and cover the same area in half the time. I charged $50 an hour and shared my thermos of coffee with those who wanted it. I stayed very busy when I wasn't working at the dock chartering flights over the glaciers and once in a while up to Mount McKinley.

That fall, I also started taking meat hunters; they would set up camp and stay there for two to three days. I would return and pick them up along with their meat and fly them back to Seward; sometimes I would just fly them out in the morning and go back in the afternoon and pick them up, especially if they were caribou hunting. There were times when I would just land on the highway between Anchorage and Fairbanks; there were so many caribou that lots of times the hunters could just shoot them from the highway and sometimes on the highway.

This was also the year I had a little mishap on a no-name lake south of Seward on the Kenai Peninsula. I had taken a couple of hunters moose hunting; they had been successful and were ready for me to fly the meat back to Seward. It was a very windy day, and the lake didn't have much protection. I didn't have any problem landing, and even though it was windy, I didn't anticipate any problems taking off. Once they were loaded, I taxied into the best position possible. There was still going to be a strong crosswind, throttle to the firewall bouncing along the choppy water. We just started to lift off; the skis were almost out of the water, and a gust of wind caught my right wing and flipped me on my side. The left wing went into the water and actually got stuck in the mud in the bottom of the lake, which was only about ten to twelve feet deep. I killed the engine immediately. Here I was, with one wing submerged, stuck in the mud; the other one was stuck up at about a seventy-five-degree angle—not a pretty sight. The only thing I could think of was to transfer some of the meat inside of the airplane to the wing that was protruding out of the water in hopes that I could get the other wing out of the mud. After about an hour of wrestling this meat around and tying it to the strut, the left wing finally became unstuck, and the plane righted itself; the floats were just barely able to keep the plane up right. But the wind, now working in my favor, blew the plane ashore. In just a matter of ten minutes, I was standing on dry land, surveying the damage on my poor PA-11 airplane.

I knew where there was another PA-11 at the Seward airport, so I decided to try to get into town to see if I could borrow the wing off of it; we had to hike up over the mountain. Flying over the area as many times as I had, I knew there was a pretty good-sized lake that we either had to cross or go around. One of the hunters and I took off on a hike, about five miles up over the mountain and down the other side, to the edge of the lake.

The lake was a half a mile to three quarters of a mile wide and probably another three- to four-mile walk to get around to the other side; we hadn't walked more than a couple hundred yards, and there was a boat tied to a log. It was a pretty good-sized boat; it looked like an old military craft and had a motor—the works. We looked around to see if we could find any sign of a camp. Nothing. So we decided to borrow the boat; the motor started right up, and we were under way.

There was a little village just beyond the lake, where we were able to borrow a pickup; we drove back to Seward, which was about sixty miles. We took the wing off the other airplane, which, by the way, was black. My airplane was yellow. I hired four kids; we loaded the wing on the pickup and drove back to the little village, carried the wing up, and strapped it on the boat. Then we motored back across the lake, tied the boat up where we had found it, and started our hike back up over that mountain, this time carrying the wing of an airplane.

The wing was not all that heavy, but it was very awkward to carry, and the wind was still blowing thirty to forty knots, which didn't help a thing. Banged, bruised, and skinned up, we eventually made it to the airplane. We removed the old yellow wing and replaced it with an old black wing; once that was accomplished, I ferried the four kids, two hunters, and two loads of moose meat back to Seward. By the time I landed my last trip, it was dark.

I had about ten hunters in four camps that I was supposed to go back to that day; they all had to wait one more day, but I knew I would not have a problem when they saw me land with two different-colored wings—another day in the life of a bush pilot.

Chapter Fifteen

In the middle of February 1954, I was at the Anchorage airport picking up some parts for my boat when a couple of hunters just returned from Kotzebue and a polar bear hunt. They started unloading their airplane next to where I was parked; they pulled out this beautiful white polar bear hide and unrolled it right between the two airplanes. I, of course, asked as many questions as I could; and of course, as most hunters, they were eager to share their experience with anyone who would listen.

On my trip back to Seward, I was formulating a plan on just how I could get time off from my other obligations to spend three to four days on a polar bear hunt and whom could I get to go with me. The season at that time went until the middle of May, and I knew of two hunters in Seward who had been on at least one and maybe two polar bear hunts. Frank Lewis, my friend who went brown bear hunting with me, agreed to go. A local guy, Jack Foldigger, also a military pilot, agreed to go too if he could borrow somebody's airplane.

By the middle of April, we had everything in place. Jack had talked the local Cessna dealer in Anchorage into letting him borrow a Cessna 182, and I have no idea what kind of a story he spun to pull that off, but he did.

We left Anchorage at daylight on Friday morning; destination was Kotzebue, clear on the other side of Alaska, which was slightly over 650 miles—a hell of a long flight in a Cub. The temperature in Kotzebue was reported to be ten below zero, with clear sky's and a slight breeze out of the southwest, but we had no way of knowing what the weather was between Anchorage and Kotzebue. Honestly, we were so ignorant of what it could be like that we never even worried about it. For instance, if we had encountered a strong headwind anywhere along that route, we might not have had enough fuel.

We had to fly across the very center of Alaska, some very inhospitable country. We had to first cross the Alaska Range just south of Mount McKinley (Denali), then due west to McGrath. We topped off our fuel tanks at a little community on the Kuskokwim River. After leaving McGrath, we flew northwest over the huge Yukon River Basin, then onto Kotzebue, which is located just north of the Arctic Circle. Two hundred miles north of Kotzebue is the Brooks Range, and beyond that was the North Slope and some ungodly desolate country.

As I said earlier, the trip was about 650 miles; in a plane that cruised at about eighty-five miles per hour without a headwind, the flight took Frank and me just over ten hours. In the 182, Jack flew on ahead and was there in about five hours. The scenery was spectacular; the moose and wolf population in that part of Alaska at that time was unimaginable. The Yukon River Basin later became one of my favorite places to hunt wolves in the wintertime.

We had left Anchorage at daylight and arrived in Kotzebue in just a little over ten hours, with still plenty of daylight. I remember during that flight, I sat there listening to the little engine monotonously firing all four cylinders and the prop pulling us through the frigid winter air. I thought of the many flights from Germany back to England. If I closed my eyes, I could see myself sitting in that flak-riddled B-17, praying we would soon see the English coastline and that emerald-green English countryside. Just like so many times ten years earlier, we spotted the runway and knew we were going to make it. As we touched down, snow swirled about the little Cub as I taxied to a tie-down area; the first leg of our adventure was complete.

Our first order of business was to find someplace to get a drink and something to eat; there was a little eating spot not too far from the runway. I'm not sure, but I believe it was called the Whalebone; they specialized in fried blubber, but I was much more interested in a nice halibut steak. A couple years later, when I'd had a few more drinks, I did try the deep-fried blubber; it actually was edible, but not a favorite of mine. But with a beer or two, it was edible. The natives ate it like it was candy, but then I've seen them eat it raw by the handful. Once we had a couple drinks and our bellies were full, we made our way to the hotel. It wasn't quite the Hilton, but it was adequate; we were so tired. All I wanted to do was get in that bed. I told the clerk to wake us up at least an hour before daylight; he laughed at me and said, "You think this is the Hilton?" But he did give us an alarm clock so we could get a bite to eat before we headed out onto the ice fields in our pursuit of our first polar bear.

The next morning, we were airborne just shortly after daylight; we had no idea what lay ahead, but what we lacked in knowledge and experience we made up for in enthusiasm. We hadn't flown for more than about a half an hour when we spotted our first bear; it was a female with two cubs. Even if we had wanted, there was no place to land an airplane within ten miles of her. So we continued to fly almost due west; it was soon obvious that we had to get out of this massive ice field as there were chunks of ice piled up some places twenty feet high. But in general, there were ice chunks just strewn about the landscape, making it extremely dangerous to try and land an airplane. In another ten to fifteen minutes, we reached an area where the ice was relatively flat and much more hospitable.

Jack was having a problem; he was flying as slow as he could but was still getting two to three miles ahead of us. He finally came up with a solution; he put down twenty-degree flaps. By doing that, I was able to keep up. Jack had two passengers with him: one in the front seat and one in the back. He was flying off to my left about a quarter mile, and I noticed that his airplane was going up and down and making erratic movements.

"Hey, Jack, are you okay over there?"

"Not really. One of the guys dropped a cigarette in the backseat, and it's on fire. We tried to pour some water on it, but our water bottles are frozen solid. Bill's trying to piss on it right now."

"You can't just brush it out?"

"Hell no, Denny! I have two cans of camp stove gas behind the backseat. I have to make sure there are no sparks. Bill said he thinks he got it, but I'm going to find a place to land and check it out just to make sure. Boy, is that Cessna dealer in Anchorage going to be pissed!"

"Jack, I'm going to stay airborne and continue to look for a bear. I'll fly north along this ridge of broken ice for eight to ten miles. Then I'll turn around and head back this way if you haven't caught up to me by that time. Give me a call when you get back in the air."

"Okay, Denny, it shouldn't take me but a couple minutes."

Jack was back up with me in about fifteen minutes; we continued on north for approximately another twenty miles, then came to some open water. That's where we saw our first polar bear that we felt was in an area where we could land the airplane close enough to the bear that we could find him; we landed the airplane approximately a half a mile from the bear. We then covered the engines to keep them from cooling off too much, and then we started walking in the direction we had last seen the bear; what we also didn't take into consideration was the fact that he was walking. The bear could walk probably three times faster than we could; all we ever saw of that bear were his tracks. We returned to the airplanes a little smarter than when we left and were convinced that this polar bear hunting wasn't quite as easy as it looked to be—one lesson learned and many more to go.

Within a few minutes, we were back in the air again. We had one more dry run before we finally made contact. Jack was flying a couple hundred yards in front of me and off my right wing when he spotted a bear coming out of the ice pack; the bear seemed to be headed for the open water, which was perhaps a mile to a mile and half to our west. We decided to land in an area just short of the open water; then we would just have to trust our luck that the bear would come within range. We parked the planes a couple hundred yards apart so we could cover a broader area; we agreed the bear belonged to Jack if he was close enough to shoot. Otherwise, if it came to the area where Frank and I were parked, then it would be ours.

We moved away from the planes in the direction the bear was coming from, perhaps a hundred yards, and found a couple of chunks of ice to hide behind; we had a crosswind out of the south, and the bear was approaching from the east—not an ideal situation, but acceptable. We weren't in position for more than ten to fifteen minutes when I spotted the bear off to my left headed directly toward Jack and his two friends. I looked at Jack. I could tell they hadn't spotted the approaching bear; it looked like they were in deep discussion. They were probably trying to figure out what they were going to tell the Cessna dealer back in Anchorage when they turned in the plane with one of the seats burned and the plane smelling like a urinal.

Jack finally looked in my direction. I was frantically waving my arms and pointing toward the bear, which was now no more than two hundred yards directly in front of Jack and his two buddies. Jack grabbed his rifle leaning up against an ice block and quickly got himself into position; one of the other hunters also had a rifle and was frantically trying to inject a bullet into the chamber. No simple task is a simple task when you have bulky, big old mittens on. As Frank and I watched, the bear was now probably about a hundred yards from the three hunters. Frank took aim and pulled the trigger. Nothing. He had forgotten to put a bullet in the chamber; he frantically pulled the mitten off with his teeth, ejected a shell into the chamber, hastily took aim, and fired. The bear was now less than fifty yards away; we could hear the impact as it struck the bear, but there was no indication that the animal had in fact been hit. Jack fired three more times, and his friend fired once and maybe twice. I can't remember for sure. But it was enough; when the bear finally expired, it was less than twenty feet from Jack and his crew.

When all the smoke had cleared and we started the skinning process, we realized it was a female—not something we would've chose to do, but we couldn't tell the difference. Jack was elated; this was his first polar bear.

By the time we got the bear skinned and loaded in the airplane, we decided to call it a day and headed back to Kotzebue. That night, after we had dinner and a few drinks, Jack took a lot of ribbing about shooting a sow; and his friend was asked more than once to demonstrate just how he had extinguished the fire in the backseat. That discussion was without a doubt the highlight of the evening.

The next morning, we left again at daylight, this time heading north by northwest; we had made friends with one of the natives. He said he had just returned from that area and that there were lots of seals and open water, which meant there would also be an abundance of bears; we flew for about an hour and a half before we got into the area he told us about. This was our first experience in what I would call a polar bear killing field; we could spot little black spots, which were seals, lying by a hole in the ice. Every once in a while, we would spot a big spot of blood on the snow, obviously a successful hunt by one of the polar bears. It wasn't long until we spotted a couple of bears; the problem was to find a place to land the plane out of sight of the bear and yet close enough so we could get within range without being seen. So we kept flying north; we must have passed up at least five to six bears before we found the situation that we felt provided us with a favorable opportunity.

We were able to land about a half a mile away on the other side of a ridge of ice; we then worked our way through the scattered chunks of ice. We still had cover when we spotted the bear, and we were just over a hundred yards from our intended quarry. I was quite sure this was a male; after seeing how difficult it was for Jack to kill his bear the day before, I decided to try for a neck shot. If I was successful, he would drop in his tracks; if I wasn't, then I would probably need some help from Frank. The shot was true to its mark; the bear collapsed in a pile—not nearly as exciting as what Frank had experienced the day before, but I certainly wasn't complaining. The bear was a medium-sized male. I was extremely satisfied with my first polar bear.

I couldn't even imagine that over the next fifteen years, my hunters would take in excess of three hundred polar bears. I think I took only an additional three or four bears for myself, and I have no idea how many bears I had to shoot that my hunters wounded and were going to do serious damage to all parties involved if they weren't stopped.

As I soon learned the polar bear was a much more dangerous animal than the brown bear, even though they were comparable in size, I never tried to keep track because, at that time, I didn't even think about it. But I would estimate that at least 80 percent of the time when a polar bear was shot, his first instinct was to attack, and it did that with great ferocity. I've had hunters react in many different ways, including staying right where they were and continuing to shoot until the animal lay dead on the ice like they were supposed to. Or in some cases, they take their first shot; and when the animal turns and charges, they drop their gun and run. Believe me, that is no defense for an angry polar bear. I have also had a situation where we snuck up on an unsuspecting bear; getting into position, it was time for the hunter to take aim and shoot. The hunter would get so nervous he would start to shake, I have seen that happen on at least two occasions; the hunter would then hand me his rifle and asked me to shoot the bear.

We skinned out the bear; even though I knew this was no trophy, this time, we took the hide, the head, and all four paws. We spent another hour trying to locate another bear but were never able to spot one that we felt was close enough to where we could land the airplanes. So we decided to wrap it up for the afternoon and headed back to Kotzebue.

Frank decided he really didn't care if he got a polar bear, not at this time; but one of Jack's buddies, we could tell, was going to be very disappointed if he didn't get a bear. So we decided to take one more day and see if we could find him a bear. On day 3, we decided to go basically the same route, only a little farther north. This day, it was a little windier. In most cases, it wasn't cause for concern; but in a situation like this, where you had to land in between chunks of ice and open water, a crosswind could make it very tricky and lots of times just too dangerous to risk.

For the first hour and a half, we spotted probably six to eight bears; several of those were very large, but none of them in areas where we felt comfortable landing. Now later on in the years, I have to say I have landed in a lot worse areas than we saw on this day; but we were not comfortable and were well aware that if you had an accident in this godforsaken country, even if you lived through the crash, you would probably freeze to death before anybody could rescue you.

About an hour and a half to two hours into the hunt, we spotted a small bear in a good area. Jack's friend decided that was good enough for him; the bear was preoccupied with eating an old seal carcass. We landed about a half a mile downwind. Frank and I stayed with the airplanes while Jack and his buddies successfully stocked and disposed of the young bear. We decided that once we got under way, we would fly due east until we encountered the coastline, and we could fly south along the coast until we got to Kotzebue because at this time we had no idea where we were.

But wherever we were, there seemed to be an abundance of polar bears, definitely more bears in this area than due west of Kotzebue; we were airborne for maybe an hour when we first spotted land. It was a point that stuck out into the Chukchi Sea, Point Hope. I decided it would be a good idea to top off my tanks on the Cub before we headed south to Kotzebue; as I later learned, the wind always blew at Point Hope, and this was no exception. We had a stiff crosswind, which is always tricky to land in with skis, and the Cessna was more difficult than most. I landed without much of a problem, but when Jack came in, one of his skis caught on the outer edge and twisted the landing gear. With a couple of bars, we were able to straighten the landing gear enough to where it was usable; we fueled up and returned to Kotzebue, spent the night there, and took off for Seward the next morning. When Jack turned in the Cessna, from what I understand, there was a very heated discussion. Jack never did tell me the details, but I can imagine.

Chapter Sixteen

The year 1954 was a very busy year for Denny; the fishing season started shortly after the return from their polar bear hunt. Denny had picked up a couple of seiners and hired a couple of men to help him; with a lot of hard work, they had a very successful fishing season.

Denny was already thinking ahead to next year; he definitely wanted a bigger boat. His dream was to fish the Shelikof Strait between Kodiak Island and the mainland. The fish were abundant, but the weather was terrible.

He took a number of hunters: some meat hunters—mostly moose and caribou, some goats, and black bear. Two of the men Denny took moose hunting were from Detroit, and they were telling him about this beautiful new car that Chevy was coming out with called the Bel Air. And if he was interested in one, they could get him a heck of a deal if he wanted to fly back to Detroit and pick it up. He thought about it for a couple of months, had a visit with his friendly banker, and decided it was within his budget. Then he called Detroit and placed his order; they said it would be ready by May 15, 1955.

But first things first; he had to get ready for the upcoming fishing season. He had talked to the cannery where he sold the salmon; he told them about his idea of a bigger boat. They agreed he could probably double or triple the amount of fish he caught if he didn't have to make a trip back to the cannery every time he got eight thousand to ten thousand pounds of salmon in one of the seiners. They put word out in Seattle to see what they could find that he could afford; in March, he got a telephone call from one of the managers at the cannery. They had found a seventy-three-footer, with twin Jimmy diesels, that was very seaworthy and was for sale for $12,000 in Seattle.

In April, Denny caught a flight to Minneapolis, spent about a week with his mom and dad, visited a few friends, then flew on to Detroit, picked up his new Bel Air, and headed for Seattle. Within three days, he was parked at the end of the pier, waiting for the owner of the seventy-three-footer to show up. A couple cups of coffee later, the gentleman who owned the boat arrived. The boat was something that Denny had never seen before; it was a PT boat, built for fighting the Japanese in the South Pacific islands. The boat was built in the Seattle area; but before it could be shipped to the Marshall Islands, the war was over, and this navy vessel was just one more piece of government surplus that was no longer needed. The previous owner had removed the three 1,000 hp Packard engines that originally came with the boat and replaced those with two Jimmy's Marine diesels; as he was getting the tour of the boat, the wheels were already turning. This boat had living quarters, a little galley, restroom facilities—all the luxuries of home. Denny took the boat for a shakedown cruise out to Friday Harbor, then returned to the pier; it handled a lot better than he had expected for a vessel of that size. He now had to get to a telephone and make a call to Seward; there were three people up there who had agreed to come to Seattle to help him bring the boat back to Alaska. He decided that instead of shipping his new car by freighter to Alaska, he would put it on the PT boat and haul it back to Alaska himself; he just had to figure out how to get it on the boat.

The next morning, his crew—Clyde and Marge Lovett and Jimmy Walker (JW)—arrived at Boeing Field north of Seattle; everybody had a quick breakfast and headed out to look at the new boat. When they saw the boat, everybody thought Denny had lost his mind; this sure didn't look like a fishing boat. When they heard it was intended to be used as a tender, then that started to make more sense. JW was in the navy during the war and had run some landing craft; this was not a lot different, just had more power and was more maneuverable.

They checked around and found a spot at the standard oil docks where they could pull the boat up to a loading dock and just drive the car right on the back of the boat; while they were there, Denny was able to pick up some charts of the San Juan Islands and the inland passage. He was also warned about the weather and the fact that there were areas along there route where rock outcroppings at low tide were within inches of the surface, sinking many unsuspecting boats and ship.

They bought provisions for the trip and decided to wait until the next morning to start.

Denny remembers they were up the next morning well before daylight, had their breakfast, and cast off right at daylight; they had the car secured on the fantail. The tide was just starting to recede; they crossed the very east end of the Strait of Juan de Fuca, and within about forty-five minutes, they were in Canadian territory. What they were supposed to do was stop at the closest Canadian community, check in with them, and declare their intentions. They would get a piece of paper that gave them permission to be in Canadian waters, and they could be on their way. Now Denny honestly doesn't remember if they were aware of that situation or just didn't care or if they just didn't realize they had to check in; bottom line: they did not for whatever reason.

With the tide going out, they had about a three-foot chop; at about twenty knots, they kind of glided right over the top. If they slowed up much below that, it was rougher than a cob. About twelve hours later, they were at the upper end of the Strait of Georgia; they were north of Nanaimo on Vancouver Island and just south of Powell River on the mainland side. They hit some vicious riptides created by the massive amounts of water rushing into the islands; they started tossing them around like a cork. Besides extremely rough turbulent water, there was about a thirty-mile-an-hour wind. They were all up in the pilothouse watching for debris, rock outcropping, or anything else that might be a hazard. Jimmy's eyes got about as big as a coffee cup.

"Thompson, your car's about ready to go over the side!" Jimmy shouted.

Denny turned and looked. Sure as hell, the car had broken loose from all but one of the tie-downs. He backed off on the throttle and turned the wheel over to Marge, saying, "Just keep it as straight as you can." The three of them made their way back to the Bel Air, which was within a couple of feet of going over the starboard side; one of the lines was still hooked to the front axle, so they grabbed that and wrapped it around one of the chocks on the opposite side of the boat and took up the slack little by little until they got the car back near the center of the boat. They then proceeded to put two more ropes on the car and this time secured them where there was no way the vehicle could move an inch. Denny presumed one of the lines got just a little slack and started to work back and forth; and the way they were being slammed around and the weight of the car, eventually, something had to give.

Once they all got their nerves settled down, Marge went down to the galley, got them all a cup of coffee, and made up about a dozen ham-and-cheese sandwiches for the evening; they had to fight this riptide for about another half hour. Once they got past Powell River, it widened out considerably, and the tide became quite manageable. They debated whether they should pull in to one of the little towns or a bay and anchor for the night, or if they should just keep steaming forward and take their chances. If Denny remembers right, the debate didn't last very long; they all came to the agreement that they should just keep moving and slow it down considerably, even at a much-reduced speed, and they would cover a couple hundred miles during the night. The Lovetts decided they would like to take the first watch because it was relatively easy sailing for the next four to five hours; at that time, they would enter the Queen Charlotte Strait, where the channel in places was a mere couple hundred feet wide and the cliffs on either side of the channel extended upward to the stars, so it seemed. The cliffs were quite high on both sides, and then there were areas where the trees came right down to the water. By this time, the tide had slowed considerably, and they were completely protected by the hills from the strong west winds that had buffeted them in the Strait of Georgia. Jim and Denny took over from the Lovetts at midnight, made a fresh pot of coffee, and finished off the rest of the ham-and-cheese sandwiches.

By the next morning, they were into some open water, the Queen Charlotte Sound; the wind and the waves were coming right off the

Pacific Ocean and tossed them about like they were just a hunk of driftwood. They were only in that for a couple of hours, and then they were able to duck behind some more islands and continue up the inland passage.

From the upper end of the Strait of Georgia to Ketchikan was another two days; every twelve hours, they had to fight the tides and the rip currents. Some of those tides rushing through the narrow passages between the islands at times slowed them to almost a standstill if they hadn't had those two big diesels, and there were times when they would've definitely been going backward.

They were northwest of Prince Rupert, British Columbia, Canada, when they hit a submerged log. Denny could feel it sliding along the keel of the boat, and before he could get her shut down, the log got tangled up in the props. They were very fortunate neither shaft was bent, but both props were badly damaged. One prop could be used slightly at an idle, but in these tides, that was not going to keep them out of trouble; there were a number of fishing boats in the area, one of which they were able to flag down. He was kind enough to tow them to the nearest town, Petersburg, about two miles.

They were able to dock on what they call a grid; it was a number of timbers crisscrossed in water shallow enough that they could drive the boat onto the grid during high tide, and when the tide went out, the boat would rest on the timbers. They could then get under the boat and do whatever was necessary. They had just tied up when a Canadian Mountie came along; he wanted to see their paperwork that gave them permission to be in Canadian waters, which Denny did not have. He gave them a summons and sent them to see the magistrate of the little town; after a little explanation about their predicament, Denny thought the magistrate felt they had enough trouble without him adding to it, wished them luck, and sent them on their way.

Denny was able to get a hold of his insurance company and explain to them what the situation was; they airfreighted two new props into Petersburg. When the tide went out, they were able to get the props changed during low tide, a total of two days from the time they hit the log. Denny was backing out of the grid on high tide; they topped off the fuel tanks, and they were once again under way.

It took them about another day to get to the north end of Chichagof Island; that was their last protection from the wind and rough waters of the Gulf of Alaska. They set their course, a straight line to Seward, Alaska; three days later, the tired crew of four tied up in Seward, glad to be home.

Chapter Seventeen

Every spare moment I had for the next month and a half was spent getting ready for the upcoming fishing season. I had to build holds to store the salmon, which would be transferred from the seiners to the seventy-three-footer and then delivered to the cannery while the seiners continued to fish.

I had another idea that I was certain would work if I could just get it rigged up. I wanted to put my J-3 Cub on the fantail of the seventy-three-footer, haul it on the deck, and tow the two seiners behind; my goal was to fish the Shelikof Strait between Kodiak Island and the Alaskan Peninsula. This area had more pink salmon than any other one spot in Alaska.

But the abundance of fish came with a price; this area had some of the most severe currents and most miserable weather you could imagine, which made it very miserable and dangerous to fish. But first, I had to give the seventy-three-footer (the *Paula*) a new name; after a couple minutes of serious consideration, I decided to leave it as is. I didn't have time to paint a new name on the bow.

I had done enough flying over salmon-rich waters to realize it was quite easy to spot large schools of salmon; my idea was to spot the salmon and guide the boats into that area, therefore removing the wasted time looking for the fish and not waste your time on a small school of fish; when a mile away, there might be hundreds of thousands of salmon you would've otherwise missed.

On about June 15, we had completed work on the seventy-three-footer; we had hoisted the J-3 Cub aboard the seventy-three-footer and set it back into the water three times just to make absolutely sure it was going to work properly. The holds for storing the salmon were reinforced one last time. I estimated we could carry in excess of a hundred thousand pounds in one load.

The season opened on June 20. On the nineteenth, we pulled out of Seward and headed for Kodiak and the Shelikof Strait; we—the old PT boat with an airplane on the fantail and towing two seiners behind—must have been quite a spectacle as about half of the town came down to the pier to watch us leave. We were fortunate; the weather was reasonably good, no more than a slight breeze and a slow-rolling sea. The trip was uneventful but took several hours longer than I had anticipated; we entered the Shelikof Strait in the early evening. We decided to stop at Port Williams for the evening, fuel up the *Paula*, and be ready to go early the next morning.

During the night, we had a blow; it stormed for about four or five hours. But by sunrise for that area, you could consider it quite calm. We left Port Williams shortly after sunrise and moved about fifty miles farther south, where it was reported there were large schools of salmon; we had never set the J-3 Cub off the boat in open seas, so we still had a few things to learn. We eventually got it figured out; we had to anchor the bow of the boat, then use one of the seiners to pull the fantail around, then set the plane off on the leeward side of the boat. Once we were ready to go, one of the guys would take me to the plane in the dinghy, and our rather complex operation would be ready to make history.

At that time, I didn't have a lot of experience taking off and landing in the ocean, where the waves were much different from those in a small lake; in most cases, I had a nice stiff headwind to help me get airborne without a lot of taxiing. By 10:30 a.m., I was airborne and on the hunt for our first school of salmon. I remember it took me about forty-five minutes before I spotted a number of seagulls gathering in an area about a quarter mile off the mainland shore; my hunch was that right beneath all those birds was a large school of salmon. I would estimate it may have covered five to ten acres—exactly what I was looking for. Of course, in those days, we didn't have radios. So I had to go back to where the seiners were waiting and guide them to the fish; the fish were moving northeast just off the mainland coast.

That allowed us to set up our nets in front of the oncoming school of fish, which the boys did quite efficiently; by nightfall, we had filled both seiners to the gunwales and topped them out. Now we had to transfer those two loads of fish onto the *Paula* and get them to the cannery within twenty-four hours. We estimated about twenty thousand pounds of fish if you figure each fish averaged about two to three pounds; that figured to be ten thousand fish. Each one of those had to be speared either in the head or the tail individually and thrown into the hold of the *Paula*; that process then had to be repeated when we got to the cannery. Now they just suck them out of the boat with a big vacuum. But back in those days, each fish had to be handled twice.

The device we used was called a fish que; it was like a pitchfork, but with only one tong. I remember after the first couple of days, my hands and forearms would get cramps so bad at night that I couldn't open my fists without prying each finger individually one at a time. The first week, we were very fortunate; the weather was favorable, and we caught and sold more salmon than I had even hoped for. That first week, just my share of the catch almost paid for the seventy-three-footer. But then the weather changed, and we really got a taste of what it's like to fish the Shelikof Strait.

For two days, the wind was so strong and the sea was so rough that we didn't even venture out; we were anchored in a little bay, and that's where we stayed, and that wasn't all bad because we had some maintenance that needed to be taken care of and some nets that needed to be mended. When the weather broke, it still wasn't as nice as it was the first week, but at least we could fish. To get the J-3 Cub in the water, we had to pull into a small protected inlet during high tide; once I was airborne, I realized what it must be like for a butterfly to be caught in a tornado. The wind tossed me around so bad that it kept knocking the ash off the end of my cigar, and I couldn't keep it lit, and I couldn't take my hand off the stick to relight it. I was in a terrible fix because all I had with me were matches; the next day, I made sure I had a lighter.

Even though it was rough flying, I was still able to locate large quantities of salmon; for several days, we were able to put two loads from each seiner into the seventy-three-footer. That's approximately thirty thousand and one hell of a lot of work. If I remember right, it was about week 3 when I had my first encounter with a kamikaze seagull. I remember pursuing this school of salmon where I had learned over the first couple weeks that, in some cases, if I got down close to the water, I could spook the salmon in a certain direction. I was attempting to move them in the direction of the seiners. I was probably only about ten feet off the water. I had been flying around seagulls for the first three weeks with no problems, so I wasn't paying a lot of attention to the birds because they seemed to be pretty good at getting out of the way; all at once, it felt like I flew into a cliff. The plane shook violently; and the windshield was instantly covered with blood, guts, and feathers.

I immediately climbed to gained altitude, thinking I would probably have to make an emergency landing on the coast, which was about a half a mile away; as I climbed and turned into the wind, there was enough rain that the mess on the windshield started to clean itself up. The plane seemed no worse for wear; there was no vibration and the prop looked to be intact. After about ten minutes, the windshield was clear enough for me to once again resume my duties; however, this time, I gave the seagulls a little more respect.

The season was nearing an end; we had about five more days of fishing. The weather had taken a turn for the worse; it seemed like every other day, we had a new storm to contend with. Some days, we were not able to fish at all, but this day was definitely on the favorable side. We set the Cub in the water, and the rest of the entourage slowly started to work their way south to southwest, waiting for me to locate the next group of salmon; as the season went on, the fish seemed to be closer and closer to the shoreline.

As I remember, we located one large school of salmon, made a good set, and filled the boats in less than a couple hours; once we had transferred the fish to the *Paula*, we still had plenty of time for at least one more set. The wind was starting to come up a little bit, and the seas were getting a bit rougher, but still fishable; it took me quite a while to spot a large school of salmon; they were farther south than we had hoped, but still within reach. I flew back and notified the boats, and we commenced to set our ambush; it took almost an hour for the boats to get into position and lay out their nets; the weather was gradually deteriorating as the afternoon wore on.

By then, we had four- to five-foot waves; my window of opportunity to get back on the *Paula* for the evening was rapidly closing. By the time the boats were able to close their nets and brought their fish aboard, it was late; the tide was going out, and the areas I could land were getting fewer by the minute, not to mention the clouds were getting lower. I was skimming over the top of the waves just a few feet off the water flying north along the coast, looking for an inlet or little bay.

We had talked this situation over and had decided that if this situation arose and I couldn't land where we could bring the J-3 Cub aboard the seventy-three–footer, then my best bet was to find a piece of quiet water, someplace up an inlet that was protected from the wind and just spend the night in the airplane. It was not my preference, but at this time, it looked like the only safe solution. I only had to fly up the coast about ten miles, and there was a small well-protected inlet fed by a small river or large creek. I landed on the first stretch of calm water and taxied inland for about another half a mile; there was kind of a slew with grass to the waterline. I was able to taxi the plane up onto the bank on the wet grass, almost to the point of high tide.

I'd been cramped up in the airplane since early that morning, so I decided I'd walk up and down the shoreline and get a little exercise. I hadn't walked more than a couple hundred feet when I spotted my first bear tracks; they appeared to be a day or two old. I considered returning to the airplane, discretion being the better part of valor, but decided I would go a little farther just to see what was around the bend; what was around the bend were more bear tracks—only this time, I could see who was making them. A medium-sized brown bear was headed for the creek—smart choice for the bear since the creek was alive with salmon. At that point, I decided exercise was not as important as getting back inside that airplane, not that the airplane would be much protection if an angry bear decided to disassemble the wood and aluminum structure covered with canvas and fiberglass—a relatively minor task for one of these powerful creatures. But as a rule, they're not looking for trouble. They just want to fill their belly with salmon.

Before I got in the airplane, I retrieved a couple cans of Spam, a jug of water, a small bottle of vodka, which I had just for medicinal purposes. I climbed in the front seat with my lap full of goodies, retrieved my GI can opener from my pocket, and commenced to go to work on a can of Spam. I paused for a moment, realizing that a bear could easily smell the Spam. I just hoped they were like 90 percent of the human species who couldn't stand the stuff and that they much preferred those nice juicy fresh salmon, making their way up the creek by the hundreds. I cut off a chunk of Spam and placed it between two crackers. I had taken a couple bites of the Spam and crackers and was looking the terrain over when something at the edge of a patch of alder brush caught my eye. About seventy-five feet away, there watching my every move was a rather large bear. I couldn't see the whole animal, but looking at his head, I could tell he had been around awhile.

At that point, I decided a couple of shots of that vodka in a cup of water would be good for my nerves and my immune system, strictly medicinal. Sure enough, I poured myself a drink and took a sip, then looked for the bear; he was gone. I was quite sure not very far, but I couldn't see him. I finished my Spam and my drink. By then, I couldn't see anything; it was totally dark. I grabbed a blanket out of the backseat and tried to make myself as comfortable as possible; if you've ever been in a J-3 Cub for more than a half an hour, you'd know that's a difficult task, especially since I've been flying since almost daylight—a good eighteen hours ago. Now I was confined to this cracker box for at least another six to seven hours.

I don't know how long I had been asleep when I was brought back to my senses by a couple of bears, who were vigorously debating who had the right to fish a certain spot in the creek; once I realized this didn't have anything to do with me, I was able to relax and fall back to sleep. The next thing I remember was the easy rocking of the airplane;

the tide had come in, and I was now afloat. I pulled my flashlight out from underneath the seat; it appeared to me I hadn't moved very much, maybe a little closer to the brush, but was still in the same general location. I looked off to the northeast; there was a very faint glow in the sky, which meant the sun was about to make its appearance. The moon was just a sliver in the western sky, and there were stars everywhere. There didn't appear to be any clouds as far as I could see. I decided to wait just a little longer before I got out and turned the plane in the proper direction so I could take off. I needed to have good visibility when I took off; you never know what kind of debris an incoming tide will bring with it.

An hour later, I was tied up to the *Paula*; while I grabbed a little breakfast and grabbed a few miscellaneous items, including some candy bars and some more water, the crew was fueling the airplane. I had decided if we could fill the seiners with two good catches, that was going to be it for the day. I had no desire to spend another night in the J-3 Cub.

We had all agreed three more days would wrap it up, and we would head home. The next three days were very good; we caught in excess of seventy thousand additional fish. I had nothing to compare to, but it was much better than I had expected, so I was happy.

The 1955 fishing year was better than I could have dreamed; all the crazy ideas seemed to work, and I had new ideas for the next season that I couldn't wait to try. The remainder of 1955 went quite well. That year, I had my first Safari Club hunter from the Los Angeles chapter; he shot a big sixty-five-inch moose and two very nice caribou, and later that year, he sent a friend of his up to shoot a bear. We actually shot two bears: a big black bear and a nine-foot brown bear; he was extremely happy and booked another hunt for the next year (that's kind of how it got started). I shot a couple of goats that year and determined that was another species I was an expert at. Goat hunting, other than a lot of climbing, was quite a bit of fun; and the goat meat is very good eating. If you don't believe me, just ask a grizzly bear.

Chapter Eighteen

The year 1955 (Denny tells of his rescue of his friend.) was the year I almost lost a good friend, Jack Foldigger; it was the latter part of November. I had just put my airplanes up in the hangars for the winter. All my hunters were gone, and the days were getting very short, and most of the seasons were closed. Jack had taken a hunter out to Montague Island in Prince William Sound to do some deer hunting.

I'm not exactly sure what happened, but when the hunter was taking his rifle out of the airplane, it discharged. The bullet went through the shinbone and the calf of one of Jack's legs, completely shattering the bone and ripping the muscle into shreds.

There was no radio; the hunter had seen a logging camp down along the beach when they were flying in. Once he had done everything possible for Jack, he walked out to the shoreline and then down the shoreline for about eighteen miles to where the sawmill was located.

They contacted the coast guard, who immediately dispatched a cutter and a team of about a half a dozen men; the intent was to rescue Jack and bring him back to the hospital.

I haven't mentioned this before, but there was a terrible storm, with winds of fifty to sixty miles an hour and very low visibility; the waves in that area were at least six to eight feet. The cutter couldn't get close to the beach, so they had to launch a lifeboat with six men on board; the lifeboat was about halfway to the beach when it capsized, dumping everyone on board in the cold, icy water.

The men all made it to shore and eventually made their way to the camp where Jack was stranded, but there wasn't much they could do; they had lost the lifeboat and all their supplies, so about the only thing they got accomplished was to fill a tent full of six soggy demoralized coast guard men.

The coast guard contacted Denny to see if he thought he could do anything to help. He decided to get his plane out of the hangar, fly down there, and take a look to see if he could actually do anything in this kind of weather. The ceiling was less than three hundred feet, and he had to fly across about ten miles of open water. Denny could not see the horizon and had only the whitecaps to use to be able to judge his altitude. Camp was not far inland from the beach. It was on the shore of a little lake only about two hundred feet long; using the advantage of the strong winds, Denny was able to set the plane down. Almost like a helicopter, he taxied over to the camp; the wind kept the plane pinned right up against the shoreline.

A couple of the coast guard guys came out to help hold the airplane while the rest of them helped Denny move Jack out to the airplane, put him in the backseat, and strapped him in. Jack was sometimes awake and sometimes in a coma. Denny then instructed the guys to hold the airplane as steady as they could until he was ready to taxi for takeoff. Denny accelerated to full power, then signaled the guys to turn her loose; they hadn't traveled a hundred feet when a gust of wind shot him skyward, but he still clipped the top of a pine tree in his effort to gain altitude. Jack said, "Hey, Lieut, that was a close one!"

He delivered Jack to the hospital; this was now the third day, and gangrene had set in. So they had to amputate the leg just below the knee.

To this day, there is no doubt in Jack's mind that he would've died in that tent if it wasn't for "Denny Thompson." I know that to be a fact because I met Jack at Mud Bay, northwest of Naknek in Bristol Bay a few years ago, and he told me the story in person. Jack and his partner were camped about fifty yards back from the beach, waiting for the herring run to begin. Denny and I were bear hunting; we were scouting out the area north of Bristol Bay. Once our bear hunt was complete, he intended to move his boat out to Mud Bay for the herring season. We were flying along the beach when Denny spotted Jack's camp, and he decided to land and let me meet one of his old friends. Jack and his buddy were in a little tent; they had a campfire blazing just a few feet from the tent, and they were setting on a couple chunks of driftwood half buried in the sand, having a drink. I had a couple extra cigars in my pocket, so we all lit up a stogie; that was just enough to make me one of the boys. I looked at my watch; it was 10:30 a.m. We, of course, were asked to join them. Denny told Jack to make his a light one. Jack said, "Since when does a drink bother your ability to fly?"

Then he looked at me and said, "I believe the lieutenant here could fly in his sleep." And that's when he told me the story of the rescue.

But this isn't the end of the story. After rescuing Jack, Denny had again put his airplane in the hangar; two days later, an officer from the coast guard contacted him, telling him their men were still stranded on that island. The weather was showing no signs of improving, and they wondered if Denny would be willing to help them rescue the rescuers. Denny couldn't pass up this opportunity, so he agreed.

The next day, he flew all six men one at a time down to the logging camp, where they were able to get back on the cutter. The men had run out of food and fresh water; at least one of the men had pneumonia and probably wouldn't have made it if they had waited for the weather to clear because it stayed bad for at least another week.

For Denny's heroic efforts and superior flying ability, he was awarded Man of the Year. This was not the last time Denny would use his extraordinary ability as an aviator and risked his own life to rescue someone in a perilous situation.

In 1956, Denny, of course, was still working on the docks; he had a very good arrangement. He basically could work whenever he wanted as long as he paid his dues to the union. Denny worked day and night getting the plane and boats ready for the upcoming season. He planned to take the Super Cub (the PA-11) over to Kotzebue and leave it there during polar bear season; then he could catch a plane out of Anchorage and be there in a couple of hours instead of him flying six to seven hours every time he wanted to go polar bear hunting. After a couple years, they had enough polar bear hunters that they just stayed in Kotzebue for the entire season.

By then, Denny had two hangars at Seward and an empty lot where he could bring the boats up out of the water and store them for the winter; by the early part of December, he had everything stored for the winter, with most of the repair work and maintenance well under control. He and Jean decided to take the kids back to Minnesota for Christmas; the grandparents hadn't seen them in a couple years.

On December 15, they loaded up their Bel Air and drove the four-thousand-plus miles to Staples, Minnesota; that is about five days each way, and that's hard driving. They spent about two weeks in Minnesota and were back home in Seward shortly after the first of January. Denny had sent out letters to everybody he had hunted with in the last couple years to inform them that he was expanding his hunting operation to include polar bear hunts. When they arrived home, he had several letters from clients requesting additional information on polar bear hunts; by the end of January, Denny had three polar bear hunts lined up for the coming spring. One of those was with one of the gentlemen from Detroit; the other two were from the Los Angeles Safari Club, and Denny expected to hear from several other hunters before the season started.

Chapter Nineteen

Jack and I decided to take the airplanes over to Kotzebue, put them in a hangar (if there was one available), and get everything ready for their first hunt, which was scheduled for the latter part of February. When we arrived in Kotzebue, the weather was beautiful—very little wind and not a cloud in the sky. But it was cold, about fifty below zero. We decided if the weather was this good the next morning, we would go scout the area to see if we could find any bear; and if we found one that was really to our liking, we might decide to do a little hunting. Polar bear hides, with their skull and claws, were very easy to sell. The next day turned out to be one of those Chamber of Commerce days; other than, it was about fifty-five below zero when we got up.

Remembering the good luck we had north of Kotzebue toward Point Hope, which was the direction we flew, we were only out about an hour when we started to spot some bears; we tried several times to land behind a bear and tried to get close enough to get a good shot, but each time, the bear just kept getting farther and farther away. We realized we had to change our tactics or spend the whole day just getting a lot of exercise. The next bear I spotted was a nice-sized bear. By looking at the tracks, I figured it seemed to be going in a straight line as if it knew exactly where it wanted to go; we found a spot about a mile ahead where we felt for sure the bear would come through that general area and hopefully would be close enough to shoot. We landed and taxied the airplanes behind a couple large chunks of ice, found ourselves a small chunk of ice to hide behind, then started to scan the area where the bear would make his first appearance.

I don't think we had been there any more than fifteen minutes when Jack spotted the bear coming through a gap in one of the pressure ridges; if it stayed on track, it would come within fifty to a hundred yards of where we were hiding. We checked our guns two or three more times to make sure they were loaded to their capacity and then waited; within a very few minutes, the bear was within range, probably 120 yards or less. It seemed to sense something wasn't right; it stopped for a moment to look for danger. It somehow sensed. We both fired; the bear never hesitated for a moment. He turned and charged. He seemed to know exactly where we were even though we were well hidden behind the ice.

In a situation like this, it always seems to take forever to do the most menial things, such as ejecting another shell into the chamber. I know it didn't take more than a second, but it seemed like forever, and the bear was wasting no time. It had no hidden agenda; his objective was quite clear: bash our heads in, then tear our insides out. We both fired again; one of us hit his left front shoulder, and the other one went right into the boiler room. His leg gave out, and he took about two somersaults before he was able to regain control; as soon as he regained his footing, Jack and I both fired. This time, we both tried for the right shoulder at front; this time, when he went down, he stayed down. We practiced skinning this bear just to see how fast we could actually skin him out and get him in the airplane. We decided against skinning out the head at this time; to do that right would take time. We could save that chore until we got back to the hangar.

Once we were loaded up and airborne again, we still had plenty of daylight, so we decided to do a little more scouting; one of the things we discovered was the network of green rivers that crisscrossed the entire ice pack. It is where, for some reason I'm not entirely sure of, the ice would split and separate sometimes five to six feet wide, other times fifteen to twenty feet wide. When it first happened, it would be open water; but within a day or two, they would refreeze, and they would be an aqua green. They would usually run in a fairly straight line until they intersected with another green river running in a different direction; in some cases, they would provide a very good area for landing, but we were never sure how deep the ice was. We learned through experience that the ice thickness had to be a minimum of ten inches to support the plane; we eventually learned that if it supported a polar bear, it would support the plane. The green rivers were the favored areas for the bears primarily because they were also the favored areas for the seals—the number 1 item on the polar bears' menu. We spent the next couple of hours learning a little bit more about the movement of the polar bears and how we felt we should hunt with our first client, who was due to arrive in two days.

The first polar bear hunter was a Mr. Zimmerman from San Diego, California. Mr. Zimmerman was in his eighties the first time I hunted with him and in his midnineties the last time I hunted with him; over that span of about twelve years, Mr. Zimmerman hunted with me at least eight different years, including once in Africa.

Mr. Zimmerman arrived at the Kotzebue airport via an Alaskan airline; we picked him up at the airport that afternoon. Before we were scheduled to hunt, we had set up a little target out behind the hangars where every hunter would have to try his gun to make sure it hadn't been bumped during the flight. Mr. Zimmerman checked out in good shape, his rifle was on target, and he appeared to be a very adequate shot.

The next morning, we took off just as the sun was starting to make its appearance in the eastern sky; the snow was so cold as we walked to the airplane that it squeaked beneath our feet. The moisture had frozen to every stick, twig, and blade of grass; as the sun cast its rays about the landscape, every little ice crystal glistened like a diamond.

The ravens were squabbling over something; the sled dogs were tearing at their chains, trying to get free, as they watched a very large snowshoe hare make its way across the runway. We double-checked everything we could think of, wanting this first hunt to be flawless.

"Mr. Zimmerman, do you have some sunglasses with you?" I asked.

"I do, Mr. Thompson, and I also have my rifle and a box shells. Do you think that will be enough?"

"If that's not enough, Mr. Zimmerman, we're going to be in big trouble. These polar bears don't seem to retreat once the shooting starts. They have one thing in mind, and that is to eliminate the source of their distress, and they seem to be able to identify our position and waste no time. They usually come on the dead run. Besides the shells you have in the gun, try to have another three or four in your pocket or someplace easy to get to in case you have to reload. You won't have a lot of time."

The snow swirled about the airplane as we lifted off the runway into the cold arctic air; we turned due west and climbed to about five hundred feet. The large chunks of ice that were strewn about cast eerie shadows in the early-morning sunlight; those shadows also made it much more difficult to spot the bears, but that situation rapidly improved as the sun climbed higher into the morning sky. We had only been airborne for about thirty to forty minutes when we spotted our first bear. I dropped down to about a hundred feet to take a better look. Mr. Zimmerman said he would do if I felt that was the best we could do.

"Let's just keep looking. We haven't been in the air for an hour yet, and I think we can do a lot better than him."

Mr. Zimmerman nodded his approval, and we climbed back up to five hundred feet and continued our search. I could tell by the look on Mr. Zimmerman's face that something was bothering him.

"Mr. Zimmerman, you seem to be concerned about something. What is it?"

"I'm wondering, when we do find a bear that we like, how do we find a spot to land in all these chunks of ice? I had no idea that this frozen ocean was such a mess."

I explained to Mr. Zimmerman that those were called pressure ridges; and it's when the wind or the tide, or a combination of both, causes the ice to either separate or create so much pressure that the ice buckles and pushes these giant chunks of ice upward, causing small mountains of ice sometimes thirty to fifty feet high. There were many places in those pressure ridges where you absolutely could not land a plane. I estimated probably 5 to 10 percent of the area out here was flat enough to land on; but most of the time, we could find a place close enough to the bear, but not always. Over the years, I have lost several monsters in the pressure ridges.

It wasn't long until we came upon one of the big green rivers running north by northwest; we hadn't followed it for more than ten minutes when we spotted a big red spot on the bright white snow. It was the remains of a seal; about fifty to a hundred feet from the seal, we could see where the bear had rolled in the snow and cleaned the blood off his fur and perhaps had taken a nap. But now he was on the move again, apparently looking for some dessert; we could see his tracks quite easily and decided at that point in time the most prudent thing to do would be to follow those tracks. We idled the plane back a bit so we didn't make quite as much noise; after about ten minutes, the green river branched off, one branch going due north, with the other west. We had to circle the area twice to make sure which branch our bear took because there were three different sets of tracks at this juncture; two of them had turned west, and the third one was heading north. It didn't take us long to determine that the northbound bear was the one we had been following and definitely had bigger tracks than the other two. We hadn't flown for more than a couple of miles when we spotted our quarry, perhaps a half a mile ahead; we immediately turned to the west and made a big detour around the unsuspecting bear. Now we had to find a place to land that was not too far from the green river and try to get into position before the bear arrived; the closest spot that I could land was about three miles north of the present location of the bear and about a quarter of a mile to the west. I asked Mr. Zimmerman if he felt he was up to the walk; he assured me he would be there if I could just get him out of that airplane.

We landed and taxied up to the very edge of the pressure ridge, threw a blanket over the engine to keep it from cooling off too fast, then started our trek through the maze of broken ice. We got ourselves situated behind a couple blocks of ice, which were no more than twenty feet from the edge of the fractured ice (green river); the last we had seen the bear, he was on our side of the river. At that point, it really didn't matter what side of the river he was on because the channel was only about twenty feet wide and looked to be adequately thick enough to support either us or the bear; now all we had to do was wait. I have learned over the years that when it comes to polar bear hunting, you usually don't have to wait very long. They cover a lot of ice in a very short period of time. Mr. Zimmerman got right down to business, ejected a bullet into the chamber, then stuck another one into the magazine and looked around until he found himself a piece of ice that was just the right height so he could use it for a gun rest. Over the last couple hours, the sky had become overcast; he removed his sunglasses and exchanged them for his regular glasses. He looked at me and gave me a thumbs-up; he was ready.

We didn't have very long to wait, maybe twenty minutes. Jack had stayed airborne and had climbed to about a thousand feet and was slowly circling the area, keeping an eye on the bear; just in case he decided to stop or take a detour, he would buzz us and try to give us an indication of where the bear had gone. Mr. Zimmerman had his eyes glued on a bend in the river, about a hundred yards to our south—the first place we expected to catch sight of the bear. I looked up to see where Jack was to see if I could get any indication as to how far off the bear might be. Jack was about a half a mile south of us; he dipped his wings a couple of times. I took that to mean the bear was getting close.

"Hey, Denny, here he comes!" said Mr. Zimmerman.

Sure enough, about ninety yards away was the biggest polar bear I had encountered yet in my short career; he was moving along at a fast walk, still on our side of the river, which meant he'd have to almost run over us to get past us.

"Mr. Zimmerman," I whispered, "take your time. But don't wait too long."

I expected him to start shooting immediately; the bear was now no more than fifty yards away. I pushed the safety off my rifle and got ready. I glanced over at Mr. Zimmerman; he seemed to be cool as a cucumber. He had his finger on the trigger and was watching the bear intently; the bear was now less than thirty yards away. Needless to say, I was beginning to get a bit nervous. Then without warning, flames exploded from the end of the old .30-06. The explosion rocked the death-still silence of the cold arctic air, and the bear dropped like he had been hit with a freight train and never moved a muscle. Mr. Zimmerman slowly stood up and ejected the empty cartridge from the chamber. I was still watching the bear intently for any sign of movement, but there was none.

Mr. Zimmerman had placed the shot about a foot behind the bear's ears and broke his neck, killing him instantly. I was impressed. Jack buzzed us about twenty feet over our head and then proceeded to land so he could help me skin out the bear and get him loaded in the airplane.

"Mr. Zimmerman, you had me a little worried there for a minute." I usually didn't like to shake hands with these guys before I shoot, but in this case, I was concerned that was what we were going to have to do. But that was a nice shot—a little risky, but I'm not complaining. We had just about completed skinning the bear when Mr. Zimmerman asked about shooting a wolf.

"Denny, how far do you think we have to go to get a wolf?"

"I'm not sure, but I suspect we wouldn't have to go very far. There are reindeer all over the area north and east to Kotzebue, and wherever there's reindeer, there's going to be wolves."

"We had scheduled two days for the polar bear hunt, I believe," said Mr. Zimmerman. "So if you're willing, I would like to take my second day and try to get a wolf."

"That sounds good to me. I'll ask some of the men in the village. They will be able to tell us. If the weather holds, that works for me."

"I don't want to be picky, but if it works out, I'd like to get a black one. I know there's not nearly as many black wolves as there are white and gray wolves. But I guess that's probably why I want one."

"Well, Mr. Zimmerman, if that's what you want, we will do our utmost to get you a black wolf. No guarantee, but that will be our goal. They're out there, not near as many. But when I'm flying around, I do see one once in a while."

That night at the restaurant, there were several native hunters who were quite eager to share with us their knowledge of the wolf population in the surrounding area. It sounded like we had several options; on our way back to the motel, we happened to meet a fish and game man who was stationed here in Kotzebue. His advice, if we had the time, was to go up on the North Slope, just south of Barrow. There were more wolves up there than probably anywhere else in Alaska, and very few people hunted them that far north. It was an area I had heard about many times but as of yet not had the opportunity to go there. So now was my chance to see some new country, and the best part of it was that I would get paid for it.

The next morning, we were up well before daylight; there was a local guy who picked up the Russian weather forecast for Eastern Siberia. That gave the locals a pretty good idea of what to look for weather-wise for a couple days in advance; the weather forecast that day was just like yesterday's: slight overcast, snowstorms a couple hundred miles south of Kotzebue, but nothing in our area all the way to Barrow. We learned over the years that there were occasions when they got it wrong, but as a rule, it was very helpful.

We departed for the North Slope just as the sun was peeking over the eastern skyline; we had to race the jackrabbit down the runway. We won. As we lifted off, I glanced back at the little village just as the first spears of light were touching the rooftops, transforming a very cold, desolate place into a moment to remember. The little shacks and poorly constructed stores and shops were magically transformed into objects of beauty; the ice crystals sparkled like diamonds, and the long shadows cast by the early-morning rays of the sun created for a few moments a sight to remember. Our ETA at the North Slope was an hour and a half to two hours; it just depended on when we started to see wolves. We stayed to the east end of the Brooks Range, then across the Colville River Basin, then across the small narrow range of very rugged mountains called Lookout Ridge; everything from this point to Barrow was downhill and very flat.

We had already seen a number of wolves, but none in areas where you could easily land an airplane. I had made up my mind that we were not going to take any chances in this area; to be stranded up here overnight was almost sure to be a death sentence, and we always kept one airplane in the air. I estimated we were about fifty to sixty miles south of Barrow when we spotted a pack of wolves, six in total; two of those were black as onyx. It looked like they were on a reindeer carcass. We circled several times, staying about a half a mile away, until I located a small frozen lake behind a ridge about a quarter mile from the wolves. Once we were on the ground, we had to sneak down a brush-covered draw; if that provided us adequate cover, this would bring us within about 150 yards of the wolves. Jack stayed about a mile away and circled slowly, keeping an eye on the pack. I set the Cub down on the little frozen lake bed and immediately cut the engine as we slid across the powder-soft snow. So far so good.

We quietly exited the plane, being careful to not make any noise. Now we started to sneak through the brush and down the frozen creek bottom. I glanced up at Jack to make sure he was still in position. I knew if the wolves moved, he would immediately let me know. Mother Nature was cooperating; the snow was not crunchy, the creek bottom was low enough, and the brush was thick enough that we could stay completely out of sight. As we got closer, we could hear the wolves squabbling over whose turn it was when we finally decided to take a peek; to our surprise, we were no more than eighty or ninety yards from Mr. Zimmerman's desired quarry. A very large black wolf was on our side of the pack. It seems like a relatively simple task now to just take your shot, throw your trophy in the airplane, and go home—not so in sixty-five-below-zero weather. Nothing is simple. Just to get the safety off and get your finger on the trigger is sometimes a monumental task; however Mr. Zimmerman handled it like an old pro. After several minutes, he was in position to take the shot; again, he was on the mark. The old male took two leaps and collapsed; the rest of the pack disappeared like smoke in a brisk wind. They went in several different directions and disappeared into the brush.

We made no attempt to skin out the wolf there on the tundra; we managed to drag him back to the plane and get him loaded. I couldn't see much of Mr. Zimmerman's face underneath his parka, but what I did see looked like a big smile.

The flight back to Kotzebue seemed like it only took a few minutes; my first polar bear hunter was extremely happy, and I had learned that you didn't have to have a bloodhound to track a polar bear, and I could now add wolf hunting to my list of expertise. The next morning, we got Mr. Zimmerman on his airplane back to Fairbanks.

We had one day before our next hunter arrived; we spent that doing a little maintenance on the airplane. That spring, altogether, we had six bear hunts—all successful. We also took four more wolves—all of them in the Yukon River Valley, much closer to civilization and, as a rule, not nearly as cold.

Chapter Twenty

By May 1, we were back in Seward; we had some major changes we wanted to do on the seventy-three-footer, and we had lots of nets that needed to be worked on, among other things—typical work that had to be done to get ready for the 1956 fishing season.

I still had my longshoremen job; plus my charter service (Seward air charter) was much more in demand. The number of tourists who were arriving by ship was increasing each year; that seemed to be the source of most of my charter flights. I could carry six passengers in the Widgeon; at $50 a head, that become a profitable venture. On about June 20, 1956, our little caravan—the seventy-three-footer, with a J-3 Cub tied on the fantail and towing two twenty-six-foot fishing boats—left Seward, Alaska. Our destination was the Shelikof Strait and what we hoped would be a prosperous fishing season.

Although 1956 was very much like 1955, our operation was a little smoother, and we had two monstrous catches that we didn't have in 1955; on two occasions, we had more fish in the net than we could load in the boats. So rather than let the fish go to waste, we allowed two other fishing boats to take what we couldn't haul. By the end of the season, we had taken fifty thousand more fish than we did in 1955. There were a couple of situations that were a little out of the ordinary that did occur, which, I suppose, deserves honorable mention.

As I remember, it was shortly after lunch, probably about 1:30 p.m., when I spotted a nice school of salmon working their way north along the mainland coast. I immediately flew a couple miles northeast, where the fishing boats were waiting for instructions; we decided to anchor one end of the net to the shoreline, then string the thousand-foot net perpendicular to the beach. When the salmon start hitting the net, the boat makes a big loop, entrapping as many salmon as possible. Now this was all done with me flying as slow and close to the boat as possible. I would open my window, and we would shout back and forth—no radios. As the net started to close, the salmon started to boil, as they were forced into a smaller and smaller area; they, of course, panicked and started jumping and flopping on the surface of the water. This commotion caught the attention of a couple brown bears that were evidently in the brush not very far from the beach, watching this operation with much curiosity, probably trying to figure out just what we were doing. But once all those salmon started to flop around in the net, the temptation to demonstrate to us just how to catch a salmon was more than they could endure; the crew on the boat could see what was happening as the bears emerged from the brush and made their way toward the beach. The poor guy standing on the beach, making sure the end of the net stayed anchored in place, had no idea what was going on behind him. With his back to the brush, he had no idea he was about to be visited by a couple of very hungry brown bears.

He was intent on making sure that end of the net stayed anchored to the beach and was watching the salmon fill the net when all at once, out of the corner of his eye, he caught some movement. He turned his head just in time to see these thousand pounds of bears galloping down the beach, heading in his direction, then go plunging into the water, not fifty feet from where he was standing. That was when he felt his feet were getting very warm and came to the realization that he was in the process of peeing his pants to the extent he filled his boots, with the liquid spilling over. Both bears, one about fifty feet away and the other one about three hundred feet away, bear sat down in the water up to their armpits and started feasting on salmon. We couldn't close the net with the bears in it, and we sure didn't want to turn the salmon loose. So what the hell were our options?

I buzzed the bears a couple of times; they would run up on the beach, stand there for about thirty seconds, and then head back into the salmon; finally, one of the guys brought a skiff in and a couple of fish ques. They got as close as they could, much closer than they wanted, to the bears; then they speared a couple dozen salmon and threw them up as far as they could up on the beach. They then got back in their skiff and headed back to the boat. I then chased the bears out of the net again with the airplane; this time, they found the salmon we had tossed up on the beach and seemed quite content to watch us work while they enjoyed a free meal. It was not at all unusual to see several, sometimes half a dozen, brown bears along the beach; but this was the first time we had to compete with them to get a load of fish, but it was not the last.

Shortly after the encounter with the bears, just a couple days later, I had another run in with the suicidal seagull. I was searching the area just east of Katmai Bay; it seemed this was always an area with an overabundance of birds. This time, I was about fifty feet above the water, intently watching the choppy seas below. Then I glanced forward and immediately pulled back on the stick, but I was idled back so far that the plane was slow to react. Immediately in front of me was an albatross at least as big as a turkey buzzard, but with a much longer wingspan—I'm going to guess at least ten feet. I have heard sailors tell about them flying right into the side of the ship, with no attempt to avoid it. They spend most of their life just sailing around the ocean with no obstacles to avoid, but a few high waves; if I had not pulled the nose of the airplane up, I believe he would have hit me dead on. The prop caught one of his wings, so the rest of the bird glanced off the underside of wing and hit the strut and hung there for just a couple of seconds before it spiraled into the water below. I venture to say that if that old albatross had hit me head on, I probably would've been the one spiraling into the sea. Other than the strut having a small dent, the plane sustained no damage.

Besides having an awful lot of fish to handle that year, I can remember one other situation that gave me several moments of anxiety; it was one of those days that was marginal at best. It was pretty rough that morning when we set the plane in the water; it just seemed to get gradually worse as the day wore on. The fishing was good, almost too good; we had more fish than we knew what to do with. It was tough to transfer them from the seiners to the *Paula* because of the choppy seas. By the time they were ready for me to bring the plane aboard, it was way too rough, and we had a load of fish on the *Paula* that had to be delivered to the cannery yet that evening. I decided about the only option left was for me to fly about a hundred miles to the closest area I could land and get a room or fly about two miles into a little protected bay and spend another night with the bears; since it was almost dark already, I decided a night with the bears was about the only option I had left.

The tide was coming in. I had a huge area to select from for a spot to spend the evening. I chose an area that was protected from the wind, but as far away from the brush as I could get; there was a huge old tree stump that had washed up on the beach sometime in the past, which made for a very secure tie-down.

I had stowed a few provisions in a sack in the back of the airplane for just such an occasion. I had a few cans of my old standby Spam, a frying pan, a little bit of Crisco, salt and pepper, and a small fishing pole and half a dozen hooks.

I decided to collect a little driftwood and make myself a fire so I could have something hot to eat. If I was successful with the fishing pole, it would be fish for dinner; if not, then I guess Spam would have to do. There was a little grassy slough maybe one hundred yards from where the plane was tied to the stump. I could see the salmon jumping and flopping around in that area. I figured they were probably spawning. I put the biggest treble hook that I could find on the line and headed for the slough; they normally won't bite when they're spawning, but they're so thick that all you have to do is throw the hook over the fish and drag it back. Almost without fail, you will snag one of the fish, which is precisely what I did—one cast and one fish, a nice three-pounder. I would have enough not only for dinner but also for breakfast.

I had started a fire before I went fishing; while I was collecting wood for the fire, I could see several bears on the other side of the inlet, at least a couple hundred yards away—nothing to worry about at this time. The fire was crackling and popping, with flames jumping four to five feet into the air; by the time I returned, the sky overhead was covered with stars that appeared to be just out of reach. But off to the southwest, the sky was black; a giant cloud bank appeared to be getting closer each time I looked at it. The sun had not totally disappeared over the horizon, and the moon was just starting to make its appearance; this was going to be one of those nights in Alaska when it never really got dark unless the storm made it this far north; if that happened, all bets were off.

I was just finishing up my fish, getting ready to put everything back in the airplane, when I heard an excessive amount of splashing taking place over by the slough. I couldn't see as well as I would have liked to, but well enough to see a big brown bear picking up fish out of that slough and delivering them to a couple of cubs that were waiting just at the edge of the water—a very touching scene for the average environmentalist but a little unsettling for someone who knows the ferocity of a mother bear with a couple cubs.

Very quietly, I collected as much driftwood as I could find and piled it on the fire, then stowed all my gear in the plane. I felt that I had enough wood on the fire to keep it going for at least the next three to four hours; however, if the storm arrived, the fire could be quenched in a matter of minutes. I eased into the airplane as quietly as possible; the old bear, every once in a while, would stand upright and look in my direction. Probably not seeing any imminent danger, it would then go back to fishing; the cubs seemed to be having as much fun pouncing on the flopping fish as they did eating. Every time the fish would move, the cubs would swat it or pick it up and toss it in the air. I suspected they would eat their fill, and then she would lead them back into the brush, where she could have a nice long nap while she digested her fish dinner. In my way of thinking, that made perfect sense, and I was quite sure that's exactly what she would do.

Now that I had a belly full of fish, I was getting very sleepy; and sometime shortly, after I climbed back into the airplane, I was sound asleep; it had been a very long and trying day. I'm not sure how long I had been asleep before the storm hit, but all at once, there was thunder and lightning. Shortly after that was a torrential downpour. I could hear the wind roaring overhead, but where I was parked, we were pretty well protected. I dozed off several times during the storm. I think the quiet after the storm caused me to wake up again; this time, I could see some clear skies. My fire, of course, was ancient history—not even an ember or wisp of smoke remained.

I don't believe I ever completely woke up until the airplane started to rock back and forth; this got my attention immediately; the moon and stars were peeking through the clouds adequately to allow me to watch a brown bear scratching his back on the starboard strut. I couldn't tell if it was the old sow with the cubs or a newcomer, but the way the plane was rocking back and forth, I was quite sure it wasn't something I wanted to continue. I didn't feel real comfortable in opening the door and telling the beast he shouldn't be doing this. I even thought about throwing out the remainder of my fish; that didn't make a lot of sense since he had a whole river full of fish. Then I came up with the ingenious idea of starting the airplane. I didn't really want to start the engine, just turn it over a couple of times. I kept an eye on the bear as I hit the ignition switch; if you ever think you could outrun or outmaneuver one of those big old bears, you should see how fast he moved when that engine turned over. In a second, he was forty to fifty feet from the airplane; there, he stopped, stood on his back legs, and looked at this funny contraption, which made a very convenient place to scratch his back. I hit the switch one more time; the bear disappeared at a gallop into the darkness.

I sat there for the next hour as the moonlight faded into daylight; the tide was rapidly coming in. I felt that within an hour, I would once more be afloat.

As the light improved, I could see at least one bear in the slough and at least three on the other side of the inlet. I eased myself out of the plane, trying very hard not to draw the attention of the local residents. I wanted to check the strut where the bear had been scratching his back, just to make sure there wasn't any damage, and nature was calling. Once all my chores had been attended to, the water was lapping at the back of the floats. I untied the plane from the old stump; with a little pushing and shoving, the plane was once more afloat. With a little nudging in the right direction, I had her headed out to sea; by this time, the light was more than adequate. The engine sputtered a couple times, then ignited. I glanced at the bears; the only one that seemed to be paying any attention was the one in the slough. He watched intently as I taxied out into the main channel and bounced over the choppy waters until I was airborne. Fifteen minutes later, I was taxiing up to the *Paula*.

A few days later, we were headed back to Seward, with another successful fishing season under our belt.

The rest of 1956 was good. I got a lot more into brown bear hunting; before the season was over, we had taken in excess of a dozen brown bears. Most of those were down in the area where we had been fishing and farther south down around Pavlof Bay. We took a couple of black bears that fall and at least a dozen moose and caribou. I was now looked at legitimately as a professional hunter.

Chapter Twenty-One

In 1957, we started off with a bang; by the end of January, I had a dozen polar bear hunts booked, and I knew there'd be more as the season drew near. A large proportion of those bookings were from the Los Angeles Safari Club members; it seemed everybody who had shot a moose or caribou was now rebooking for the same or upgrading to a brown bear or a grizzly bear. Even though they were not considered dangerous game, the challenge of the hunt and the beauty of the beast rapidly made the Dall sheep and the mountain goat one of the prize species to go in the trophy room.

I worked day and night to get all my equipment in top-notch shape; we were definitely going back to the Shelikof Strait once polar bear season was over with.

I had no idea what was going to develop; the polar bear was also becoming the sought-after animal to be added to the trophy room, and there were rumors that polar bear hunting was going to be banned in the United States. Even if you shot one in Canada, you couldn't bring it into the United States. Pretty stupid, but that's what happens when you get tree huggers and politicians calling the shots. But for now, just the threat was good for business; by the time the season was open, I had sixteen hunts scheduled. At this time, I was getting $1,500 per hunt, and that went up to $2,000 by the early 1960s.

On about February 10, we had a high-pressure system settle in, and the weather was clear, but awful damn cold. A young man, Raymond Cappasello, had approached me about helping me with some of my flying. I checked him out and decided to start him out on the polar bear hunts. His nickname was Cappy. With clear weather all the way to Kotzebue, we decided to move the planes.

We met our first polar bear hunters of the year at the Kotzebue airport on February 15, 1957. Cappy and I had scouted out the area the day before and located several pockets of seals, and where there are seals, there will be bears. The hunters were two men in their midfifties from Chicago; they both had fancy hand tooled leather gun cases.

When we went out behind the hangars to see if they could shoot, the first guy, Tony Rizzio, pulled out a German-made Mauser .375 with some fancy gold and silver inlay. His two shots were within two inches of the bull's-eye, and he seemed to be very familiar with the gun. The next man, Robert "Bob" Kramer, was a big man 6'5" or 6'6"; with all the clothes he had on, he looked like a giant. I found out later that he had played ball in his younger days for the Chicago Bears. He unzipped the leather case and pulled out a beautiful .416 Rigby—"the real thing." I thought to myself, "These two guys have more money in those two guns than I have in my airplane." Bob also did well; he clipped the bull's-eye with both shots. That night, after a couple of drinks and a few hunting stories, they bought us dinner at a not-very-fancy restaurant—at that time, the only one in Kotzebue.

The next morning, we were up before daylight and got some breakfast, and I warned them about drinking too much coffee; it was not easy to drain your lizard in fifty-below-zero weather with about five layers of clothes on. Just as we were starting to get some daylight as we were rolling down the runway, we had a stiff crosswind out of the south, which would actually help us get to our quarry a little faster; but if the wind persisted the whole day, it would make our trip home this evening much slower.

We were not in the air for more than an hour when we spotted a big set of tracks; they had to be quite fresh, or the blowing snow would've covered them. We hadn't tracked the old boy for more than five or six minutes when I spotted him about a mile ahead; he had evidently found the seal's airhole and was getting into position to ambush the next furry little creature that came to the surface. We had a great place to land, maybe a quarter mile west of his position.

Cappy stayed in the air, and Bob and I landed. We quickly covered the plane's engine so it wouldn't cool off quite as fast; if the engine gets cold, the oil gets just like syrup, and you can't turn the engine over. I would carry like a bocce pot; we sometimes had to light this and put it under the engine to heat the oil. if it took us longer than we expected or we ran into a problem.

Once on the ice, we checked out all the gear, and we both loaded our rifles; we then worked our way through the pressure ridge and the tangle of ice blocks, many of them bigger than the airplane. When we came out the other side, we were a little off target, and the old bear saw us. And here he came; he was about two hundred yards away, closing in fast; he obviously thought we were seals or perhaps walruses. It made no difference to him—it was just a meal. He probably thought, "Man, am I lucky! I caught these seals out on the open ice, and I am going to eat good today."

"Hey, Thompson, that son of a bitch is coming after us, isn't he?"

"Looks that way to me. Are you ready?"

"I will be in a second."

"Get behind that ice block. You can use it for a rest."

The bear was now less than a hundred yards. The Rigby roared; the recoil almost made Bob lose his footing. I could see blood on the snow, but the old giant never even flinched.

"Shoot again!" I yelled.

This time, the four-hundred-grain chunk of lead hit the front left shoulder; and the bear, now only thirty yards away, was trying to figure out what was wrong. As the bear struggled to his feet, Bob fired his third shot; this time, the old bear stayed put. We waited a few minutes; he reloaded his rifle, I got my knife out, and then the work began. There lay about 1,200 to 1,400 pounds of bear; and we had to roll him around to get his beautiful white coat—not an easy task at fifty below zero. To date, this was the biggest polar bear we had taken.

In the meantime, Cappy was checking out the surrounding area, trying to locate another bear for his passenger. My football player and

I eventually got the hide off and loaded it in the airplane; we were bouncing down the ice for liftoff when I heard, "Denny, I think I left my rifle back there by that chunk of ice!"

"Are you sure?" I asked.

"Did you put it in the plane?"

"No, I don't think so."

I pulled out the throttle, slowed the plane down, and made the turn, taxiing back to where we had parked previously. We took a little stroll through the ice field; and sure enough, leaning up against the ice block was Bob's very expensive rifle. Fortunately, he thought about it when he did because once you get in the air and are a half an hour away, your chances of finding that exact spot in this mass expanse of ice is remote at best.

We rendezvoused with Cappy and his hunter; they hadn't spotted anything other than a couple of medium-sized bears; we were getting short of daylight, and we would have a headwind all the way back to Kotzebue. So we decided to call it a day, and it's a good thing we did as it was dark by the time we landed. In those days, the old airport didn't have much for landing lights; once you were close to the airport, they were adequate, but you couldn't see them from very far away. Sometimes if there was a problem with the lights (and that was quite often), they had buckets along the runway with diesel and gas in them. They would light those, and they would become our runway lights.

I think one of the most rewarding times was after the hunt; everybody had a couple of drinks, and we were sitting around the table, listening to the hunters relive and tell the story of their hunts. The sparkle in their eyes and the excitement in their voice were as rewarding as the actual hunt. And of course, the stories got a little more exciting, with an extra drink or two, as the evening crept closer to midnight.

The next day, we wound up by Point Hope before we found a nice bear; after seeing his buddy's big trophy, Tony wasn't about to settle for a runt. Eventually, we found a very nice bear for Tony. They were both extremely happy and over the years sent me a number of hunters; some of them took multiple trophies.

We had one other experience that year that was more exciting than I would have preferred. We had tracked what appeared to be a big bear—at least that's what it looked like. We eventually spotted him and made our routine detour so we could get ahead of the bear and set up our ambush; we landed approximately a mile in front of the meandering bear, always hopeful that you've chosen the right spot. This was probably our ninth or tenth hunter that year. Cappy and I were both pretty cocky; most of the hunts were about the same. The bears usually charged after the first shot; as a rule, the hunter usually got the job done. Once in a while, Cappy or I would have to help out with a shot or two; that primarily was the routine.

We were in position just in time; here he came, about two hundred yards out—at their typical fast walk, almost a lope. The plane was only about fifty yards behind us. For some reason, I turned to look at it, and there about sixty or eighty yards behind us was another bear heading directly toward us; he had come out of the ice pack someplace behind us. I suppose it spotted us and thought we were edible, and I guess he was going to take possession before his buddy could get there.

I grabbed the hunter by the shoulder, spun him around, and yelled, "Shoot!" He dropped to one knee and put his rifle to his shoulder; it seemed he took forever to shoot. The bear stumbled but kept coming; he was now only about twenty yards away. I shot; then he shot again. The bear went down. I shot him one more time in the neck just to make sure; by then, he was lying only about eight feet from where we were standing.

I turned to check on the first bear, expecting him to be hightailing it in the other direction, not so. He had actually picked up speed and was now less than a hundred yards out. I only had two shots left in my rifle, and the hunter had none; he was fumbling around, trying to get another shell in his rifle. The bear was closing in fast. I managed to get one more shell in my rifle but dropped two shells in the snow. I guess there was a possibility I might have been a little nervous. I started picking them up. I glanced at the bear. There was no time; he was not over a hundred feet out; just then, the hunter fired. Then I shot; we both immediately shot again. This time, the bear went down; the hunter hit and broke its front shoulder. As he was falling, my second shot was a little high but luckily hit the spine. I put one more shot behind his ear to end the drama. The bear was no more than fifteen feet from where we were standing, and both guns were empty; the hunter and I just stood there for a couple of minutes, staring at the bears.

"Thompson, that's the most exciting thing that's happened to me in my entire life, including my wedding night."

"You better load that rifle again, just in case," I said.

Cappy was watching this whole drama unfold while he circled overhead. I waved at him, motioning him to land; we were going to need some help getting these two bears skinned and moved in the airplanes. I don't think Cappy shut up the whole time; he was more excited than we were. And you should have heard him that night at dinner; everybody in the place stopped what they were doing while Cappy told the store. After listening to him, I'm not sure how we survived.

We had a couple more hunters that season, but nothing out of the ordinary; one thing I was totally convinced of was that I needed a bigger Super Cub. That was going to be one of the first items on my agenda when we got back to Seward.

Chapter Twenty-Two

Denny located a PA-18 with floats in Orlando, Florida, and only had a hundred hours on it. He caught a flight to Orlando to check it out; the PA-18 was for sale for $6,500. He offered the gentleman $6,000 cash and was the proud owner of a new floatplane. Denny took off from Florida, flew up the coast, and headed due west across the southern United States; there were not many facilities to accommodate floatplanes across the desert in the Southwest. To get fuel, he had the land in a river or lake where there were fishing facilities to be able to find fuel for the airplane.

Once he got to Nevada, he turned north and flew north along the east side of the Sierras. Once he got into Oregon, he headed northwest toward the Seattle area; his intentions had been to fly up the Alcan Highway, then due west through the Wrangell Mountains into Seward.

When he got to Seattle, the weather was good along the coast, and the weather report said the weather was going to hold for at least a couple more days. So Denny decided to take a chance and fly along the west coast of British Columbia and on up to Seward. The trip from Florida to Seward took a total of five days, and now Denny had the airplane he needed to become a serious contender for the growing number of hunters who were choosing Alaska for their next adventure.

It wasn't but about two months later when Denny got a call from his banker; they had just repossessed a Super Cub with very low hours. He made Denny an offer he couldn't refuse. Mr. Thompson was now the proud owner of *two* PA-18 Super Cubs and the distinction of being one of the best-equipped guides in the area.

Now Denny started to think about a lodge, someplace where his hunters could stay, and a better, more central location. Seward was okay for goats, moose, and black bears, but definitely not for brown bears, grizzly, and caribou. Wherever he relocated, he could still hunt the Kenai Peninsula if he wanted to. One more challenge was to find the best location, then get a lodge built. But first things first: Salmon season was rapidly approaching, and there were a number of things that had to be done to the boats; for the next two months, Denny worked at the docks, worked on his boats, and took about ten hunters brown bear hunting.

Back in those days, flying and hunting the same day was legal; as a rule, the hunters would stay in their hotel overnight. Denny would pick them up at the airport or their hotel, and they would go hunting and scout the area out until they found a bear to their liking. Then they would find a place to land and then try to get close enough to get a shot. Sometimes this was very simple; a couple of hours and they would have their trophy. Then came at least a half an hour of picture taking, another hour of skinning, and they would be on their way home; sometimes they would be home in time for a late lunch.

However, there were more than a few times when the hunter would choose a bear that was in a difficult spot or an area where Denny couldn't land. They would have to walk a mile or two just to get to the spot where they had last seen the bear, who, at that time, had probably decided to move someplace else; now the challenge was to find the bear in the brush without being eaten. Hunts like that usually took much longer; not only didn't you make it home for lunch—in some cases, they were lucky to get there for a midnight snack.

They tested every hunter before they put him on the bear to make sure he could shoot. However, many times, when the hunter was in position and the bear was fifty or a hundred yards away (sometimes even closer), the hunter would just freeze and couldn't move; other times, they would get so nervous that the gun would be bouncing up and down like a yo-yo. There was no way in God's green earth they could hit a barn, let alone that bear.

Sometimes Denny could get them calmed down; other times, they would hand him their rifle and tell him to shoot the bear. The worst situation was when they would take the shot and just wound the bear. He always tried to be ready for that situation; most of the time, the brown bear would disappear into the brush. Wherever there were brown bears, it seemed there were brush and tallgrass. Other times, the old bruin would come at them on the dead run; as a rule, Denny was the Lone Ranger, the only one left at the firing line that could function when the smoke cleared. And the bear lay dead, sometimes virtually at his feet; several times, he could touch the bear's nose with the barrel of his gun when it finally expired. More than once, Denny would find his hunter fifty to sixty yards away, shaking like a leaf, sometimes with his gun in hand; but most of the time, it was lying on the ground, where he had taken his first shot.

But what Denny always thought was amusing was listening to the story of the hunt four or five hours later at the bar after everybody had a couple of drinks. He first thought the hunters were just intentionally lying, but as the years went on, he believed most of those stories were the way they believed it really happened. And then of course, there was a good hunter who made a good shot, killing his quarry, with no drama. But when he got to the bar and had a couple of drinks, the stories he told were usually only bits and pieces of the real hunt, but the drama just riveted everyone to their seat. Now that's what you call a hunter.

Denny remembers one such hunter. He won't mention his name because he may still be alive. They flew down to King Salmon and stayed at the King Salmon Lodge overnight. They had a very special guest, Ted Williams. He was there to fish. They left the lodge the next day at about 7:30 a.m. and flew south the Cinder River area; in about a half an hour of scouting, they located a very nice big brown bear at a perfect spot, along a creek strewn with dead salmon from last year's salmon run. They had a great landing spot about two or three hundred yards over a little hill. Piece of cake. They landed and walked over to the edge of the creek about eighty yards from the bear. He had a good rest, two shoots, and that was it. The bear was dead on the other side of the little creek. They skinned him and were on their way home.

The weather was bad south of Anchorage, so Denny decided they had better stay another night in King Salmon. They took a little nap, then headed down to the bar to await the opening of the dining room for the evening meal. He and the hunter had both had a couple drinks and ate some popcorn when Mr. Williams came in with a basket full of walleye pike and trout. By then, there were a dozen people sitting at the bar and tables. Mr. Williams said, "If I can get the cook to fix these fish, would you guys like to join me tonight for a good old-fashioned fish fry?" Of course, everybody's response was yes. They nursed a couple more drinks and ate another bowl of popcorn over the next couple hours. The hunter kept asking Denny about the different hunting adventures he had. Of course, all hunters were always eager to share their stories, and they have a tendency to embellish the facts just slightly.

The dinner bell rang, and for the next hour, they enjoyed one of the finest fish dinners Denny has ever had; besides the fish, Mr. Williams also provided each table with a bottle of wine—a class act to say the least. Everybody was sitting around after dinner having another couple drinks. Mr. Williams shared some of the highlights of his fishing trip, of the ones he caught, as well as of the big ones that got away. Knowing that they were going bear hunting that day, he asked how they did. To make this tale a little easier to follow, Denny is going to call this hunter Tony.

"We had a good day," Denny said. "Tony here got a beautiful big brown bear. Haven't measured it yet, but I'll bet it's over ten feet." Everybody congratulated Tony on a nice job, and Denny thought that was about it, but he was now about to hear what really happened.

"Mr. Thompson here is being a little modest," Tony said. "Of course, I realize he does this every day, and I'm sure today's hunt was just a normal romp in the woods with bears for Lieutenant Thompson, but not for me. Let me tell you what really happened. We scouted the area for about an hour before Denny here spotted this big bear, and I'll bet he measures more than ten feet. This bear was down in a deep ravine. The banks were very steep and covered with brush. We circled the bear two times, trying to pick the best way to approach him. During that time, we spotted four other bears in the immediate area.

"Finally, Denny here had a plan that sounded good to me. We landed behind this little hill, then had to sneak through the brush, trying to find an opening where we could see down into that ravine. The first time we reached the edge of the ravine, we couldn't see a thing. The brush was too thick. All the time, we were trying to be as quiet as possible. Then we had to backtrack and try another approach. We went upstream about a hundred yards and found a bear trail going through the brush toward the edge of the ravine. We had to crawl on our hands and knees. We were almost to the edge when Denny stopped and lay flat on the ground and motioned for me to be very quiet. He pointed to his ear to tell me to listen. What I heard was not good. It was the breathing of a big animal. Denny pointed into the brush to our right. After about two minutes, I could see what he was looking at. About ten to twelve feet to our right. I could see patches of brown fur through the brush. There was a brown bear taking a nap.

"We slowly backed out of that area, careful not to make a sound. By the time, we cleared of the brush, we were both ringing wet with sweat. Denny said, 'Let's try one more thing. Let's see if we can get right down in that creek. I don't like that, but I think it's about the only way we're going to get a clear shot. If that doesn't work, we will find another bear.' We had to go at least a half a mile downstream before we found a way to get into the creek. Most of the time, we could keep out of the water, but not all the time. The creek was crooked, one little bend after another. Denny whispered, 'Be ready. You never know what we will encounter when we go around these bends in the creek.'

"We had moved up the creek quite a ways. By now, we were not sure exactly where the bear was. We were just about to go around the next bend in the creek when all hell broke loose just around the bend. We could tell there were two bears mixing it up. It sounded like a war. Denny grabbed me by the arm and pulled me up against the bank. Not two seconds later, this big brown bear came charging around the bend in the creek. He was pickin' 'im up and puttin' 'im down, moving just as fast as he could. When he went by us, I could have touched him with my gun barrel. Not twenty feet behind him was a second bear, even bigger. He was so intent on killing the first bear that he didn't even see us.

"Denny said, 'Get ready.' I was so excited I forgot why we were there. it took me a moment to realize what he meant. The first bear tore up the bank and was out of sight. That seemed to satisfy the big bear, and he stopped right on the edge of the creek, about seventy-five yards downstream. Denny whispered, 'Take your time. He's not going anyplace.' I had a good broad side shoot and fired. The bear turned on a dime and charged—not at all what I expected. I shot again. The bear was still coming. He was now maybe twenty-five yards away. This was my last shoot. I fired, as did Denny. The bear dropped like a rock. One of us hit him in the neck."

While he was telling his story, you could have heard a pin drop; after it was over, everybody offered them drinks. Mr. Williams congratulated him on a great job. Denny had seen lots of guys stretch the truth, but this was one of the best he could remember.

Sam Levits with his huge brown bear taken in 1977

Chapter Twenty-Three

Susitna Lodge

It was 1958, one year before I started the lodge, but it was actually when the work really began. First, I had to locate a site people could find quite easily. I also had to have room to build a landing strip in an area where there weren't clouds or fog most of the time and where the wind was primarily right down the runway. I found a spot on the Denali Highway, about sixty miles off the Fairbanks–Anchorage Highway, on a little lake. This was the perfect spot. I could land on the lake with the floats or on my runway, which I had yet to build. Prevailing winds were favorable, and there was lots of room at both ends of the runway with no obstacle.

I had to file with the state for an eighty-acre homestead, then have the property surveyed. All of that took time. By 1959, everything was in place to start on the lodge; the owner of the First National Bank of Alaska loaned me $50,000 on his signature. But first things first. He had an entire year of fishing and hunting to try to accumulate the rest of the money to build the kind of lodge he had in mind.

By the end of January, we had sixteen polar bear hunts on the books; by then, most of the hunters were aware that if the bear hunt went well and we had enough time, we would work on a wolf hunt. North and east of Kotzebue were nothing but tundra for miles, with no trees and only some brush on the creek and riverbanks, with most of them not more than five to six feet tall. There were also lots of reindeer, which seemed to feed the wolf population adequately. This was the first year we had the new high-powered PA-18 Super Cubs. They were much faster, could carry a bigger load, and were just all around a better plane.

The weather was good. It was cold, of course, but not too windy. There were no storms and no bears either, at least in the areas where we were used to finding them. The first two hunting parties had to stay an extra day; after spending the first day, we found nothing worth shooting. On the second day, we decided to go farther west. Sure enough, when we got out to about two hundred miles, we started to spot some good bears; but by then, we were getting very low on sunlight. We had only perhaps an hour and a half of daylight left, but at least we knew where to go tomorrow.

On day 3, we left Kotzebue before daylight; we had to try to get both polar bears that day, or someone was going to go home very disappointed. We did in fact get both bears.

Our fourth hunting party was with a couple of young guys out of Los Angeles. During the first day, we got them a couple of nice bears: a nine-and-half-footer and a ten-footer. Since they had an extra day, I asked them if they would they like to try for a wolf; there was no hesitation. I had heard some more stories about some extraordinarily big wolves up on the North Slope, so I suggested the North Slope for our wolf hunt; they thought that was extraordinary. The next morning, we were all up before daylight, ready to go; but it seemed one of the boys did a little too much partying the night before and couldn't make it. So the three of us loaded up the two airplanes and headed north; we spotted reindeer and wolves from twenty miles outside of Kotzebue, all the way to the Colville River Basin.

There was an abandoned military landing strip at a little place called Umiat. Wien Airlines used it for an emergency landing strip; there was a Quonset hut that they kept heated, so we decided to stop there for a few minutes and get warmed up. Just outside the door, hanging on the wall, was a thermometer; it read –67°. Our hunter saw that and looked at me in disbelief.

"That can't be right, can it? I know it's cold, but is it really sixty-seven below zero?"

"I'm afraid so. Believe it or not, it even gets colder than that. I've heard of temperatures in the eighty-below-zero range up here talked about more than once. This is an area you don't want to make mistakes in. They could cost you your life."

We sat around a little oil stove for a few minutes, but we didn't have the luxury of wasting a lot of time; the days up here were even shorter than in Kotzebue.

"Okay, gentlemen, I think we'd better get going. There should be some wolves in that river basin. We just need to find where they're at and flush them out."

Cappy and I headed for the door, but the hunter stayed put.

"Guys, it's just too damn cold out there. Will you shoot me a wolf? I don't think I could hit one anyway, the way I'm shaking."

"Okay. Cappy, we better get at it. We are running out of daylight."

We got in our airplanes and were airborne in a matter of a couple of minutes. Cappy headed upriver, and I headed to the north. I hadn't flown for more than a mile when I spotted a big old black wolf all by himself; he came out of the brush along the river and took off across the tundra. I turned and followed him for just a little ways and set the plane down behind him; then I taxied up as close as I felt I dared, shut the plane off, grabbed my rifle, and exited the plane. The wolf ran for about another fifty to seventy-five yards, stopped, and turned broadside just like in the script. I used the strut of the airplane as a rest; my old .270 performed again. I taxied the airplane up to where the wolf was; this was an old-timer, with a couple of broken teeth and lots of scars, I suspect he got from defending his territory. It was a very large animal, and it took me quite some time to wrestle him in the back of the Airplane I'm sure he weighed more than I did, unless you considered all the damn clothes I had on.

I could hear Cappy heading back to the airstrip; the sun had now disappeared over the horizon, and it was getting darker by the minute. I taxied the airplane into the wind and just started to pick up speed when I hit a large clump of grass buried in the snow; it tore the ski right off the airplane, and I came to a very sudden stop. I made a quick appraisal of the situation and decided there was absolutely nothing I could do that night to fix that airplane. I had to get a fire started, or I'd be dead before midnight. The only place where there was anything that you could burn was along the riverbanks; there was willow and alder brush on both sides of the river, nothing very big, but there was usually a lot of dead stuff lying around. I grabbed a can of camp stove gas out of the back of the plane and headed for the riverbank, which was almost a half a mile away.

I picked the spot that was down over the bank that was protected from the wind. I broke off a pile of twigs and branches, and within fifteen minutes, I had a nice fire; in twenty minutes, it was all burned up already. So the rest of the night, I was either huddled around the fire or collecting wood; this went on for the next eighteen hours before I even saw a trace of light in the eastern sky. I was so tired I was ready to collapse. I had not sat down all night. I knew if I sat down for just a minute, I would fall asleep; and within an hour, I'd be stiff as a board, frozen solid.

The sun was just starting to peek over the horizon when I heard an airplane; it was Cappy and the hunter flying down the river, looking for me. Not only was the one ski torn off, but the prop was also bent; after I got warmed up, we had to dig the ski out of the snow and take the prop off, then go back to the Quonset hut and do some major repairs. We put the prop in the vice and were able to get it—not perfect by any means, but usable. Then we jury-rigged a couple of 2x6s and bolted the ski to the bottom of them. Long story short, we ferried all that back out to the airplane and got it attached; as unbelievable as it may seem, I took off and flew back to Kotzebue no worse for wear, other than my old beaver skin parka having most of the hair singed off the back side. I guess I was standing a little too close to the fire during the night.

Our hunter went home with a beautiful polar bear and a black wolf pelt, and God only knows what kind of a story he told his friends. All is well that ends well. This all happened about two hundred miles north of the Arctic Circle.

The rest of our hunts that season were pretty routine except for the last one; although it started out like most of the rest, we were now flying about an hour and a half northwest every morning just to get to the bears. That morning was no exception; we were about two hundred miles out when we picked up the tracks of an exceptionally big bear. We started to follow him; he was going due north. We had been on that track probably forty or fifty miles when, lo and behold, there was our bear lying dead on the snow with two Super Cubs parked right alongside it; a couple of the other hunters in the area had beat us to the punch. We had flown over several other tracks that looked interesting. So we decided to go back and try to pick up on one of them, and hopefully, we wouldn't have to follow it too long. We passed up two nice tracks. I was quite certain I had seen a bigger track farther south; we flew about another ten minutes, and there it was—the tracks were going west toward Siberia. We only had to follow him for about another ten minutes; he had caught a seal and was just in the middle of dinner. He was right on the edge of the pressure ridge; the closest spot we could land was on the other side of the ridge, about three quarters of a mile away. We looked the situation over carefully and decided it was doable.

The hunter and I landed, and Cappy stayed in the air; we made our way through the maze of broken ice and came out about eighty yards downwind, just about the perfect position. The hunter seemed to be reasonably calm. I had no reason to suspect that he was going to have one of the most serious cases of buck fever I had ever encountered. At first, I thought he was just being cautious; but after about ten minutes, I realized he was having a problem. He kept whispering to me about what a beautiful animal this bear was, etcetera, etcetera. Finally, I had to threaten to tell all his buddies he was too scared to shoot the bear; he thought about that for a minute, and I guess he came to his senses and realized why we were there. He was shooting a .338 Remington, plenty of gun to do the job; if he just didn't shoot the bear in the ass, and that's exactly what he did. From a docile-looking creature eating dinner, he turned into an enraged wounded animal with mayhem on his mind; he spun around, spotted us, and here he came. I was not about to stand around and watch what might happen next. I started to shoot; at that point, I couldn't be concerned about what the hunter was doing. My focus was to stop that bear; my second shot broke his left front shoulder. He went down momentarily but was back up, continuing the charge on three legs. The hunter finally decided to shoot again; this time, the shot was dead center. The bear turned to his left. The hunter took one more shot; that was all that was needed as the bear collapsed in the snow.

Cappy landed right next to the bear; by the time we got it skinned out and loaded in the airplane, it was starting to snow. We knew we were north of Point Hope, but I felt we were at least three hundred miles north of Kotzebue. I just felt the safest option was to fly due east until we hit the coastline, and we could follow it south to Kotzebue; there was no doubt we were going to arrive in Kotzebue well after dark. The sky was much darker to the south. I truly hoped that didn't mean heavier snow. I had my taste of more than a couple whiteouts and didn't like any one of them. I landed and just waited one out; a couple of the other times, I was able to just fly along at ground level and was able to get out of it—scary.

I told Cappy to get behind me and just stay on my tail if it got bad and not take his eyes off my plane for even a second. The first seventy-five to one hundred miles wasn't bad. We could fly at one hundred feet and still see the ice packs; as the light faded and the snow got more intense, I had to drop down to twenty or thirty feet to be able to see. There were times when I couldn't see at all. I would just hold the plane level, hoping that we would eventually get a spot where we could see the ice pack again, which occurred several times in that last fifty-mile stretch to the coastline. We were about fifteen feet above the ground when we finally crossed over some brush forty to fifty feet back off the coastline. I immediately turned south and started to follow the coastline, but within ten to fifteen miles, we were just skimming the top of the brush. I decided to land. I knew there were a couple of villages right along the ocean in this area, but I had no way of knowing how far away they were. Cappy landed right behind me. We got out and talked for a couple of minutes. I explained that I wanted to continue to taxi south along the coastline in hopes of coming across one of those villages. I taped a big red rag to the tail of my plane in hopes that Cappy would be able to see it and not run into the back of me if I had to suddenly stop.

We taxied down the coast for about forty-five minutes; we almost ran into the team of huskies and a native that was headed north. We stopped and talked to him for a couple of minutes; he said we had about four to five miles yet to go. The village was right on the coast, so we couldn't miss it; he felt for sure several of the elders would be glad to have company for the night. He also felt that by sunup, the storm would have passed, and we would have clear sailing in to Kotzebue.

As we got close to town, we could hear the commotion of dozens of dogs barking; another hundred yards and we were right on the edge of the village. There was one yard light about in the center of the village on a little pole perhaps ten feet high; as we stepped out of the airplanes, several doors opened. A couple of natives slipped into their parkas and stepped out into the cold, curious as to what we were doing in the middle of their village with a couple of airplanes. I explained what had happened and what our situation was and asked if it were possible that we stayed with them for the night until the storm cleared up enough that we could fly again. They seemed to be elated that they would have company for the evening. I had several extra cigars, which I handed out to all the men I saw; even one of the older ladies asked if she could have one.

They split us up in three different huts; in all three cases, the women immediately fixed us a hot meal. They never stopped asking questions; they wanted to know where we came from, what we were doing, and what it was like to fly. I told them the next time I was in this area and I had some time, I would take them for a ride in the airplane; that seemed a bit frightening to them, but they were quite sure they would like that. They were still asking questions when I fell asleep.

The next morning, as predicted by the man on the sled, the weather was still cloudy; but the storm had passed. Visibility was several miles; after last night, it seemed like we could see forever. Whiteouts are scary—about the worst situation, I can imagine.

As soon as we wrapped everything up in Kotzebue and made our way back to Seward, I had at least a half a dozen brown bear hunts scheduled, which had to be taken care of before the salmon season opened because we were definitely going back to Shelikof Strait at least this one more year.

Chapter Twenty-Four

I had a young guy by the name of Bill Sims I had been working with. I was teaching him to fly; flying for him seemed to be natural. He had good instincts and a burning desire to be a bush pilot. He had only about twenty-five hours of experience; the first time I took him on a bear hunt, I had two hunters. They rode with me, and Billy carried all the tents and camping gear; we flew down to Bear Lake, a hundred-plus miles south of Kodiak Island, just north of Pavlof Volcano, but south of Port Heiden—The mountains to the southeast where absolutely great bear country.

Every year of my hunting career, I probably took on an average of eight to ten nice bears from this area. At that time of the year, the bears are just coming out of hibernation; they primarily headed for the streams, creeks, and rivers, which were normally lined with dead salmon from last year's spawning run. The bottoms of the bears' feet, at this time of the year, are soft and tender because of inactivity during the winter. Therefore, when they emerge from their long sleep, they usually take the shortest route to the best food source; and that's where they'll spend the next couple of weeks until the bottoms of their feet start to get tougher.

When we arrived at Bear Lake, we spent perhaps a half an hour just scouting the area; during that half hour, we counted forty or fifty bears. It was a smorgasbord; we just had to determine which ones we wanted to hunt and what would be the best and easiest route to get to our quarry. Both hunters got very nice bears, and in three days, we were headed back to Seward; we had such good luck at this spot that we decided to leave our tent and camping gear here at Bear Lake and just bring our next group of hunters back to the same area.

They were even more successful; one of their bears squared off at eleven feet. It did in fact make the record book—not number 1, but definitely qualified to get in the book. Altogether, we took seven bears from that same campsite that spring; we took a couple north of Port Heiden, and if I remember right, I think we took another five bears north of Bristol Bay in the Dillingham area and two grizzly bears just outside the Mount McKinley Park area.

One of those was kind of an interesting hunt; while we were flying around scouting the area, we spotted several nice-looking bears. One of those was a beautiful silvertip grizzly; naturally, he was the most difficult bear to get to and the one the hunter wanted. We had to land down at the bottom of this canyon, hike about a mile and a half up the canyon, then climb up the side of the canyon, which was about three hundred to four hundred feet, to get into position where we could be above where the grizzly was feeding on an old moose carcass. Once we reached our destination, we expected to be about five hundred yards east and at least a couple hundred feet higher than the old bear. The terrain was primarily brush covered with just intermittent open areas between the patches of brush; we felt once we had located the grizzly, we could work our way down the hill, using those open areas but staying behind the brush for cover.

As we settled into position and started to look for the grizzly bear, it wasn't long until I picked up the moose carcass, but no bear; this wasn't entirely unpredictable. A bear will usually gorge himself, eating every morsel possible, and then go off into the brush and take a nap. The duration of that nap can be anywhere from an hour to perhaps three or four hours; you just never know. We decided to sit for a little while to see if we could spot any type of movement in the brush; if we knew precisely where he was located, we might be able to spook him out into the open. I was scanning the area carefully with my binoculars. I had been watching the area for maybe about a half an hour when the hunter nudged me.

"Hey, Denny, is that a bear down in the canyon?" he asked.

I immediately looked at where he was pointing; sure as hell, there was a bear going up the canyon, basically the same route we had just taken. I put the glasses on him and watched him for a few minutes; not only was he going up the same area we had just walked an hour ago, but he also had his nose on the ground as if he was trailing something, like an old coonhound. I glanced back at the moose carcass—no activity there at all. I told the hunter to keep an eye on the area where the moose carcass was. I was going to watch this grizzly in the canyon and see what he was up to; he had been in the shadows ever since we first spotted him, but now he came out into the sunlight. Sure as hell, he was a silvertip. It was hard to believe there'd be two silvertip bears in this close proximity to each other, but it was also hard to believe that he would leave the moose carcass and go down into that canyon just to check us out.

The more I watched him, the more I was convinced it was the same bear we had spotted on the moose carcass; but I couldn't be 100 percent sure, which meant if we went crawling around the side of this mountain, it was possible we'd stumble onto the bear that was asleep down by the carcass. And that wouldn't be good. I decided to move just a little bit to my right so I could keep an eye on the bear moving up the canyon; he was getting very close to where we turned and climbed up the hill. If he made that turn, there was very little doubt he was tracking us. If that was the case, I needed to move to a much better vantage point; where we were now sitting, he could get within twenty or thirty feet of us before we could even see him—not near enough room in my estimation. If he came out of the brush on the dead run, one shot would be all you could get—if you were lucky. There weren't many choices; the whole side of that mountain was covered by brush, except for kind of a bald rocky knob on the other side of where the moose carcass was. I still wasn't totally convinced the bear in the canyon was the same bear we had seen on the moose carcass. I was watching the bear move up the canyon intently. I was just about ready to give a sigh of relief, quite sure he had passed the point where we had made the turn; then he stopped, sniffed the ground like an old bloodhound, found our trail again, and headed up the side of the mountain. I had heard stories of bears tracking men but had never experienced it before; to say the least, it was somewhat unnerving.

I turned to my hunter and said, "We need to get moving. If this old son of a gun is going to be after us, we have to get in a better position to defend ourselves."

"You really think he's coming after us?"

"I have no idea if he's coming after us or if he's just curious. But I don't intend to sit in the middle of this brush patch and ask him when he shows up. Let's go."

We hightailed it down the hill, stayed about fifty yards to the left of the moose carcass, and worked our way up the hill; approximately two hundred yards beyond the carcass, we took turns glancing behind us just to make sure he wasn't closer than we thought. We had just about reached our destination when I spotted him coming out of the brush in the area where we had just been sitting; we ducked down behind some of the brush. He spent at least a minute sniffing around the area where we had been sitting; he followed our tracks down the hill. When he got to a point within a couple hundred feet of the moose carcass, he made a mad dash for the carcass and chased several ravens that had decided to come in and have a little lunch; he checked the entire area around the carcass and then decided to eat a little more moose meat. I looked the area over. I felt that we could get fifty to seventy-five yards closer, but the wind was not in our favor. And if we snapped just one twig, God only knows what he might do. He could disappear into the brush, never to be seen again; or he could come charging up the hill like a runaway freight train, giving us very little opportunity for a good shot, as he plowed through the brush.

The hunter was looking this situation over very carefully. "Denny," he whispered, "that's not a bad shot right where we're at. I don't think we're more than two hundred yards. That's what my rifle is cited in at. I can use this pile of rocks over here for a rest."

"That's up to you, if you feel comfortable. Take your time."

He got situated behind the rocks, disengaged his safety, and was just ready to shoot when the old bear turned, almost facing us.

"You've got the perfect shot," I whispered, "right in the center of that left front shoulder." His .338 roared like a cannon, echoing up and down the canyons; the impact knocked the bear completely off his feet—something you don't see very often. He rolled around in a circle, biting at his shoulder, for about thirty seconds. He let out one powerful nerve-shattering roar, and one scary hour was over with.

There's no knowing what might've happened if we hadn't moved; the ending might've been much more exciting, but for me, this was exciting enough. The bear was definitely one of the best grizzlies I had taken to that point; he was big, and his coloring was as good as I'd ever seen. We got him skinned out and back to the airplane, and we were back home before dark.

Chapter Twenty-Five

The fishing season for 1958 was good; it seemed it got a little better every year. I don't think it had near as much to do with the abundance of fish as it did with our experience; we now had a system, and the little things that threw us a curve at the beginning were now just routine. I hit two gulls this year: one was so bad that I actually had to land and clean the windshield; the other one hit the wing so hard that it tore some of the fiberglass on the leading edge of the wing. That night, after we set her up on the fantail of the *Paula*, I had to do a little repair work on the wing.

There were a lot of problems that year with the beluga whale; they were everywhere, many more than I remember seeing in the past years. If they got mixed in with the school of salmon, we couldn't set the nets; they would tear big holes in them, so I had to try to skim back and forth across the water between the salmon and the whale and spook the salmon one way and the whales the other. It worked most of the time, but not always; sometimes we just had to let that school of salmon go.

About midway through the season, we had a stretch of bad weather—windy and rainy for a solid week. I took some extra provisions and stuck them in the back of the airplane that morning before they set me in the water; it was rough flying all day, but they caught lots of fish. It was time for me to either get back aboard the *Paula* or find some quiet, peaceful water up an inlet someplace and camp out for the night. No chance of getting back aboard the *Paula* as the seas were way too rough, so campout it was. The weather was so bad I didn't even consider trying to catch a fish or get a fire going, so a can of Spam was the menu for tonight. I saw a couple of nice bears, but they stayed their distance, and the whole evening was uneventful; the next day was very much like the past couple days, windy and rainy. They had to make a run into the cannery that evening, so there was no way we could get the Cub back on. The *Paula*, my destiny for the evening, was up a little cove and shared some peace and quiet with the bears. I didn't have to go very far up the inlet to find protection from the wind; the fishing boats were anchored about a half a mile from shore.

I decided to walk down to the beach. I felt sure the crew would be able to see me and send a skiff in to pick me up. I hiked down to the beach and commenced to wave my arms and shout. I did that for the better part of an hour with no results; no one spotted me. I don't even think they looked in my direction. So before it got completely dark, I decided I had better make my way back to the airplane. That night, I decided if the weather stayed the same, I was going to find them a deep-enough channel so we could pull the *Paula* out of the weather, and they could set me and the Cub on the fantails, and I could get a hot meal for the first time in about fifty hours.

The next day, we worked our way up the coast about forty miles; there was a nice bay, and it was jam-packed full of fish. We, all three boats, harbored there for the night; the next morning, we had high tide. The first thing we did was set nets in that little bay and made a killing; we had two loads a piece per seiner caught and loaded on the *Paula* before noon, and I never even set the planes in the water.

It was a couple days later; the weather was clear and kind of balmy that morning when we got up. The water in the strait was calmer than what we were used to; anytime we got a day like this, we look at it as a gift. Everyone felt energized. As the sun rose over the mountains to the east of us, it looked like a bright red ball of fire. There was always a few clouds that seemed to hang around Mount McKinley; other than that, I don't believe there was a cloud in the sky.

We set the Cub in the water. I took along a few provisions and a couple of sandwiches, then took off to the south in search of some salmon. I don't believe I was airborne more than twenty or thirty minutes when I spotted a nice school of fish making their way north about a quarter mile off the mainland. I made several circles over the school of salmon, which got the attention of the seiners; they moved into position and set the nets. Within an hour, they were closing the nets. Both seiners were full of fish within two hours. While they were transferring the fish to the *Paula*, I flew south not more than ten to fifteen miles and spotted another large school of fish; the boys weren't ready yet, so I continued to look for more fish. In the next half hour, I spotted two more large groups of salmon. In four years of fishing the strait, I had never seen this amount of salmon in such a small area. I flew back to the boat to tell the crew what was out there and what I felt we should do to take advantage of the opportunities.

The water in the strait was even calmer than it was that morning when we got out; it makes everything you do on a boat just that much easier. Pete Kramer, the oldest guy in our crew, had been fishing these waters for at least twenty-five years; he warned us, saying, "Something's wrong. This isn't normal."

We should've paid attention, but we didn't. I got airborne again and located the closest school of fish; they filled the nets again and transferred the fish to the *Paula*; before they were done, I had another large school of fish located not more than a mile from where we were anchored.

This was promising to be the biggest day ever; one more catch and we would have more fish in the *Paula* than at any time over the last four years, and we would still have eight hours of daylight left.

By now, I could see a buildup of clouds way off on the western horizon; it looked to me like it would be well after dark before that storm would arrive. I felt two more sets and we would have more fish than we had ever caught in one day; that was a goal we had all talked about, and it definitely felt within reach that day.

The next set took just a little bit longer than we figured on, but we still had plenty of time to make the fifth and final set and shatter all our previous records for fish caught in one day. I had to go about ten miles before I found the next school of fish, and they were crowding the bank just about a hundred yards off the beach. I had glanced at the approaching weather front several times and was surprised at how rapidly it seemed to be approaching, but it seemed we would still have plenty of time. I had to circle the fish for about a half an hour before the guys could get set up. I was just thinking about heading back to the *Paula* and get the Cub aboard the boat before the storm hit when, out of nowhere, a blast of wind hit me and just about turned me upside down; within minutes, there were four- to five-foot waves.

I fought to maintain control of the plane. It was bouncing me around worse than any German flak I had ever encountered. I estimated the winds were at least seventy-five to eighty miles an hour; the sky was starting to get blacker by the minute. A return to the *Paula* was totally out of the question. I couldn't even see the seiners. I had no idea how they were faring. I knew I only had minutes to find a place to land and get out of this wind, or I'd be torn apart. I had to fly north because I couldn't buck the wind coming from the south. I wasn't more than fifty feet off the water and rapidly losing the battle when I spotted a little inlet that went inland far enough to give me some protection from the wind. I was able to fly up this little creek, not more than one hundred feet wide and rapidly narrowing. I found a little gravel bar, beached the plane on that, cut the engine, and hoped I would stay there until the rain let up; it was raining so hard at times that I couldn't even see the prop, and it was only six feet in front of me.

Now that I was reasonably safe, my concern turned to the fellows that were on the boats; they were out in the open. There was nothing much they could do but turn the boats into the wind and just ride it out. By then, it was dark and no letup in the storm; the rains were torrential. I could hear the wind roaring overhead, but where I was sitting, I was pretty well protected. I must've dozed off several times; when I finally came to my senses and realized I was no longer on the gravel bar and was instead bobbing up and down in the choppy waters, the rain had let up, and the howling wind was not howling quite as loud.

I grabbed my flashlight. I could not find anything that looked familiar; the hundred-foot-wide creek I had landed in now appeared to be in excess of a hundred yards wide and moving rather rapidly. There was brush and small trees in every direction I looked; now it started to make sense. I was in the middle of a flash flood; if I didn't do something and soon, I would be washed right out into the strait. My only option was to crank up the engine, taxi upstream, and try to find some backwater out of the current. I had to do that while holding my light out the window in hopes that I could see where I was going. After about twenty minutes of dodging floating logs and brush piles, I got close enough to the bank and found a little cove where the water wasn't moving. I cut the engine and looked at my watch; it was 3:00 a.m. I still had two to two and a half hours before it started to get daylight.

About every half hour to forty-five minutes, I had to start the engine and move the plane back into the quiet water; it was still raining, but not nearly as hard. Likewise, the wind had diminished, slightly more than the average for this area, but a far cry from what it was just five to six hours earlier.

Daylight finally arrived; little by little, I could see what was going on. The water in this inlet appeared to be five to six feet higher than the ocean and was rushing downstream at a breakneck pace, carrying all the trash and debris that had washed off the hillside. The backwater where I was sitting was starting to go down slightly. I had to be careful not to be stranded; it was about 7:30 a.m. when I finally decided I could see well enough to take off without running into some of the debris, which seemed to be just about everywhere. I clipped a couple of submerged chunks of debris with no adverse consequences; the floats finally pulled free of the water's icy grip, and we were airborne.

Now that I was back in the air, my first concern was to find the boats. I had to fly almost a half an hour north before I spotted the first boat; all hands were aboard and accounted for and were under way. The second boat was another two miles to the northeast, and it did not have power. I had to fly back and get boat 1 to help boat 2. The *Paula* rode out the storm and was in good shape; we did break our record for one day, but when I look back, all of the fish in the Shelikof Strait wouldn't temp me to go through another day like that.

It was a good year, very profitable, but I had some very close calls with the airplane; it was kind of like flying over Germany and being shot at every day. Sooner or later, you're lucky rabbit's foot will stop working, and that's how I felt about flying the Shelikof Strait. The strait had been very good to me, but it was time to move on.

I had been approached by a rancher on Kodiak Island; he was interested in buying the *Paula*. He wanted her for moving cattle from one part of the island to another. I looked him up and made a deal, selling the *Paula* for $10,000; he paid $2,000 down and the rest that fall when he sold his cattle. I never saw the other $8,000. The story goes that he had a load of horses aboard the boat and got caught in a storm. It was high tide, and he had to beach the boat on a mudflat. The waves from the storm and the high tide pushed the boat so high up the beach that they were never able to get it back in the water; as far as I know, it's still sitting there.

This was our last year of fishing in the strait or any other part of Alaska for almost twenty years. Professional hunting and guiding was now a full-time job. The only thing about fishing that was fun was picking up your check; the rest of it was just backbreaking, hard, dangerous work. At least hunting had its moments when it was interesting, entertaining, and sometimes spine-tingling dangerous. Every day was different; you may hunt the same animal in the same area, but it would be a totally different adventure.

The rest of 1958 was spent acquiring the land for my new lodge; plus we had dozens of hunters for moose and caribou that fall and a number of brown and grizzly bear hunts in the fall. Late that season, if I remember right, we took another trip back to Minnesota to see our parents and show off our two young sons Denny Jr. and Lee. They both became excellent pilots and mechanics and still both live in Anchorage, Alaska.

Susitna Lodge Denny's first lodge built in 1959
Denny guided out of here until 1970

Fred Bear Hall of fame Bow hunter, Denny and a
couple local boys enjoying Fred story's

Chapter Twenty-Six

Full-Time Professional Guide

The years 1959 and 1960 were very interesting, with 1959 involving working on the lodge from daylight to dark.

One day, an old guy from Los Angeles drove into the parking lot; he introduced himself as Grandpa Hawken—to this day, the only name I know him by. He wanted to go caribou hunting. I told him I was too busy. I had to get this lodge done before winter. He stomped around and cussed at me and the weather and anything else he could think of; he then went to his truck and sat there for maybe an hour. Then he came over where we were working on some steps and suggested I didn't know what I was doing. I agreed but told him I would have it done by winter. He suggested he could help; he was a carpenter and would help me build my lodge in trade for some hunting. I asked him to show me what he could do; he went back to the trailer and pulled out a big box with all kinds of tools and finished the steps we were working on in half the time it would've taken me. I had tons of interior work, such as the bar and kitchen, that had to be done. I agreed to take him hunting once we got some of the carpenter work caught up.

As it worked out, Grandpa Hawken was a great help; he was probably one of the grouchiest old men I ever met. He never smiled and always complained about something; he was a genuine pain in the ass but did very good work and really improved the quality of the lodge. But it seemed like every couple of weeks, he had to get drunk for about two or three days. He lay around in his camper except for an hour or two a day, at which time he would walk around and watch what we were doing and inform us in no uncertain terms that we didn't know what the hell we were doing; in most cases, I would probably agree.

The lodge had eight rooms upstairs and a bar, kitchen, and dining room downstairs. The bar had a big fireplace and was called the Wolf Den; there was a nice porch on three sides. The Wolf Den and the porches seemed to be where everyone congregated and told the biggest lies they could think of; and I'm here to tell you some of them had quite an imagination.

Probably the biggest favor Grandpa Hawken did for me was the introduction of Royce Myers and his wife. Royce was a bartender at the world-famous Brown Derby in Los Angeles. Hawken and Myers were old friends, and when he told Royce about my new lodge in the wilderness, Royce was intrigued. He and his wife showed up in their brand-new airstream several months later and made a deal with me to manage the lodge and help keep track of the hunting parties and the everyday stuff that had to be done; plus Mrs. Myers was a good cook, so she took care of the kitchen.

One big negative for 1960 was my divorce with Jean. I was never home, and Jean didn't want to move into the wilderness. So a separation seemed the most appropriate solution.

By the spring of 1960, the lodge was complete, and the staff was in place. The beginning of the fabulous 1960s was about to begin. San Francisco had the flower children, and Alaska had me, Denny Thompson.

This could probably be considered the heyday of Alaska hunting; there was abundant game and minimal regulations. Polar bears were still legal and abundant, and there were still areas in Alaska that had not been hunted yet; times were good.

Mr. Myers helped introduce me to some very prestigious people, and my reputation grew. I worked very hard to live up to that billing but never forgot where I came from. Nor did I fail to realize how fortunate I was to complete that thirtieth mission and be able to walk away from that flak-riddled B-17 and return home in one piece so I could pursue my dreams. Now here I was, living my dream.

Chapter Twenty-Seven

The year 1960 was a big one; the new lodge was open. We had sixteen hunters booked for polar bear hunting and twice that many for brown bear and grizzly. I don't know how many goats and sheep or moose and caribou hunts we had booked. But that summer, we never got a minute's rest.

The polar bear hunting seasons started out with two hunters from Dallas, two of the biggest bullshit artists I think I've ever met; they were fun to be around and good hunters, but they had forgotten what the truth was many years ago. It was the end of February. I don't remember the exact day, but I do remember that morning, we grabbed a little breakfast at the Igloo—not much of a café, but it was all that was open at that time of the morning. Bacon and eggs was $14 a plate—that was in 1960. You could probably buy the same thing in McGregor, Iowa, for a dollar and get free coffee.

We walked out of the Igloo just as the sky started to show a glimmer of light on the eastern horizon; we made our way down to the tie-down area and pulled the planes out and got them started. The temperature was a balmy thirty-five below zero. Two days previous, the wind had blown like a hurricane—a totally whiteout for the whole day, which meant any tracks we saw that day would be no older than about twenty-four hours. We took off with the sun to our back and headed northwest; due to the bad weather, Cappy and I had not been able to scout the area out. So that morning, we were just flying on dumb luck, hoping we didn't have to fly all the way to the Russian coast before we picked up some bear tracks.

And we were in luck! After being in the air for not more than about fifty minutes, we picked up our first set of tracks—not a very big bear, but we felt quite sure where there was one, there would be more. We were into our flight nearly an hour and a half before we spotted a set of bear tracks that made us sit up and pay attention. We didn't follow him more than five miles when we spotted him making his way north through a maze of broken ice; we stayed back at least a half a mile and made a couple of slow lazy circles and watched the bear to get an indication where his destination might be. Once we felt comfortable where we thought he was headed, I made a detour around the bear, and we landed approximately a mile and a half in front of what we considered his most likely route. My hunter removed his rifle from the case. I was watching the area where I felt the bear would make his appearance; the hunter was trying to put shells in his rifle but dropped several in the snow.

"Hey, Thompson, I don't have the right shells for this rifle!"

"Are you absolutely sure?" I asked.

"I'm afraid so."

"Let's get out of here. I don't want to be here when that bear arrives with just one gun."

We were back in the air in just a few minutes; we told Cappy what happened. He had his hunter check his gun to make sure his shells worked; once that was confirmed, he landed in front of the bear. I continued to stay airborne and keep an eye on the operation. They were successful and bagged the bear; it was a nice ten-and-a-half-foot bear; the hunter I had with me was very quiet on our trip back to Kotzebue and took an unmerciful amount of kidding from his partner that evening. The next day, he used his partner's gun, and we were successful in getting him a bear. The rest of the polar bear season that year is kind of a blur. I believe everyone got their bear with no major mishaps. I know we got several big bears, but I can't remember if any of them went in the record books that year. We also took fifteen or twenty wolves.

Chapter Twenty-Eight

The Susitna Lodge

With no fishing this year, I had a lot more time to dedicate toward hunting. I booked more springtime bear hunts and spent a lot more time that year looking for new areas. I spent some time in the Brooks Range looking at the Dall sheep population and a lot of time in the Wrangell Mountains, looking for both sheep and goats. But by far, the best sheep were in the Alaska Range. I also spent some time on the peninsula south of King Salmon and Naknek in the Cinder River area; there seemed to be more brown bears in that area than any other place in Alaska—and these were big bears. Through the years, I proved that by taking numerous big bears that made the record book.

New requests for information were coming in daily. Royce was a great help, and his wife did an outstanding job in the kitchen.

After we got the lodge at Susitna up and running, when I had time, I would fly into new areas. I would scout them out, trying to determine where the best place might be for my next group of hunters. It was on one of these days that I decided to scout out the moose population north of Wasilla; hunting there five years earlier was exceptionally good, but the last two years were not very good. So I decided I would check that area out first. I took the .270 and my 12-gauge shotgun, which had about six inches cut off the end of the barrel. I knew I would see wolves, but most of the time, they were in the timber. You couldn't find a place to land, and you couldn't shoot them from the plane. There were a couple of areas on the side of the mountain with an occasional tree or two, but mostly just brush and tundra and lots of open areas and places to land; and in some cases, it was open enough that you could shoot from the plane. There were normally several herds of caribou in this area and in the past a very healthy population of moose, but as of late, the wolves had taken their toll. Last fall, I had estimated the caribou herd to be one-third what they were five years earlier. It was hard to estimate on the moose, but I know they were down at least 50 percent; the wolf pack was much bigger than normal. Last fall, as I was coming home from a grizzly bear hunt, I flew over this area and counted eighteen wolves in one pack; with those numbers and a smart leader, if they could find it, they could kill it.

I arrived at the area a little after 10:00 a.m. The snow was three to four days old. The landscape looked like a postcard. The fir trees were coated in snow. The sky was clear. The sun was bright. The mountainside sparkled like diamonds. I had to fly over forty to fifty miles of forest. I spotted eight or ten moose. I should have spotted thirty or forty, but the snow in that area appeared to be clear up to their bellies, which was an advantage for the moose with their long legs. The wolves would have to really struggle to plow through that depth of snow, so they tried to avoid the areas of deep snow.

Once I reached the more open country, I flew northeast to where a couple of river valleys merged. There was lots of open tundra, and the snow was only a fraction of what it was in the timber; the wind kept these areas swept pretty clean of snow. This was good caribou country, with an occasional moose in the river bottoms. I flew maybe eighty miles, then west ten miles, then back whence I came; in that area, I spotted several small caribou herds, forty to fifty head each. With each heard, there was at least three or four wolves staying very close; most of them were eating on a recent kill, and in every case, I spotted other carcasses that were just killed since the last snow. It appeared the wolves would make a kill and eat on that for a day or until it froze so solid they couldn't eat it anymore; then they would kill again. They're no different from us; they prefer a hot meal.

On my way back, I spotted a bigger herd, 150 to 200 head, almost completely surrounded by wolves. I was sure that must have been the pack I spotted last fall. As I circled the herd, they milled about, and the wolves started to reassemble as a pack. As I looked closer, I could see carcasses in all directions; it looked like the pack had this herd corralled and was just killing whenever they wanted. As they recongregated, I was able to move them into a treeless area, where I could get within twenty to thirty feet. I was able to shoot six big wolves, including the leader, from the airplane and drive the pack several miles from the herd of caribou. As soon as the wolves were chased away, the herd started to move, putting as much distance as possible between them and the wolves; the pack split up into small groups of four or five and headed in different directions.

I skinned and loaded the six wolves in the plane and continued to check out the area; about three quarters of the way back to the lodge, I came across the small pack of five. They had just, in the last ten to twelve hours, killed three moose, a cow, a calf, and probably her last year's half-grown calf; they were lying about a quarter of a mile apart, which meant they killed one, then pursued and killed the next one and then the third. This proved to me this old idea—that they only kill what they can eat was so much BS when hunting was good. I believe they just killed for the sport of it. All five wolves were eating on the yearly; by the time they would finish eating that one moose, the other two would be frozen so solid they would be like a cake of ice and wouldn't thaw out until next spring.

The wolves were in pretty deep snow and couldn't move very fast. So I grabbed my double-barrel shotgun, circled around, came in about twenty feet above the ground, and zeroed in on the big black wolf. I opened my door just enough to stick the barrel of the gun out the door. I flew over the wolf and shot both barrels, banked to the right, pulled up just a little, reloaded the shotgun, then made another circle. I came in again; this time, I picked out a big gray and repeated the routine. There was another wolf about a hundred yards ahead, making tracks as fast as he could. I opened the double-barrel through the empty shells out the door and stuck two more shells in the shotgun and snapped the barrel closed. The moment I did that, the shotgun fired; the gun was between my legs, pointing at the floor. It blew the whole side of my mukluks off but somehow never hit my foot; it went through the firewall and blew a hole in the muffler of the plane. I had no idea where the third wolf went and really didn't care. I knew I had to land, check out the plane, and retrieve my two wolves; the black one, I could tell, wasn't completely dead. So I landed about twenty feet from where he was lying.

This time, I stuck the barrel out the window when I loaded the shotgun. I checked the triggers and then closed the gun; everything worked like it was supposed to. I opened the door and commenced to get out of the airplane; when I stepped out of the plane, my one foot broke through the crust on the snow and went down about eighteen inches. I had one foot in the snow and was dragging the other one out of the plane, a real clumsy position. And here he came—the black wolf came alive, like someone had jabbed him in the ass with a hot poker. I could see hate and mayhem in those yellow eyes as he leaped through the snow, getting closer by the second.

I didn't have time to put the shotgun to my shoulder. I just shot from the hip as I was falling into the snow; the wolf was only about eight feet away and looked as big as a horse when I shot. The blast from the shotgun caught him in the neck, and that was all she wrote; he crumpled up in a pile about four feet from where I lay in the snow.

I loaded the shotgun and then checked the airplane for serious damage; there was a little facial damage. The muffler would have to be replaced; other than that, it was flyable. The other wolf was dead. I skinned both of these wolves, loaded them in the plane, and headed back to the lodge. I came to the conclusion that I had enough excitement for one day and thought a good hot toddy and a cigar back at the lodge would be just what the doctor ordered.

But I did decide to hunt wolves in that area every chance I got until the population was more in balance with the moose and caribou herds. Within five years, there were still wolves in that area; not as many, but the moose and caribou had tripled. If left alone, the wolves would have eventually killed every animal in that region; they would have died off for lack of food and perhaps even cannibalize some of their own species.

My best day shooting wolves, with one of us flying and the other one shooting (or, as we called it, the gunner), was thirty-four wolves. We took nineteen from one pack and still didn't get them all; at that time, they were paying a $50 bounty for each wolf that you killed, and you would get another $45 for the skin. January was usually our best month for hunting wolves. I know of at least two different times that we killed over two hundred in one month.

One time, the Department of Fish and Game did an experiment where they closed a specific area that was not very far from the lodge; no wolf hunting was allowed. In five years, the wolves had virtually wiped out the moose, caribou and dall sheep in that area.

Chapter Twenty-Nine

The Susitna Lodge was a very good setup. We had the gravel landing strip for the planes with wheels; plus there was a little lake just a couple hundred feet from the lodge for the floatplanes and the two PA-18 Super Cubs. I also still had the PA-11 for emergencies, and we could accommodate eight to a dozen hunters quite easily. From this location, we could hunt all around the park and the huge Alaskan mountain range, the Kenai Peninsula, and the Wrangell Mountains. We hunted a much larger area than that, but those areas were close and convenient to get to.

By this time, I had earned the reputation of being one of the guides to go to if you wanted a sheep or a goat; in fact, I was called the goat man because of my ability to reach the goats and sheep in very difficult areas. Most of those hunts required landing on the glaciers, where many of the other guides were reluctant to go to; some just flat-out refused to go into these areas because of the difficulty and danger.

Sometimes I would land on a little glacial Lake or on the glacier itself at the foot of a sheer cliff that may rise out of the ice for another thousand feet or more; the goats or sheep would all look very small as they stood on their rocky perch, hundreds of feet above us. My first order of business would be to glass the area carefully, picking the largest of the rams. My next challenge would be to make sure the hunter was looking at the same animal that I was. Several times, I had hunters shoot the wrong animal; but when we retrieved it, they were so proud of their trophy that I didn't have the heart to tell them they had shot a much inferior animal.

Sometimes we would land in a lake at the foot of a sheer granite cliff; and on the face of that cliff, there would be several goats, which appeared to be glued to the face of the cliff because we could see no evidence that there was anything they could stand on. If the wind was calm and there was no water movement in the little lake, the hunter could stand on the float of the plane and lean across the fuselage, using it as a rest, and shoot the goat three hundred to four hundred yards above us; the goat would fall directly into the water. We would taxi over to the goat and drag him aboard if he wasn't too heavy. We would load him in the plane, and sometimes we'd be back at the lodge in time for lunch. But believe me, that was a rare occasion; usually, there was a lot more work involved.

I remember one time we were in the Wrangell Mountains when I spotted a billy not on the face of a cliff, but in some real rugged rocky crags; the rock formations were like a gigantic windfall—columns of rocks lying every which way, with some standing perhaps thirty to forty feet tall. There were several other goats in the surrounding area that were much easier to get to, but this was a big old buck with long horns. This, of course, was the one the hunter wanted; and this old guy is right in the middle of that pile of rocks. I'm not talking about a truckload of boulders. I'm talking about half the side of that mountain—perhaps six hundred to eight hundred acres, maybe more—covered with rocks and boulders, some larger than your house. And this damn goat was in the middle of that mess, standing on the highest rocks he could find.

We had to land about a mile away because of cracks and crevices in the ice, then work our way along the back side of a ridge until we were close enough to the location of the goat; then we had to ease up over the top of the ridge and, bang, shoot the goat and be on our way. That was our plan. But as you hunters know, very frequently, stalking plans hardly ever work out exactly as planned—and this one was about to become a record breaker for change of plans. As quietly as we could, we climbed to the top of the ridge, being very careful to stay behind several large boulders. I knew if this goat even so much as suspected we were in the area, he would disappear into that maze of rocks, and we would never see him again.

The weather was nice, about forty degrees—cool enough to keep the mosquitoes and the no-see-ums grounded. The sun was trying hard to find gaps in the clouds. But the clouds weren't very cooperative and were quite low, some lower than we were, recklessly racing across the landscape, frequently plowing into the side of the mountain, and hiding everything from view. As I peeked around the rocks, I could see the old goat standing on his lofty perch just slightly over one hundred yards below us.

"Adam, he is dead ahead," I told the hunter, "approximately a hundred yards straight ahead of us. Why don't you use that rock as a rest for your rifle? Stay low. Don't show any more of your body than necessary. These guys have eyes like an eagle. They will pick up the very slightest movement."

"Denny, should I make any adjustments because I'm shooting downhill?"

"No, don't worry about that. At one hundred yards, just put her slightly behind his front shoulder and just a little below center and pull the trigger."

Adam got in position and laid his rifle over the rock. I was watching the goat and Adam. He was being very careful; the low wispy clouds were racing across the mountainside, like ghosts in a race to see who could be dashed against the rocks the quickest. I glanced at Adam; he was ready to shoot. I expected the explosion any second. I looked back at the goat; then I understood why there was no shot. The clouds had raced to his rescue; they covered him like a white sheet, totally obscuring him from view.

Adam glanced at me with a questioning look. I whispered, "Be ready. The clouds will pass." As did the goat; we just caught a glimpse of him as he left his perch and slid into the maze of boulders, moving off to our right. About a half a mile to our right was another big outcropping, about the same height as the ridge we were on, but separated by a little gully about fifty feet deep.

"Denny, what do you think?"

"Let's drop down behind this ridge again and get down by that outcropping as quickly as we can. My guess is that's where he's headed. Maybe we can beat him there and be in position by the time he arrives."

We dropped off the back side of the ridge about one hundred yards, where the walking was much easier; it took us only fifteen to twenty minutes, and we were climbing back to the crest of the ridge. The hillside was covered with loose rock and giant boulders the size of a house—great cover. But unless you were very careful it was extremely noisy, it was very easy to dislodge a rock and send it rattling down the steep hillside. Once we reached the top of the ridge, we found a great spot to observe the entire area. We crawled up on our bellies to the very crest of the hill. It took us about ten minutes before we finally spotted the old billy; he was only about halfway between where he started and where I felt he intended to go. There were a few little shrubs and some mountain grass that he seemed to be enjoying as he worked his way in our direction. I knew of course there was no guarantee that this was his intended destination, but I knew if I was the goat, that was where I'd be going. We watched intently as he disappeared into the rocks and reappeared again numerous times, but he always seemed to be headed in our direction; the sun seemed to be winning the battle with the clouds. As I lay there with the warm sun on my back, I started to get sleepy. I could hardly keep my eyes open. I glanced at Adam. He didn't seem to be having any problem; he had his binoculars on the goat and was watching his every move.

"How far away do you think he is?" Adam asked.

"My guess is he's about 250 yards out."

"You think he'll keep coming?"

"I think so. This is a great spot. He has a commanding view in all directions. I would guess he lives right here in this general area. He's an old buck, probably doesn't tolerate other goats except during breeding season."

We lay there for the next hour while he had lunch but all the time slowly working his way in our direction; he was now about 150 yards away, but we couldn't see anything but an occasional ear or horn or maybe a patch of white in between a couple of rocks. Then he totally disappeared; we didn't see him at all for a half an hour. The wispy clouds were back; it was now afternoon, and the chances of getting socked in by low clouds was increasing by the minute.

"Denny, I think I see him," Adam whispered. "He's on the right side of the rock outcropping. the clouds, again, completely obscured the rocky crag we were watching. Then they thinned to where we could just see a thin light silhouette of the rocks just as it disappeared in the clouds again. I thought I saw the outline of the goat, almost at the top of the rocky pile."

"Adam, be ready. I think I saw your goat almost at the very top."

It was at least ten minutes before the clouds thinned again to where we could start to see some of the rocky outcropping; they thinned more. I was quite sure I could see the goat; then it faded for just a moment. Then the sun broke through the clouds and illuminated that entire rocky outcropping, and very near the top stood the old monarch; the report of the rifle echoed across the canyon. The goat collapsed on the spot. It was a beautiful old buck and turned out to be good enough to get in the record book.

We had quite a hassle to get the old guy off the rock pile and down through that little hollow and up and over the ridge; then we had the better part of a mile and a half to carry our trophy back to the airplane. But when we got home, back at the lodge, I found out Adam was a very good cook. The next night, we had barbecued goat, with all the trimmings. I have to say, it rated at the very top of meals we ever fixed at the lodge.

Chapter Thirty

The location of the lodge gave us some distinct advantages; we were halfway between the Fairbanks–Anchorage Highway and the Denali Park and about halfway between the cities of Anchorage and Fairbanks.

We got a lot of people who just drove into the lodge and wanted to go hunting; they wanted to get a moose or caribou or both. We usually could accomplish that in one or two days; we would take them out, spot a moose or caribou, land someplace close, and sometimes let them hunt on their own, depending on the individual. If they looked like they knew what they were doing, we could turn them loose and come back four to five hours later, pick up the meat and the hunters, and that was it. But sometimes we would get that hunter that you know, with just one look and a five-minute conversation, that if you turned him loose, we would probably never see him again.

We had to stay with those hunters until the meat was safely back in the plane and they were safely delivered back to the lodge. Back in those days, the legal and acceptable way we hunted was to pick up our hunter; we usually knew where we were going before we started because we were always flying, covering thousands of square miles, and we kept track and talked all the time about what we saw and where. We then would scout out a couple areas with our hunter and find what we thought was a good animal; if the hunter agreed, we would set the plane down as close as we could without spooking the animal. Sometimes we would have to walk a mile or more, but most of the time less. I have had hunts where they would lean across the back of the airplane and make their shot.

In some cases, we could taxi right up to the moose or caribou, load the meat in the plane, tie the horns to the struts, and be back at the lodge in five to six hours. We could do that two or three times a day. In the summertime, we had twenty hours of daylight or more, and flying and hunting the same day was legal for everything we hunted in those days.

I remember at one time, I had 138 hunters in camps in the bush, and I was the only pilot. I had two aircraft: one was the floatplane and the other on wheels. The bartender mapped every camp as I placed them. I never lost a hunter that I know of.

The years at the Susitna Lodge all kind of blended into one; it seemed we were always running about a hundred miles an hour, going from dawn till dark. So the sequence of events, I'm about to tell you, will probably not be in the proper order; and I won't even attempt to remember the year. except for a couple extraordinary events that happened during that time, which I do remember precisely.

It was a blustery day at the lodge in mid-October, with occasionally a little snow squall. The sun would come out for a few minutes; then it would rain or snow again. I guess you could say pretty typical Alaskan weather. I was taking a German hunter from the Lake Clark area down to the Lake Iliamna area; he had already shot a nice moose and was now after a caribou. On that route, there was a series of small lakes, most of them no more than ten to fifteen acres in size, some bigger and some smaller. We were flying at about five hundred feet when I spotted the sun reflecting off something shiny about a mile off to our left. I decided to take a look just in case.

As we got closer, we could see a man and two small boys, probably ten or twelve years old; they were huddled up on their plane, which was lying upside down in the lake. They were waving frantically, afraid I wouldn't see them. I circled them once so they were sure I did see them, and then I flew to a decent landing area about a half a mile away and dropped off my hunter. I then returned to the stranded threesome to pick up the boys and bring them back to where my hunter was working very hard to get a fire started. I landed downwind, then taxied alongside their plane so they could grab the wing and the struts, and hold the plane alongside so the boys could get into my plane. They were so cold they could hardly move. I thought several times they were going to fall in the lake before they got aboard the plane.

I hadn't realized it till I got close, but they were friends of mine from King Salmon. The German hunter had a bottle of good Irish whiskey he sent with me to give to the man stranded on the airplane. I left the whiskey with the pilot and ferried the boys back to where the hunter had a rip-roaring campfire started. When the boys tried to thank me, they couldn't even talk because they were so cold. I went back to get their father; he had drunk at least a third of that whiskey by the time I got back. Once I got them all safe and sound on dry land and all huddled around the fire, I asked him what happened; he said he wasn't sure. I think he tried to land downwind, and a gust of wind caught his tail and just flipped the plane on its nose, and then over it went upside down in the lake; they had been stranded on that plane since the day before, shortly after lunch—approximately twenty-six hours. They had spent the whole night on that plane. I was surprised they all made it. For years, every time I would run into one of the boys, they would thank me for saving their life. They were convinced if they would have spent another night on that plane in the middle of that lake, they would've perished.

The doctor said three to four more hours and they would've been goners. The hunter seemed to be thrilled with his small role in the rescue and told everybody that would listen.

Doctor Uhlb from Ohio took this Record brown bear in about 1963

Denny Thompson with a Big Black bear taken by Herb Klein

Chapter Thirty-One

Denny lived in the lodge during spring, summer, and fall; but about the first of November, he would head for Anchorage, where he had a home. If he had any flying during those winter months, he would fly out of Anchorage airport; they had facilities for both floatplanes and regular planes with wheels. The winters at Susitna were brutal, with lots of snow and extremely cold weather. Forty to fifty below was not uncommon.

A hundred years ago, this area was a thriving gold mining area. The dredges were tearing up the countryside, and they were taking their gold to town in bushel baskets; at least that's what I was told by some of the old-timers. No question, there was plenty of gold mining taking place sometime in the past; evidence of that is indisputable, but I was never able to confirm the bushel baskets of gold.

It was shortly after New Year's; the weather had been atrocious—snow, wind, and cold weather seemed to be the order of business in Anchorage. I remember I was watching one of the bowl games when I got a call from a hunter in Wisconsin; it seemed he was a bow hunter of stature. I learned later that he was one of the top five bowhunters in the United States and was in the Bowhunters Hall of Fame; he had heard that I have the number 1 moose in the world and that just about every year, ten or twelve of my hunters make it into the record books. He wanted to book a moose hunt for next fall and wanted to know if I would take a bowhunter. I told him that was no problem. I had taken several people bowhunting; in most cases, they had been successful. We made arrangements and set the date, and I put it in my book.

"By the way," he said, "I would really like to get a big moose that would make it to the top of the record book for a bowhunter. It wouldn't have to be as big as the one you have to make it to the top for bowhunters." So the challenge was on to locate a big moose sometime next summer before Art Laha arrived.

I had no way of knowing that this hunt would turn into at least six different hunts and a lifetime friendship.

I didn't remember at the time, but I had met Art at Kotzebue a couple years earlier; he was hunting polar bear with Sam Pancotto and several other men from Chicago. I had hunted with Sam in 1958, the year we started working on the lodge; he got a nice moose and a couple caribou that year, then came back the next spring and shot a respectable brown bear. I found out later that Sam was the one who recommended that Art call me. Sam also hunted many more times with me; if I remember right, he took an additional ten brown bears after that first one over perhaps the next twenty years—a couple of those quite memorable. I'll tell you about that later in the book.

Right after the first of the year, I bought a truck and drove to Chicago. I picked up all kinds of provisions that we needed at the lodge; on the way to Chicago, I stopped in Wyoming. Before I left Alaska, I had loaded the truck with about fifty sets of antlers. I dropped them off at a taxidermist in Wyoming.

I picked up the provisions in Chicago, brought them back to Anchorage, and locked that up in storage until the snow melted and I could get into the lodge; that turned out to be the middle of May, a couple weeks after polar bear season.

This year, we had seventeen polar bear hunts booked. Almost all of those were two hunters; in some cases, we would have three hunters to a party. By then, we were getting quite efficient. Most of our hunters were taking their polar bears plus a wolf. We had found several areas in the Brooks Range where wolf hunting was exceptional, with wide-open country and lots of wolves, and some of them were monsters. Most of the hunts that year, I presume, were quite routine because I don't remember much about them; but there is one that sticks in my mind.

If I remember right, it was halfway through the season; the weather had been quite cooperative, cold, but not excessive. There was not much wind and only the threat of a couple whiteouts, which never really materialized. We knew we were living on borrowed time; it was only a matter of time when our luck would change.

We picked up our hunters the evening before the hunt, a couple of fancy Dans from Argentina or Brazil. I don't truly remember. When Cappy laid eyes on them, he said, "Oh my god, what do we have here? Denny, is it okay if I just skip this hunt?"

"Not on your life, my friend. It's going to take both of us to get these dudes a bear."

They were dressed as if they were going hunting in Minnesota or Wisconsin in the middle of October, and their shoes were just slightly better than street shoes, but the killer was that they both had cowboy hats on.

"Do you gentlemen have any other clothes with you? I asked. "And I don't mean a change of underwear or extras socks. Do you have any heavy clothes like we are wearing?"

They looked at each other and then back at me and shook their heads no. I suggested we head to the restaurant before they froze to death out here in the street; a ten-minute walk to the restaurant and they were ready to get back on the airplane and head south. I didn't have the heart to take them out behind the hangar and test their rifles. So Cappy and I got them something hot to drink; then we took their rifles and tested them. They both were right on the money, so we had to assume the boys at least knew how to shoot. When we got back to the café, they had spiked their coffee with some rum and were now feeling much better. Once we were finished with dinner, we made a dash for the hotel, which was only about a hundred feet from the restaurant. Cappy and I both had some extra clothes and boots; before the night was over, we had these two Argentinean cowboys looking like Eskimos.

The next morning was cold and crisp; everyone had eaten, and we were in the airplane taxiing down the runway just as the sun made its appearance in the eastern sky. The weather forecast from Russia and the

Siberian coast was good: a big high pressure anchored right over the top of us, which usually meant good weather for at least a couple of days.

Since we had good weather, we decided to go just a little bit farther west than normal, so the route that morning was due west; the weather was so clear it looked like you could see forever. After an hour and a half of flying, we could see the Russian coast. We had spotted several nice bears on the flight, but nothing exceptional. We got within about ten miles of the coast and then turned north; we could see what looked like open water fifteen to twenty miles ahead. If that was the case, there was an excellent chance that there would be seals; if there were seals, there would be bears. True to our expectations, as we drew closer, we could see the little black spots all lined up on the edge of the ice; within several minutes, we could see four to five bears trying desperately to catch one of the elusive seals before they slipped back into the water. This stretch of open water extended for maybe five miles; there was ice between the open water and the mainland in some cases, but in other places, the open water extended clear to the shoreline.

Near the north end of the open water, we spotted a big bear; he was staying back from the edge of the water at least a hundred feet, and he seemed to have some kind of a plan. I expect he had hunted the seal for a number of years and knew it was hopeless to try and catch one by running up and down the shoreline. He was headed north; we made a detour, and I landed about three quarters of a mile in front of where I estimated he was headed.

We exited the plane as fast as we could, made sure our weapons were loaded, covered the plane, and moved about fifty yards from the airplane. We found a couple chunks of ice to get behind and waited, but not for long. I hadn't even finished giving instructions to the hunter when we saw him coming, but if he stayed on his present course, he would pass to our east about 150 yards and farther away than I would've liked. I asked the hunter if he felt that was too far; he assured me he had made many shots much longer than that. The bear had passed the position where he was the closest, and now every step took him just a little bit farther north and extended the length of the shot.

I encouraged the hunter to not wait any longer; he fired. The bear shifted into high gear—one of the few beasts that did not turn and charge but took off on the dead run; the hunter took two more shots; since we were in no imminent danger, I wanted to let him kill the bear if possible.

With my binoculars, I could see there was blood on the snow. He reloaded his rifle; and by then, the bear was 250 to 300 yards away and headed directly toward the Russian coast, about a half a mile away. We watched him through the glasses as he started to climb the steep bank; several times, he slipped and fell but eventually made it to some trees and brush and disappeared. I felt he was badly wounded. I decided to get the plane and see just how far inland he was moving; then I had second thoughts about that. I really didn't want to fly over Russian territory and get picked up by radar; we were already in Russian territory, but not overland. So we decided to taxi the plane as close as we could and then go the rest of the way on foot.

I could see why the bear was having a problem; the bank was almost straight up and down and covered with blood. We finally managed to claw our way to the top; there was no problem following the tracks as there was blood everywhere. I couldn't believe that he made it this far with the amount of blood he had lost; once we reached the top of the bank, we didn't go more than fifty feet. There he was, stretched out on the snow, like he was taking a nap; his old heart had finally run out of blood.

Finally, we got him skinned out; then we dragged the hide back to the plane. When I started to put the hide in the plane, that's when I realized just how big a bear he was. The hunter had hit him twice, just a little bit too high and a little bit too far back for a quick fatal shot, but it eventually did the job. Cappy had located another bear just about a mile north of where we were. Once we were airborne, Cappy landed, and his hunter killed his bear with one shot to the neck; we were back to Kotzebue before dark with two beautiful polar bear hides and two very satisfied cowboys. They thanked us a dozen times; we tried to talk them into going wolf hunting, but they said, "No, thanks." They wanted to get on that airplane and not stop until they got to warmer weather.

Super Cub with Float's land on water or ice and snow

Alaskan Mt Range; Mt Mckenley on right

Marge

Chapter Thirty-Two

When we finished the polar bear hunts, we only had a couple of weeks until the brown bear and grizzly hunts started; we had twenty-two hunts on the books and were almost sure to have three or four people who wanted to go on a hunt drive into the lodge. At this time of the year, the sheep and goats looked pretty woolly for several months while they shed their last year's coat; during this period, we did not hunt either of those species.

During the brown bear and grizzly season, I spotted two exceptionally large moose; they were located on the northwest side of Mount McKinley near but not in the Yukon River Basin. I had arranged for Art to hunt during the rut; it was much easier to find a big bull during the rut. Over the years, I had taken several other bowhunters. I was not that impressed with their ability to kill an animal in a reasonable short period of time; it seemed to me that most of the hunters I took wounded the animal. In some cases, it took us three to four hours to track it down. Sometimes they were dead; other times, they had to be finished off with a rifle.

Alaska mountain range where Denny took his hunters for the majority of his goats and sheep

Arctic Ice West of Kotzebue and Point Hope typical polar bear hunting area Denny estimated less than 5% of the area was safe to land the plane

In those days, you did not have to have a guide to hunt moose, caribou, black bears, and goats. Several times, I heard of bowhunters wounding a moose or caribou and never finding it; of course, to be fair, I know of more than one situation where that happened with hunters who were using rifles, but not nearly as frequently. But with Art Laha, I made the exception partly because he was recommended by a good friend of mine, Sam Pencotto, and the fact he was one of the top five–rated bowhunters in the world.

Art arrived the latter part of August; if the weather in Alaska can ever be rated as perfect, this was about as close as you could get. The only problem with this nice weather was the mosquitoes, and the no-see-ums were out in force. But Art brought some new kind of mosquito repellent, which was really a big improvement compared with what we had been using.

The first day, Art wanted me to fly him around the areas where I intended to hunt; then the next day, we would actually go hunting in one of the areas where he saw the biggest moose. The first day, he wasn't even going take his bow, but I finally convinced him there was always that possibility he would see the moose of his dreams and that we may not be able to find it again the next day.

We left the lodge that morning at about eight o'clock with bow and arrows aboard. I decided to fly north around the mountain; that would mean we had the sun to our back when we turned west on the back side of McKinley and get into the area where I had seen the big moose. We turned pretty much due west in the Bitzshtini Mountains / Wein Lake area. The next fifty miles was where I had seen the two large moose earlier this summer; we had already seen at least a dozen nice moose. Several of those Art wanted to take a closer look at, but I convinced him that I knew where there were larger moose.

I had flown only eight to ten miles after I made the turn when we spotted an exceptional moose. Art about jumped out of the airplane; he was so excited. The only problem was this moose was in a heavily treed area with nowhere to land within at least five miles. We continued west and got into some areas where there were some gravel bars along the river and some small treeless tundra, which I felt I could safely set the plane down. Now all we had to do was find a moose close to one of these areas, and we were in business.

We continually saw moose; we probably went another ten miles when we spotted two very large bulls; they were in pitched battle. They were duking it out, trying to win the admiration and affection of three cows grazing a couple hundred feet away, which were acting as if they didn't know what was going on and, what's more, didn't care. They kind of reminded me of a couple girls I once knew. These two big boys were right out in the open, and there were plenty of places to land the airplane; what I had to be careful of was not to spook them when I landed.

"Art, you think either one of these bulls would be adequate? Or shall we keep looking?"

"Hell no, Denny! Either of these two will be fine if you can just get me close enough."

"You see that little gully to the east and that little clump of fir trees? I think I'll land to the west on the other side of that grove of fir trees. We should be able to sneak through there without being detected by either the cows or the bulls."

"I think I see what you mean. It looks good to me."

I set the airplane down in a little patch of tundra; we exited as quietly as we could. Inside the grove of fir trees, there were paths going every direction; evidently, this was one of their favored areas to hang out in an attempt to stay away from the mosquitoes and other bothersome critters. Walking through that grove of fir trees was easy and quiet, and it ended right at the edge of the gully; we slipped into the gully undetected. It was only about fifty yards to the other little clump of fir trees, where I hoped we would be close enough for Art to have a good shot.

"Art, how close you need to get to be effective?" I whispered.

"I can hit him at a couple hundred feet, but I'd prefer to be half that distance."

The little grove of fir trees was only about fifty feet wide and a hundred feet long; the two bulls would bang each other around for several minutes. Then they would circle each other, strut around, and try to impress their lady friends, grunting almost continuously. We were on a slight hillside; the bulls were fighting above us at least two hundred feet to our east. Art got himself situated, then looked at me to see what I thought.

"Art, I think our best tactic at this time is just be patient. As you can see by the ground they tore up, they have been all over this hillside. And it looks to me, at one time, they were within forty or fifty feet of where we're standing."

We crouched behind some bushes and watched the battle as it continued. They did more positioning and posturing than they did fighting; they were both so evenly matched it was impossible to tell which one might be the winner. The next time they engaged, one of the bulls was slightly downhill; the bull on the upper side seized the advantage and pushed the other guy downhill at least fifty or sixty feet before he could get repositioned. Now the bulls were maybe 130 to 150 feet as they continued to fight; they gradually got closer to our position. Art was ready; within a couple minutes, they backed away from each other. By then, they were just a little more than maybe a hundred feet. Art decided the bull on his right had a couple more points and a more uniform set of horns. The arrow was true to its mark; it looked to me like it should've hit the heart. The old bull never even flinched; he shook his head a couple times and grunted, threatening the other bull. Art launched another arrow; this one hit about six inches higher than the first arrow—still no appreciable reaction from the bull. He started to take a couple of steps and collapsed in a heap; the other bull looked confused. We stepped out of the woods; the remaining bull stood there, then took a couple of steps in our direction as if to challenge us. I decided it was time to break up the party and fired my rifle in the air; with that, the three cows and the bull left the area.

I left Art with his trophy, which was a very nice trophy, and I got the airplane and landed it right beside the moose. I think Art never stopped talking; he was one very happy hunter.

I had to make two trips to get all the meat and the horns back to the lodge. I believe the moose made the record book for Art, but I don't remember that for sure. When we were sitting around the lodge that night, reliving our moose hunt, Art asked me about a polar bear hunt with the bow for next spring.

"Art, I have no doubt that if the bear were in a cage, you would kill it with the arrow without being eaten alive. But out on the Arctic ice and sixty-below-zero weather, I'm not too sure."

"Now, Denny, that moose has to be almost as big as one of those bears, right?"

"That's true. Weight-wise, I guess they're probably about the same. But, Art, that's where the comparison ends. Number 1, you had almost perfect conditions that day. The temperature was in the fifties. The animal was standing not more than a hundred feet. After the first shot, he stood there for at least a minute, maybe more. And in that length of time, the bear would be on top of us. Even if you hit him in the heart, he will live for another ten minutes, which means if you shoot him with an arrow, it's almost 100 percent that I will have to finish him off with a rifle. It's very rare that one runs off and dies."

"Are you telling me you won't take me polar bear hunting with a bow?"

"No, that's not what I said. I'm saying you have a very slim chance of killing a polar bear with an arrow, without Cappy or me having to shoot the bear with a rifle to save your life—and I'm not saying that there's not a possibility you could be successful, but I doubt it very much."

"Well, Mr. Thompson, I would like you to put me on the books for next spring. Whenever you think I would have my best chance, and the bear does not have to be a giant. Any polar bear taken with the bow will make the record books."

So the negotiations were over with. Art would be back up late next winter.

In 1962, I married Marge Lovett. Like me, she was divorced and in fact contemplating moving to California. If any of you who are reading this book were ever at the Susitna Lodge, you undoubtedly met Marge.

That year, Sam Pancotto had a brown bear hunt and a goat hunt that are worth mentioning. When Sam arrived, we still couldn't get into the Susitna Lodge, so we flew out of Anchorage to King Salmon; we made the King Salmon Lodge our headquarters for a couple of days.

Then we would fly down the peninsula about 150 miles to an area called the Cinder River; that area always seemed to produce some big brown bears and was one of the better areas to hunt early in the season. We had a couple of days. Sam wasn't in any rush; we counted over forty bears. Some of those were exceptionally good, but in very difficult areas to get to. I finally got the feeling that Sam just wanted to spend this day sightseeing and looking at all the different options, which were many.

We flew on down to Port Heiden and fueled up, then started working our way back up the peninsula toward King Salmon. I was just a little west of Goose Lake when Sam spotted his bear. The bear was in the creek bed, chowing down on dead salmon; he was very good-looking. The bear's head was mostly black or dark brown, and his shoulders were very light reddish brown from about the middle of his back; from there to his rump was black or very dark brown. He wasn't a monster, but he was a nice large bear.

The problem was where the bear was located, there was at least a couple hundred feet of thick brush on both sides of the creek in that particular location.

"Unlikely as it may seem, Sam, there is a possibility that this bear might move down the creek a half a mile by tomorrow morning. If that were the case, I think we would have a very good chance of getting a shot at him. Where he's at now, the only chance we would have now is to wade up the middle of that creek. It's probably at least waist deep, and I'll bet the temperature is not any more than forty degrees."

"That's the one I want, Denny. Do you think he'll still be in this same general area, or is he likelyto take off and go to a different location overnight?"

"Can't be certain, but I bet his feet are still tender. And as long as there's plenty to eat, I suspect he won't go very far. Tomorrow morning, we will get going bright and early."

We returned to King Salmon, had dinner, and spent a little time in the bar; all Sam could talk about was that bear. The next morning, we were up bright and early, had some breakfast, and were airborne shortly after the sun came up.

Last night, before we left the Goose Lake area, we had checked the landmarks very closely in hopes that we could find this exact location without wasting a lot of time flying around. Apparently, we did a pretty good job; we hadn't been in the area more than fifteen minutes. We had made a couple passes at other bears, thinking they were the one, until we took a closer look; the third or fourth bear we spotted was Sam's bear.

He had in fact moved down the creek several hundred yards; there was still brush, but not nearly as thick, and the bear seemed to be slowly working his way toward the open area we were hoping for. My main concern was he would go into the brush and just stay there, and then we wouldn't have any chance at all. I found a good spot to land about a half a mile away on the other side of a little knoll; once on top of that knoll, we could see down into the creek bottom, but no bear. We couldn't see just where he was located, and we had to know precisely where he was before we started working our way through the brush patches to get close enough for a good shot. We sat there for at least an hour; the little knoll was a great vantage point. We could see for at least a mile in a couple different directions; while we sat there, we counted at least six other bears.

We were at least three hundred yards from the creek, beyond where Sam wanted to risk a shot; his preference was to be 100 to 150 yards. Sam had bought a brand-new .300 Weatherby Magnum; this would actually be his first animal with his new rifle. There were a couple of snowshoe hares that were cavorting around the brush patch about halfway down the hill; off to our right, there was a red fox, not quite as pretty as he would've been a couple of months ago. He was in the process of shedding last year's coat and looked a little woolly and not nearly as red as normal.

Denny in 2005 Colorado mule deer

Herb Klein with very respectable caribou

We were intently watching the creek in the few areas we could see; most of it was hidden by the brush, but sooner or later, we felt the bear would show up in one of those open areas. When that happened, we could then put our plan together and make our move on Mr. Bruin.

All at once, the covey of ptarmigan took off in a mad dash. We could hear one thrashing about and squawking; we presumed that the fox had just made his decision what to have for lunch. We glanced back down at the creek, and lo and behold, we could just see the head of our bear. He was standing up, looking in the direction of the ptarmigan, curious as to what was going on. He stood there only for several seconds, then disappeared behind the brush again. But now we knew where he was.

Sam and I talked it over and decided we would drop back behind the knoll. There was a bend in the creek just a couple hundred yards from where the bear was now located; we decided to get in position right where that creek made a bend and hoped that he would keep moving downstream to a position of our liking.

We made our way to the bend in the creek; once we were in position behind a couple clumps of brush, we could see the bear. We estimated him to be just a little over two hundred yards; he was in some deep water at the moment, and there were not many salmon along the banks. But about halfway between where we were and the present location of the bear, there was a nice little sandbar covered with dead salmon.

The closer he got to the sandbar, the faster he moved; he was just making his way up the far end of the sandbar when a wolverine with all the tenacity of a thousand-pound grizzly bear charged out of the brush and laid claim to the sandbar full of dead salmon. It took the old brown bear so completely by surprise that he retreated up into the brush.

"Hey, Denny, I'm going to shoot that little son of a bitch."

"Wait a minute now! Don't do anything drastic."

"I can't believe that old brown bear is going to give up a pile of fish like that to some new bully on the block without a fight."

"Right now, I think he's just contemplating if he should kill that little bastard and leave him for the crows, or if he should kill him and eat him."

We didn't have long to wait; the old bear strolled out of the brush, which kind of reminded me of John Wayne.

"Denny, shall I take him now?"

"No," I said as I put my hand on his rifle. "Let's watch and see what happens. Now that the old bear has come back to his sandbar, I doubt he's going anywhere very soon."

The wolverine was making all sorts of threatening sounds; he was running back and forth across the sandbar, and every once in a while, he would charge right up to the old bear like he was going to eat him alive. The bear would rear up on his hind feet, and the wolverine would make more threatening sounds and then back away. This went on for five to ten minutes; nobody was keeping time. It was really interesting to watch. Finally, the wolverine made a charge at the bear; this time, the old bear didn't rear up. When the wolverine finally stopped his charge, he was well within reach of the bear, who delivered a left hook to the side of the wolverine and knocked him clear out of the creek, up in the brush; we presumed this debate had been concluded, but to our amazement, here came this tenacious little ball of fur back onto the sandbar. It appeared he was now ready to negotiate the idea of sharing; he would stay on one end of the sandbar, and the bear could have the other end. But John Wayne had enough of this two-bit gunslinger, and there was only one solution: "You leave town, or you die, Pilgrim." The bear charged down the sandbar at the wolverine, who appeared to get the message that this dinner table was going to serve only one guest, and he wasn't invited.

Jay Mellon and Denny at Bear camp after a successful brown bear hunt

Very respectable brown bear taken in the Cinder River area

The old bear went into a raging fit, attacking magpies, crows, blue jays—anything that moved. Sam waited until he was in the middle of the sandbar and took his shot; we were only about eighty yards away, and his shot was true to the mark. I was ready to shoot. I did not want a wounded bear in that thick brush, but there was no need to worry. The shot was about a foot behind his ear, which killed him instantly—just the way I like it.

Sam and I returned from the brown bear hunt; he was all energized. He decided he wanted to go on a goat hunt in the Wrangell Mountains. I told Sam I had two other hunting parties that wanted brown bear, and I had to hunt them first. I suggested that he go with Cappy or Bill Sims, but Sam decided to wait for me.

By then, the road to the lodge was opened. Sam decided he could do some chores around the lodge and help me dispose of some of last year's liquor and start this year with brand-new stuff. I have to say he did a pretty good job. The two groups of hunters were all above-average shots, and within a week, everybody was headed home with their trophies.

The next morning, Sam and I were on our way to the Wrangell Mountains; the weather was warming up, which meant the county would continue plowing the roads into the park. This meant we would be getting some drive-in traffic, but for that day, the sun would make landing on the glacier a bit more treacherous. The mountains were still covered with snow, which made it extremely hard to spot the goats—unless they were on a sheer cliff of granite, and then they stood out like a sore thumb. I decided to hunt the area on the east side of Mount Blackburn, which was due north of Kennecott and McCarthy on the Copper River. I figured with the sun shining, the goats should be lying or standing on a clear rock, soaking up some of that early-morning sun; we were not disappointed.

We flew around the north side of the peak; as soon as we got on the east slope, we could see goats. We never counted, but I would guess in a half an hour, he spotted fifty to seventy-five goats. For some reason, if you come from the upper side, above the goats, they're a lot easier to sneak up on; and when goats spook, they hardly ever go downhill—always around the mountain or up the mountain. Since the breeding season was over, most of the old-timers seemed to like being by themselves and were usually nice big bucks with impressive horns.

We spotted a half a dozen animals that we felt fit that description; now the chore was to find a spot on the glacier above the goat where I could land. We picked a couple of distinct landmarks in close proximity to the goat we intended to hunt; the area where I wanted to land had too much of a side slope that the plane wanted to slide down the slope. I had to take off and pick a spot approximately four hundred to five hundred feet lower that was nice and level, but now we had another five hundred feet to climb, plus approximately three hundred feet to get on top of the ridge. At five thousand feet, with our winter clothes on, that was an exhausting chore. We would walk a hundred feet. Sam would have to take a breather; it took us over an hour to get to the top of that ridge; then Sam had to sit fifteen minutes to catch his breath and quit shaking.

While Sam was resting, I eased up to the top of the ridge and slowly peeked over the top. I almost swallowed my cigar; not more than a hundred feet below me was our trophy, nibbling on several old clumps of grass and slowly working his way up and to my left. I slid back away from ridge a couple of yards. I had to pick up a chunk of ice to throw at Sam to get his attention, then frantically motioned for him to get up here "right now." I guess he could tell by the expression on my face that he'd better move and quick, yet he had to be quiet. We were so close to the goat that we didn't even dare whisper; everything had to be in sign language.

Sam's problem was going to be getting in position to shoot without being seen; he peeked over the ridge, then slowly withdrew back to where I was waiting. He suggested waiting until the goat reached the top of the ridge or got a little farther away. I didn't have a problem with that idea and suggested he get in position to cover the ridge if the goat decided to cross over the ridge to our side. I crawled back up the hill to where I could see over the ridge; the goat was actually a little farther away but was almost to the ridge. I glanced at Sam, who was ready and watching the ridgeline. The goat disappeared from my view behind a couple of rocks. A couple of minutes passed; then the morning stillness was shattered by the explosion of Sam's new Weatherby. I scrambled to my feet in time to see the goat make two giant leaps and then collapse in the snow. Sam was now the proud owner of another beautiful trophy.

It was now midday; the sun was shining with only an occasional cloud. It had warmed up to a point where we could take our jackets off while we were skinning out the goat; of course, this didn't take place until we had completed our picture taking. Then it was time to return to the plane, which was about a half a mile away and five hundred feet below us. The temperature had climbed above freezing, and the sun had now reached our side of the mountain; as we were working on the goat, both of us slipped and fell several times on the ice, which was getting very slippery.

"Sam, I don't know if we are going to be able to walk down this glacier. We may have to slide down on our butts."

"If we're going to do that, I'm going to sit on this goat hide and use it as a sled."

"You're liable to wear all the hair off a spot in that hide and ruin it for a full mount."

"If so, I'll just use it as a shoulder mount. But as slippery as this ice is, I don't think it'll hurt the hide."

Cappy Capesella fueling one of the supper cubs at Kotzebue before a polar bear hunt. In the early 70's Cappy was killed by a wonded grizzly bear.

Kotzebue Alaska early 1960's where Denny and Cappy spent a couple months every spring polar bear hunting

So we got Sam situated on his goat hide; he had the head between his legs, and he was hanging on to the horns. I wished later we had taken a picture. He started to ease himself down the side of the glacier; before long, he had picked up considerable speed that he was having trouble steering himself with his feet. So he used the stock of his gun as a break and a rudder; about halfway to the plane, there was a little level spot where Sam was able to bring his goat hide sled to a stop. He looked back up the glacier to see how I was doing. I hadn't moved a step. I was enjoying watching Sam bounce along down the hill, expecting him to go tumbling off his sled; but to this point, I was impressed with his ability to keep everything under control. I started to ease my way down the hill. I have no idea how many times I slipped and fell. I finally arrived where Sam was waiting.

"Hey, Thompson, this is a blast. I just hope there's no crevices between here and the airplane."

Then he pushed off and continued his descent down the side of the glacier. Again, I just stood and watched until he was able to stop about fifty feet from the airplane; it took me another twenty minutes at least before I caught up to Sam.

"Hey, Thompson, what took you so long? Do you charge extra for the toboggan ride?"

"Nope, no extra charge. But it looks like your rifle didn't fare nearly as well as you did." Sam held up his new Weatherby; it was in sad shape. He had worn off about two to three inches of the bottom of the stock using it as a rudder; it was totally ruined, and there was no way it could be fixed.

"That's what I get for buying a cheap gun," Sam joked.

We loaded the hide, guns, etc., in the plane, then cranked up the engine and turned the nose downhill. Within a couple hundred feet, we were airborne, floating down the canyon like a leaf in the wind.

The stories that night in the Wolf Den were classic. I had four hunters who had just arrived from LA. Sam had a couple of drinks, and the boys in Chicago would have been proud. Sam dragged out his bear hide and of course the goat and, last but not least, his rifle. I won't even attempt to retell the tales that were spun that night, but I will say if there was a record book for the most embellished hunting stories ever told, Sam would be right there near the top. And those four hunters who sat there the whole evening, hanging on every word, I'm sure they felt cheated. Even though they had good hunts, there was no way they could measure up to the tales that Sam told.

Polar Bear Hunter

48 Below zero not counting wind chill.

Chapter Thirty-Three

Marge was a very good addition to the Susitna Lodge; her beautiful smile and winning disposition just seemed to make everyone feel welcome and relaxed.

The rest of 1962 was pretty routine except for the amount of drive-in traffic, which picked up considerably; with three of us hauling hunters in and out of camps, we still had to turn some people away.

By the middle of October, we had to close the lodge and move back to the house in Anchorage; from there, I took a number of wolf hunters. Other than that and nonstop maintenance, there wasn't a lot going on until polar bear season; our first hunters arrived right after the first of March.

The weather was bitterly cold. Cappy and I arrived several days early with a three-hundred-foot roll of electrical wire; we dug a four-inch trench in the ice with the pick, laid our wire in the trench, then poured water on it, which froze instantly. That protected it from automobile traffic and snowmobiles. The wire ran from the back of the hangar to our tie-down; we would cover the engine compartment with an insulated blanket, and then we would put a 75- to 100-watt lightbulb in the engine compartment, which would create enough heat to keep the engine oil from becoming so thick that the starter couldn't turn the engine over. Our first three or four hunting parties were all successful, but the weather stayed exceptionally cold; several nights, it reached seventy below zero, and it didn't warm up much during the day.

My bowhunting friend from Wisconsin, Art Laha, arrived. I asked him again if he was sure he wanted to try for a polar bear with his bow. There was no hesitation; he was committed. I decided we would hunt west of Point Hope; there always seemed to be more bear in that area, and to date, we had not hunted that area yet this year. Other than being extremely cold, the weather was good. I called the weather station to get the official reading on the temperature; it was forty-four below zero, not counting the wind chill. The weather was acceptable—bright sunshine, but a wind of about twenty-five miles per hour. Cappy and I each carried an additional ten gallons of gasoline; we anticipated this hunt to be a little out of the ordinary. If we had known how out of the ordinary, I'm sure we would've turned around and spent the day in the local pub, but we were all anxious to get our names in another category in the record books.

We flew north by northwest to an area I estimated to be approximately a hundred miles due west of Point Hope; we were not disappointed. We had seen at least ten bears already, but this was a different situation than normal; we had to find a place where we were quite sure the bears would only be twenty-five to thirty yards from our ambush position. And that day, I had Art Fields with me and Cappy in the backup plane; and with Art Fields and me in my airplane was Art Laha because Art wanted this entire episode filmed. My job was to take pictures of the bear as it approached our position and, of course, of the shot by Art that we all hoped would be fatal. We finally found what we considered the perfect situation: The bear was moving north along the west side of the pressure ridge, which was at least thirty to forty feet high, so it was very unlikely the bear would attempt to cross that ridge. There was a smaller pressure ridge to the west, and the two of them came together about a mile north of the bear's present position; we felt we had plenty of room to land and keep the plane out of sight and be in position when the bear arrived at the chokepoint, which was between the two pressure ridges. We didn't get too close to the bear for fear of spooking him, but even at our distance, I felt he was an exceptionally big bear. We landed as close as we could; we had to quickly cover the engine with the insulated blanket. The temperature was forty-four below zero, and the wind was blowing about twenty-five knots. I felt we had to keep the plane out of sight; we hustled into position. I told Art to get ready and positioned him about ten yards to our south, behind a couple big blocks of ice, and I told him to let us know as soon as he saw the bear.

In the meantime, I had to get the camera going, which was no easy task when you're wearing mittens. I had my rifle, which I fully expected I would have to use. Art Fields was off to my left, about five feet; he was putting buckshot in the double-barrel 12-gauge, just in case this adventure turned into a hand-to-hand combat situation. I felt we probably had ten to fifteen minutes before the bear would arrive. I laid my rifle off to my right a couple feet away; the barrel was resting on a small piece of ice to keep it out of the snow. I was on my knees, sitting on my heels, with the camera between my legs. I glanced to my left at Art. He was basically in the same position, fumbling with the shells and the 12-gauge. I glanced up at Art Laha; he appeared to have his bow ready and was getting into position to watch for the bear. Everything appeared to be as it should be.

I was still very nervous about this attempt to shoot one of these monsters with an arrow, and I fully expected that Art Fields or I would wind up killing the bear, but I was totally unprepared for what happened in the next couple of minutes.

Art had an arrow in the bow as he rose up to peek over the block of ice; he was totally unprepared for what he was about to see. Not forty feet in front of him was the polar bear—coming at him full speed. What we think happened is that the bear must've seen the top of Art's head sticking up above the ice as he was working with his bow. The only thing that a bear sees that is black in the wintertime is a seal or a walrus, both of which are on his menu.

Art yelled, "Here he comes!"

The bear was no farther than six to eight feet away when he went past Art. Art took a shot; the arrow hit the left front shoulder of the bear.

Neither Denny nor Art Fields hear Art's warning and didn't realize the bear was anywhere close.

Art jumped off to the side to keep from being run over by the bear; he slipped and fells as he frantically tried to get another arrow in the bow. He looked over at Denny and Art Fields and realized neither of them was aware of the present danger and screamed again.

The first indication I had that there was a problem was when the bear stepped on my camera and knocked me over backward; at the same time, with his other front foot, he stepped on the barrel of my rifle. I was now lying flat on my back, looking up at this enormous animal that has stopped directly over me, with one foot on the camera and the other on my rifle.

I can remember seeing the steam shooting out from both nostrils and the saliva dripping in my face; one swipe with his paw or one bite by those enormous jaws would have probably ended my career and life in an instant. He probably paused for no more than a couple of seconds, but to me, it seemed like hours; he then turned toward Art Fields, who was frantically trying to get his shotgun in position. He swung the barrel toward the bear and fired both barrels; the blast from the shotgun missed its mark by perhaps six inches, but it was close enough to shoot the bear's right ear off. The blast from that shotgun was evidently enough distraction for the bear because he decided he didn't want anything more to do with this group and departed.

I retrieved my rifle but the barrel was full of snow. Art Fields was reloading the 12-gauge when Art came running over, waving his arms and shouting, "Don't shoot! Don't shoot! I want him to qualify for the Pope & Young record book!" Once I was sure the bear wasn't coming back, I tried to get everybody to calm down while I removed the snow from the barrel of my rifle. Cappy was circling overhead, watching this drama unfold. Art Fields was furious with Art Laha for not letting us know how close the bear was, but Art swore he yelled at us when he first saw the bear. I don't doubt that he did, but he was probably looking the other direction at the bear, and the wind was blowing. We all had our caps pulled down over our ears with the hoods on our parkas up, so we could hardly hear each other when we were standing four or five feet apart. The 1,200-pound bear had proceeded to grind my camera right into the ice. I didn't even bother to pick up the pieces. Art felt the arrow should have penetrated deep enough that it could have gotten into the bear's lungs. I didn't think so; it looked to me like the arrow had not penetrated more than six to eight inches, and I believe it was just in the shoulder muscle, which is not fatal for an animal like a polar bear.

I suggested we finish the wounded bear off with a rifle, but Art wouldn't even consider that; he had his heart set on getting this trophy with the bow. Cappy, who had been circling overhead and watching the drama unfold, landed his plane on the ice and came running over to see if we were all okay; he was much more excited than the three of us put together. He said it had something to do with being an Italian. I finally decided to pick up the pieces from my camera, not because it could be fixed, but it would definitely add to the story, which I knew would be told hundreds of times.

We hadn't been on the bear's tracks for more than a couple minutes when we spotted it; he was in an area of scattered chunks of ice, not solid like a pressure ridge, just scattered helter-skelter. We worked our way through the ice field until we caught sight of the bear; by then, his front shoulder and the side of his head were covered in blood, but the arrow had dropped out of the bear's shoulder. That gave Art some anxiety; he had felt for sure the bear would drop dead any minute from loss of blood. There were four white foxes also following the bear; we were rapidly running out of daylight. I tried to tell Art that bears very seldom bled to death because of their extremely slow heartbeat. Art took a couple more shots with the bow, but the wind was blowing twenty-five knots, and he was too far away.

Art wanted to come back the next morning and try one last time with the bow; if that didn't work, then he agreed to use the rifle to finish off the wounded bear.

There were no landmarks or anything to go by to get back to this exact area. I decided we would stay at Point Hope that night because it was much closer than Kotzebue, and I felt if we flew out of point Hope, he would have a lot better chance of finding the bear the next morning; once we were airborne, we checked our watches, took a compass reading, and flew directly to Point Hope.

The next morning, we were fortunate to have another clear day; but lord, it was cold! It had taken us exactly one hour and fifteen minutes last night from the location of the bear to the runway at Point Hope;

that morning, we hoped to fly exactly one hour and fifteen minutes in the exact opposite direction. If were very, very lucky, we may find our bear. One hour and sixteen minutes later, we spotted our bear with a red shoulder; we tried three more times to get close enough for Art to get a shot with the bow, but to no avail. The bear was getting smarter and more cautious every time we tried. Finally, Art conceded and asked to borrow my rifle; two well-placed shots and Art had his trophy—not like he wanted it, but it was still a beautiful trophy. It was missing one ear but was large enough to get in the record books, but not in Pope & Young like Art would have liked. The way back to Kotzebue, Art asked about a brown bear hunt with the bow.

"Art, there's not much difference in the size of the brown bear and the polar bear. The brown bear's not quite as aggressive—unless you run into one eating on a carcass, then I would say they're more aggressive and much more dangerous. They will tear a twenty-foot fir tree out by the roots just to chase off a raven or a blue jay. They will not share that carcass with anything. When they get in that state of mind, the adrenaline is pumping, and I believe they're harder to kill."

"You don't make it sound very encouraging."

"Art, I'm just telling you the way it is. When you have to get within fifty to a hundred feet of an animal like that, then stick him in the ass with one of those arrows. He might have a tendency to get a little hostile. The problem with the bear—any size—is they're difficult to kill. Many a hunter over the years have been killed by a brown and grizzly bear after the bear was shot through the heart. But don't get me wrong, Art. I will gladly take you on a brown bear hunt and try our damnedest to put you in a position to get your bear."

"I don't think I can make it this next spring, but perhaps the year after."

"Whenever you're ready, I plan to be here. In the meantime, I'll watch for situations that I think would give you the best chance."

We had one more memorable hunt that spring. I don't remember who it was, but I do remember what happened. We left Kotzebue at sunrise; there was a very low ice fog, not more than ten feet thick. As soon as we took off, we were out of it. We flew northwest for at least an hour before we started to see some nice tracks; that low fog made it difficult to see the tracks at times, but we finally located the bear. When I started to land, I realized once I got close to the ground, my visibility was very limited; it would be very easy to plow into a chunk of ice.

I decided to pull up and go around one more time and check out the area where I intended to land to make sure there wasn't a chunk of ice in my chosen landing area. Once I was sure I had a clear area, I sat the Super Cub on the foggy landing strip with no mishaps. I felt we were about one half to three quarters of a mile in front of the bear; because of the fog, we didn't go very far from the plane. I made that mistake one other time and spent an hour trying to find the plane in the fog. Once we got into position, we couldn't see a thing; we had no idea where the bear was, so I decided to climb up on the plane stand on the wing until I spotted the bear. It wasn't very long before I spotted him less than fifty yards and coming right at us. I slid off the wing and hustled to get back with the hunter. We were behind a big chunk of ice; within a couple minutes, we could hear the bear but couldn't see him. It was thirty below, and I started to sweat.

A couple times, we caught just a faint glimpse of the bear; and like a ghost, he was gone. When he moved, we could hear him in the crunchy ice, but what was nerve-racking was when we couldn't hear anything. All at once, there was a change in the sound; then we heard a low growl that originated someplace just north of his anus and rumbled up his throat and out through his very impressive teeth. The hunter looked at me for reassurance. "I'll do my best." But I'm afraid I wasn't very convincing. We then realized there were two bears out there; we could just imagine they were plotting how and when to attack. We squatted down behind the ice block and waited; no way we dared chance a shot, so we just hoped they decided to go on their way. All at once, I found myself staring into this set of eyeballs not six or eight feet in front of me. I damn near crapped my pants until I realized it was one of those little arctic foxes that followed the polar bears wherever they went. He disappeared, and I never saw him move. Sometime shortly after that, everything got quite; we waited a couple more minutes, then decided to make our way back to the plane and try our luck elsewhere.

Bob Peterson with his polar bear taken with a 44 magnum west of Point Hope, Alaska

Three Japanese hunters with Denny they took three bear one shot each

Chapter Thirty-Four

In the spring of 1963, right after we got the lodge open, I was approached by a mining company, I believe, out of Canada. They were looking for mineral deposits in and around the Alaskan mountain range since we were centrally located; they wanted to know if they could use the lodge as their operations center; they would rent rooms, eat at the lodge, drink, and tell war stories in the Wolf Den.

They had one chopper all the time and sometimes two; on average, there were four to six people there all the time. The pilots were Korean War veterans; they would fly the geologists, as a rule, into some very rugged country. They would try to land in some very rough terrain and sometimes with disastrous results. They were primarily searching for gold, silver, and uranium.

The Alaskan mountain range starts down by Lake Iliamna, then runs north almost to Fairbanks, turns east for another couple hundred miles, and ends just north of the Wrangell Mountains.

There are at least a dozen mountain ranges in Alaska; the Brooks Range, for instance, in the Arctic Circle has five different mountain ranges. Then there's the White Mountains north of Fairbanks; the Alaska Range has three to four different mountain ranges. Then south of the Wrangells, you have the Chugach Mountains and the Kenai Mountains on the Kenai Peninsula. On the east side of Prince William Sound is the St. Elias Mountains. I do believe if you flattened out all the mountains in Alaska, it would cover the entire Lower 48.

It involves probably some of the most dangerous flying in the world; besides the rough terrain, the weather is totally unpredictable. One minute, you have fifty-mile visibility; ten minutes later, the ceiling drops to two hundred to three hundred feet. Visibility is a quarter of a mile or less; if you don't know the terrain, you're dead.

That is what's happened to many a good pilot. More than once, I've had to get so low that I just landed on any relatively flat spot I could find: a gravel bar in a creek or river, an old lake bed out in the tundra or up on a glacier, or a brushy hillside on the side of the mountain. Sometimes you ding up the plane a little bit, but that's better than plowing into the side of the mountain. I always told myself not to ever lose sight of the ground; many of times, the conditions got bad that I would land wherever I could. Many a night, I spent sitting in that airplane, hoping that the weather would improve the next day.

I think that's one of the reasons why after *sixty-plus years* and *twenty-five thousand hours* of flying some of the most dangerous terrain in the world, I'm still here to talk about it.

Now to get back to my reason for the explanation on flying conditions in Alaska, the geologists were flying in some of the roughest out-of-the-way areas that existed; all the easy stuff had already been discovered. It was about the middle of September, and the boys had told me that morning where they were going to be flying; that was the everyday routine. Just in case something happened, I'd have an idea where to look for them.

It was about 8:30 p.m. I was just returning with a couple of moose hunters and a plane full of moose meat; when I got back to the lodge, the first thing I noticed was the absence of the chopper. Those guys were usually on the ground back at the lodge by 5:00 p.m. They very seldom missed an opportunity to drink, and they never missed dinner.

We unloaded the plane. I took Cappy with me; we hadn't been airborne more than about fifteen minutes when we spotted some smoke on the side of the mountain. As we got closer, we could see the wreckage along a small creek, a very adequate place to land a chopper. We landed a couple hundred yards from the crash site; when we got to the helicopter, everybody was badly burned. Two of the men were dead. I went back to the lodge, and we made a stretcher out of a couple poles and a blanket; one of the men was blind but could still walk. Cappy helped him get back to the airplane while I worked with the other badly injured man. You had to be very careful how you took a hold of him; his skin was burned so bad that it would come off in your hands. He was still alive when they put him in the coast guard helicopter; but by the time he reached the hospital, he died. The other man was flown to Houston, Texas, to a burn center; we never did hear if he survived or not.

We didn't know for sure what caused the accident. But my guess was the wind sometimes comes over those ridges and down those canyons, creating a tremendous downdraft. If you're not prepared, it will slam you right into the ground.

Besides Cappy and Bill Sims, I had another young guy, Mark Rogers, who would fly for me when I was in a pinch; he had his own plane—if I remember right, a Piper PA-18 115 hp.

Bob Gomes, a friend of mine from Turlock, California, had been hanging around the lodge, waiting for me to take him moose hunting; he was running out of time, and I couldn't see a break in my schedule for at least a couple weeks. He and Mark had struck up a friendship, so Bob decided to go moose hunting with Mark; they got their moose, and Bob headed back to California with a couple freezers full of moose meat and a very respectable set of antlers.

It was about a month later when Cappy and Mark Rogers took two hunters from Michigan sheep hunting; they got their sheep and were headed back to the lodge. The ceiling had dropped to less than two hundred feet in some areas. Cappy took off first and headed down the canyon. Mark should've been right behind him, but for some reason, he flew up the canyon; we presume he realized his mistake and had to make a very sharp turn without much airspeed. It appeared the plane stalled and went nose first into the ground, killing both Mark Rogers and the hunter. Mark was a very nice young man, and that really hurt. It took the sheriff's department a couple of days to recover the bodies; in that length of time, somebody went in and stole the engine out of that airplane with the two dead men still in the cockpit.

The year 1963 did not end on a favorable note.

Chapter Thirty-Five

The next year, 1964, was a very memorable one. To start out with, I had two more bowhunters for polar bear hunting; they were a couple of friends of Art Laha from the Chicago area, if I remember right. Again, we had to try to find a situation where we could get the hunters as close to the bear as possible. In this situation, I carried a .375, which was way more gun than I was comfortable with; every time I looked at the cartridge, my shoulder started to hurt. But as close as we had to get to the bear with these bowhunters, I felt that was an absolute necessity.

We left Kotzebue just before daylight and flew Northwest; our destination was 100 to 150 miles due west of Point Hope. We were into the flight only about thirty-five minutes when we started to see polar bears; by the time we had reached our approximate destination, we had seen close to fifty polar bears already. Some were really nice bears, but in very difficult areas to hunt. I turned southwest; we spotted a couple of nice big tracks and decided to follow them for a little ways. Since the ice in this area was much less broken, we followed the tracks for approximately a mile and a half to two miles. There were two big bears traveling together; they were traveling down one of the green rivers, which was approximately fifty feet wide. Conditions were very favorable, with a good place to land and a scattering of ice blocks where we could set up our ambush.

Cappy stayed in the air while I landed with one of the hunters; this hunter must've talked to Art because beside his bow, he also brought a rifle. He had just about every square inch of the rifle covered with white tape. I can't remember what caliber it was, but I do remember it was a lever action. Once Cappy saw we were in position, he buzzed the bears in an attempt to break them up; he felt one at a time would be a great plenty. It worked. One of the bears moved to the other side of the river; our bear kept coming right down our side of the river, and when I say our side of the river, I mean the bear was headed directly at us.

When he finally reached our position, he was approximately ten feet from my hunter and me; the hunter shot his arrow into the front shoulder, very similar to what Art did. It hit the shoulder bone and penetrated only about six inches; the bear was so close I could count his eyelashes. I decided the prudent thing to do was shoot him with the .375. I felt a neck shot would be the safest; he was too close to take any chances. At that distance, he appeared to be bigger than my airplane; he looked right at me, eye to eye. I pulled the trigger; there was a click, but no explosion. This happened frequently when the weather was this cold; for some reason, the bear decided to just keep going. The hunter had dropped his bow and picked up his rifle and started shooting; by this time, I had injected a new cartridge in my rifle. I took one shot, but I don't even remember if I hit the bear. The hunter had done an adequate job; we tracked the bear for a couple hundred yards. He was losing quite a bit of blood, but by looking at him, you would never know he was hit; he found some open water, dove into the water, and swam around for ten to fifteen minutes. We were afraid he was going to die in that water; we kept out of sight, but he eventually climbed back out onto the ice. Again, he came almost directly at us; by this time, you could tell he was getting weaker. The hunter fired one more well-placed shot.

Once Cappy saw that we had everything under control, he found the other half of the twosome; once we had our bear skinned out and loaded in the plane and was airborne, he and his hunter landed. They had a similar situation; the hunter fired one arrow, dropped his bow, and picked up his rifle. He dropped the bear with the second shot.

We made it back to Kotzebue before dark; the hunters were extremely happy with their trophies, and it didn't seem to bother them that they had to finish the bear off with the rifle. All they could talk about was how huge these animals were up close. Art, of course, had told them about his hunt last year and how the bear had knocked me over and then stood there for a couple of seconds standing on my rifle. I don't think they believed Art when he was telling the story, but that day made believers out of them.

Our next hunter that spring was a gentleman by the name of Bob Petersen, owner of Petersen Publishing Company; he published *Guns & Ammo*, *Auto Trend*, and about sixteen other magazines. He arrived in Kotzebue on Wien Airlines. We had been waiting for him for two days; he was held up in Anchorage because of a volcanic eruption just south of the city. This seemed to happen every couple of years; there was no real lava flow, but it just put an extreme amount of ash in the air. The wind was out of the southwest, which carried the ash right over Anchorage and the airport. All commercial airlines in or out of Anchorage were grounded. The wind finally switched out of the north, and within several hours, the planes were back in the air; they just had to be routed around the ash cloud on their approach to Anchorage.

I remember we left Kotzebue early that morning; there was a frigid wind right out of Siberia. The temperature was forty-five below zero, not considering any windchill.

"Is it always this cold up here?" Bob asked.

"No, sometimes it's even colder. Last week, it was sixty-eight below, and the wind was about twice as strong as it is today."

"Does it ever get so cold that you just don't dare go out?"

"If it gets to forty-five below zero, we generally don't go out. We have, but so far, we've never had to cancel because of cold weather. But we have had to cancel several times because of ice fog and wind—sometimes it blows so hard up here that you just don't dare try to fly."

We flew northwest what I estimated to be approximately two hundred miles; we had seen a number of bears, but nothing that we were impressed with. We finally ran across a set of tracks that appeared to be of an above-average bear; we had to follow him for a while, I guess at least three to four miles. We finally spotted him up ahead, made a detour around him, and landed approximately two miles in front of the bear on what was a nice wide flat chunk of ice—a much better area to land than we normally had.

We had to walk approximately a quarter mile to get into position; the bear passed within about fifty yards. Mr. Petersen was using a handgun, I believe a .44 Magnum. Bob's first shot was good, but he continued to shoot all six shots until the bear collapsed. While we were skinning the bear, there was a large cracking explosion of ice, something we heard almost every time we were on the ice. But this time, it was louder than normal and shook the ice we were standing on.

"Denny, what the hell was that?" Bob asked.

"Just the ice shifting, probably creating another green river."

"It sounded pretty close, don't you think?"

"I'm pretty sure when we get airborne, we will be able the spot it."

We finished skinning the bear and were dragging the hide back to the plane. Cappy made a low pass, then circled around and landed about a hundred feet in front of us; my first thought was to be angry with him but then realized he must have a good reason.

"Hey, Denny, would you like a ride back to your plane? Or are you going to swim?"

It took me a minute to realize what he was talking about; a big crack in the ice opened up between Bob and me and the plane. We walked up to the edge of the ice. It was about five feet thick; the crack went for as far as we could see and was by then seventy-five to eighty feet wide and getting wider as we watched. The plane was only about twenty feet on the other side of the broken ice. I have often thought what could've happened if the plane had been just a few feet farther north.

"How long is this split in the ice, Cappy?" I asked.

"I think it goes at least a mile in each direction. It's hard to tell, but it's wide all the way."

"Bob, if you'll stay here with the bear hide, I'll go with Cappy, get the plane, and come back and pick you up."

Once we were airborne, I followed the new green river for approximately five miles before it ended in a major pressure ridge—just too much mass, I guess.

We had another half a dozen successful hunters after Bob.

March 27 would be our last hunt of the season, and then we were headed back to Anchorage.

Our last two hunters were from Southern California—San Diego, if I remember right. This year, we had our best luck about 150 to 200 miles west, by northwest of Kotzebue, not too far off the Russian coast. We were about two hundred miles, mostly west of Kotzebue, and we picked up a nice set of tracks; there was a low ice fog that kept us from seeing very far in front of us. Looking straight down, we could see just fine, but our visibility forward was probably no more than a quarter mile.

We must have followed these tracks at least ten miles; before we finally caught up to the bear, we were almost directly over the top of him when we first spotted the bear. I landed almost two miles in front of him because he was traveling at a much faster pace than the average bear; we covered the engine and hustled into position not very far from the plane. I don't believe we waited for more than ten minutes, and here he came; the route he was traveling was taking him perhaps 150 yards to our west. He looked like a ghost in the fog. One second, you could see him clear; then he would almost disappear. The hunter wasn't concerned about the distance; he felt confident he could hit him. We hoped perhaps the bear would stop, but that didn't happen; the hunter had a good rest on a large chunk of ice. He took his shot; the bear changed stride slightly, indicating to me he had been hit. The hunter got one more quick shot before the bear disappeared behind some large blocks of ice; we could only see him for an instant once in a while in the fog. Then he would disappear again. I looked at my watch; it was four o'clock. We had only a couple hours of daylight left. I decided we'd better get on his trail.

We tracked the bear for almost a mile; he was losing a tremendous amount of blood. His pace was slowing down considerably; we would occasionally get a glimpse of the bear between the blocks of ice, but never enough to get another clean shoot. What bothered me was that most of the time, due to the fog, we didn't know where he was; he could circle around behind us. Or we could run him into a dead-end canyon, so to speak, where he was trapped. That could be very exciting.

There were two "white as the snow" arctic foxes following the bear; they would stop occasionally to lick up a puddle of blood. Whenever you find a polar bear, there are usually two or three arctic foxes in close proximity; they tag along behind the bear. When the bear makes a kill, they will just curl up in the snow forty or fifty feet from the bear and wait for him to finish his seal dinner; once he leaves, they will then come in and clean up the scraps. That is primarily the only way they can survive out here on the ice since there is no other game available. I don't think I've ever seen a bear on a seal kill where there wasn't at least two little foxes patiently waiting for their turn.

Our bear finally just ran out of gas; we walked around a couple of chunks of ice. In the fog, we almost bumped into him—there he was. He looked like he was asleep; we backed off a couple steps and watched him for a couple of minutes, then approached very cautiously. But he was dead. We were about halfway done skinning when the wind started to pick up. I was just finishing up on the hind paws; the hunter was standing off to my right, watching and helping when he could.

"Denny, what's that?" he asked as he pointed to the west. I turned to look.

"That is the Russian coast," I said. I thought we must be getting close, but I didn't think we were that close. That must've been what the bear was headed for; he probably felt if he could get to the land, he would be safe. He came up short by only a couple hundred yards.

We started back to the plane. I felt we had at least a mile to go, but Cappy came to our rescue; he landed in a little area between some chunks of ice and was putting some gas in his plane. We loaded the bear hide in the back of the plane. I put the hunter in the backseat and crawled in on top of the bear hide, and we hitched a ride back to my airplane. We left the bear hide in Cappy's plane, but the hunter and I both transferred to my plane. I looked at my watch; it was 5:30 p.m.

What we didn't realize was that the biggest earthquake ever recorded was in progress in Prince William Sound.

When we returned to Kotzebue, everybody was talking about an earthquake that hit the Anchorage area, but we all said, "So what's new?" We had quakes there at least four to five times a year; it was still too early to get damage reports.

This was our last bear hunt for the year, so Cappy and I got our gear together that evening so we could leave first thing in the morning; our hunters had to fly to Fairbanks because of damage at the Anchorage airport. We still didn't realize the significance of what had happened; we left Kotzebue about 8:30 a.m. the next day. The reports by then were starting to tell of massive damage from the quake. But even more damage was occurring from the tsunami, which had a devastating effect all over Alaska and the coasts of Washington, Oregon, and California, the Hawaiian Islands—even as far away as Japan, Peru, and New Zealand. It was even reported that fishing boats were sunk along the Louisiana coast. The reported highest tsunami wave in Alaska was over one hundred feet high, with 139 people known to have died. The wave that hit Hilo, Hawaii was fourteen ft high.

On our flight home, as we got closer to Anchorage, we saw broken ice everywhere—sea ice and lake ice alike; it was something I had never seen. We made a couple of passes over Anchorage and the surrounding areas; the damage was pretty unbelievable. Whole areas down by the bay were wiped clean. And then other areas had debris piled thirty feet high; one side of the street in downtown Anchorage had dropped ten to fifteen feet and more in some areas. Other areas outside of town had raised twenty to thirty feet, while other areas dropped below sea level and were now covered by salt water; this happened to hundreds of acres.

I heard Seward was in real bad shape; it was about a week before I got over there to check things out. When I did, it was unbelievable. I had two hangars at the airport, but they were both gone—not a trace. They had all my military clothes and records and parts for my planes. I can't even start to remember everything that was stored there, but it was all gone without a trace.

I remember there was a big harbor tugboat sitting in the middle of the runway, at least a couple hundred yards from the closest water; smaller boats and parts of the pier scattered about, but most of that kind of stuff plus numerous buildings had been washed out to sea. The quake turned out to be 9.2 on the Richter scale, I was told; that is more than a hundred times stronger than the quake that destroyed San Francisco in 1906. But life goes on.

I couldn't wait for the county to clean the roads to the lodge, so we flew into the lodge to check it out; lots of stuff had fallen off shelves, and there were a couple cracks in the concrete, but not what I had feared. I was very lucky. We had several hunters cancel that summer; we were having aftershocks every day, and there were all kinds of reports of the possibility of another major quake, enough to scare some people out of making the trip. What we may have lost this year we made up for several times over the next couple of years; people came up from the Lower 48 to take a look at the damage before it was all cleaned up.

Chapter Thirty-Six

I had two important hunters coming in this year, both for brown bear. Not that all the hunters were not important, but these were kind of special; they were of course my friends Art Laha and CJ McElroy, the president of the Safari Club International. Actually, McElroy wanted both a polar bear and a brown, so I booked him for the last polar bear hunt of the season. My intention was to wrap up our polar bear hunt and then fly over to the Cinder River area to see if we could get him a brown bear—all of this before we went home.

The polar bear season was good—not exceptional, just good. We had fourteen hunters, and they all got their bears—all nice trophies. Mr. McElroy, or Mac, arrived late in the afternoon; he had bought a brand-new .416 Rigby just for this hunt. The next morning, we were airborne right at daylight; my plan was to fly northwest until we were due west of Point Hope, approximately two hundred miles.

Mac wanted to get a record book bear if he could. I felt this would probably provide us the best opportunity to do that; we hadn't quite arrived at the area. I intended to hunt when we spotted some very large tracks; we followed the tracks for only approximately a mile when we spotted the bear, He was right at the edge of one of the big pressure ridges; it appeared he wasn't going anywhere. It looked like he was watching several airholes in the ice, waiting for the seals. We landed about a quarter of a mile away, then stalked the bear using the blocks of ice that were scattered about the landscape as cover; we were less than a hundred yards from the bear when he detected our presence. He either saw one of us move or picked up our scent; he was an old bear, with one ear half torn off and several scars on the side of his face—not the prettiest old bear I'd ever seen. But he was big, and that's the one that Mac wanted. We followed the bear for a hundred yards or more before he disappeared into a hole in the ice; we could see the bear, but there was no way we could shoot the bear and get him out of the water. We must have messed with him for an hour before we finally had to just give up.

We got back in the airplane and started to search for another bear; we hadn't been airborne more than ten to fifteen minutes when we spotted another monster. This was actually a bigger bear than the first one and in a lot better shape. Again, the bear didn't seem to be moving in any one given direction; like the last one, we stalked the bear using the chunks of ice as cover. This one had no idea we were in the area. Mac delivered one fatal shot to the left front shoulder. The bear was a monster; in fact, I believe it went into the record book as number 1 in 1965. A year later, it was beaten by less than a half an inch; but to this day, I believe it still sits in the number 2 position.

The next morning, we left Kotzebue bright and early; we had a long flight all the way to the Cinder River area. We stayed the night in Port Heiden; it was early in the season, so we hunted the upper end of the river valley. In the foothills close to where the bears hibernate for the winter, we spent a couple hours just scouting. There were lots of bears; some of them were still hanging around their dens. I was banking to the left. I thought I had seen a big bear off to my left. I glanced down at the ground; we were only about a hundred feet high. I thought somebody had parked a bus in the brush below me; it was a brown bear, a very big brown bear. I banked around to the right and made another pass over the bear so Mac could get a good look at it. He was so excited I thought he was going to jump out of the airplane; the bear was moving down a ravine that would lead him out into the open in another couple hundred yards. I had to be careful not to land someplace where he could see us. I had to land nearly a mile below the present location of the bear. I got Cappy's attention and had him stay high enough so he wouldn't distract the bear, but I wanted him to keep an eye on the bear so we didn't lose him in the brush, just in case he decided to change course and go a different direction.

We landed and started to work our way through the brush, back up the hill toward the bear, always keeping in mind there were a lot of other bears in the area. We did not want to stumble onto one of them in this brush; luckily, he kept coming down the hill in our direction. We got into position behind a bank of snow and some brush. I think we waited perhaps a half an hour, watching the bear all the time; when he reached an area, we estimated to be less than one hundred yards. CJ McElroy made another very good shot, and the bear was down for the count: two shots and what turned out to be two world records—all within two days. Mac killed two record book bears with two shots in two days. I believe this brown bear is still in the top 15 or 20 fifty years later.

We flew directly from the Cinder River area to Anchorage and put Mr. McElroy on his flight back to Phoenix, but that wasn't the last time we'd see Mr. McElroy; he hunted with us at least another dozen times and has numerous animals in the record book to show for it.

That spring, we had a number of bookings for brown bears, which kept myself, Bill Sims, and Cappy very busy from daylight till dark. And then of course, we had our friend Art Laha from Wisconsin, who was ready and determined to get a brown bear with the bow—not something I was looking forward to, but if it meant that much to him, we would sure do everything in our power to help him fulfill his dream.

I had a couple days before Art arrived, Bill Sims had a hunter waiting for him, but he was having plane problems. So I decided to take the hunter down south of Lake Iliamna on the McNeil River; that place was usually crawling with brown bears in the spring. I never took any monsters from that area, but everything I ever got was respectable, and this gentleman wasn't looking to get in the record book. He just wanted a nice brown bear. We caught an old boar that had not been out of his den very long; he was feasting on the winter kill moose carcass. We landed over the hill out of sight, then crept up to within approximately a hundred yards; the hunter felt that was plenty close enough and made a good shot. Within about an hour and a half, we had stolen his fur coat and were making our getaway back to Anchorage.

Art arrived a couple days later. I had decided to hunt the Cinder River area again. I felt it provided us the best opportunity to get Art close enough to a brown bear to get a good shot with the bow. We flew to King Salmon and got a couple rooms at the King Salmon Lodge; there was Art, myself, and Cappy. We brought two airplanes as far as King Salmon, but from there, we would all ride in my Super Cub to Cinder River.

There was an area on the river where the banks were pretty high on both sides of the river—some brush, but not so thick you couldn't sneak through it. We started seeing bears before we got close to the river, but I had an area in mind not far from where Sam had shot his bear that, I felt, provided the best opportunity to use the bow. We flew over a small hill, and there was the river.

"Denny, are those somebody's cattle, or are they bear?"

"I'm afraid they're all bear, Cappy."

"My god, we can't hunt among all those critters. We'll be eaten for sure."

With that first glimpse of the river, there had to be fifteen to twenty bears within about a mile. Most of them were in the river eating dead salmon. But there were a few others up on the banks, most of them moving downstream, kind of wandering around aimlessly like they had just gotten out of bed and weren't quite sure what to do.

"I think we'll go downstream a ways and see if we can't find a spot with fewer bears." I banked the plane to the right. I idled back. I was about four hundred feet above the river; the farther north I flew, the fewer bears we saw. There were still bears every hundred yards or so, but nothing like upstream. He finally spotted a couple of bears in about a half a mile stretch of the river; there was a decent place to land within about a quarter mile of the river. The river had high banks ten to twenty feet high; the river was only about thirty to forty yards wide, and there was scattered brush fifty yards back from the edge of the river, which would give us very adequate cover. The rest was dead grass two to three feet tall.

We slowly made our way to the riverbank; along the bank, there was pretty thick brush, with a spot here and there where there was no brush. Then there were paths made by the bears and caribou along the top of the bank; some of those trails were more than two feet deep. The bears had been traveling those trails for hundreds of years. The paths went along the top of the riverbank and then down into the river every couple hundred yards.

As we got close to the bank, we could hear a couple bears squabbling about who had first dibs on a big rotten fish on the sandbar. When we arrived at the edge of the riverbank, we were on our hands and knees, creeping up to the edge where we could look down into the riverbed. Cappy crawled up to the edge of the bank and peeked over the bank; then he backed away.

"There is a monster bear right across the river," Cappy whispered. "I think thirty yards at the most."

"Art, are you ready?" He nodded yes.

We all slowly worked our way to the edge of the riverbank; the bear was a nice reddish black—a nice trophy, even for a rifle. We had discussed where we thought Art should try to hit the bear to do the most damage and that he should try to get at least two arrows in the midsection of the bear before he got away. If he charged, we didn't have much choice but to shoot him with the rifle; but if he went off into the brush, there was a good chance he might die within an hour or two. Cappy and I checked our rifles; we both had shells in the chamber, and we felt this was about the best possible chance a person would have to kill one of these animals with the bow. Art was just back a couple feet from the bank, waiting for the bear to look the other way; the bear did just that. Art raised up to a full standing position, pulled the bow, and released the arrow—all in one smooth fluid motion. Art was reaching for his second arrow before the first one struck the bear in the rib cage, just behind the front shoulder; the arrow was buried clear up to the feathers. It was a good hit; the bear squealed and spun around. Art released a second arrow, which hit the bear on the other side and a little farther back—still a good shot.

All at once, our vision of the bear across the river was blocked by a huge brown bear with an attitude; he was coming up that riverbank right for us like a runaway train. Rocks were flying, brush was crashing, and he was making all kinds of threatening noises.

I grabbed Art by the shoulder and pulled him backward, threw my rifle to my shoulder, and fired. Cappy shot just a split second after I did; the bear raised straight up. He towered over all of us by three or four feet; he then fell over backward into the middle of the river in two feet of water, dead. Both of our shots had hit him in the neck; the bullet holes were no more than two inches apart. He was so close. The blast from the rifle barrels singed the fur on his neck. We, of course, couldn't move a thousand-pound bear. So we had to skin him in the river in two feet of freezing cold water.

Evidently, the bear we had to shoot was on our side of the river, right up against the bank, so none of us were able to see him when we were checking out the bear that Art shot with the bow. Cappy went back to the plane and brought us back a thermos of coffee; we all sat on the bank, had a cup of coffee, and relived the near death-experience. If the bear had fallen forward, he would've landed on top of us—he was *that* close. The other bear, the one that Art shot with the bow, disappeared into the brush with two arrows well embedded in the bear's midsection; we decided to skin this bear and give the other one time to expire.

Cappy and I both worked on the hide; we were done skinning in about forty-five minutes. This was a big bear. Once we had loaded the hide in the airplane, we decided to check out Art's bear; the brush was thick, and we had no idea where the bear was hiding or if he was still on the move. I decided to get the Super Cub and see if I could spot the bear from the air to see if he was still on the move or if he was hiding in the brush. Once I was in the air, I had to check out four different bears before I found the right one; he had moved out of the area. He was almost a mile from the river and still moving. By then, it had been about two hours; he had to be bleeding internally, even though not much was showing from the outside.

I picked up Art and Cappy. Once we spotted the bear again, we picked a spot where we felt the bear was headed, landed, and got into position. The bear finally arrived but never got close enough for Art to take another shot with the bow. Art asked how long I felt before the bear would die. I told him I thought it could be an hour or a day or two. Art decided the bear had suffered enough and asked if he could borrow my rifle; we had to track the bear for approximately another half hour before we finally caught him in the open. Art was able to finish him off with one shot. There was no doubt that bear would have eventually died, but who knows when. That was the last bow hunter I ever took for bear.

Denny and Chief Walnnga and a baby walrus on the Bering Sea

Trickly landing over open water and broken ice west of Kotzebue 160 miles very typical some time much worse with the ice fog so thick you could halrdy see

Chapter Thirty-Seven

I believe it was 1967, Arthur Carlsberg and Dick, his brother, were our hunters; the weather had warmed slightly. It was only twenty below zero when we took off that afternoon from Kotzebue. We decided that day to go to Point Hope, so we were closer to where we wanted to hunt the next morning. We had been in the air approximately forty-five minutes when we ran into a bank of ice fog. Bill Simms and Dick Carlsberg were about fifteen minutes ahead of us and were able to make it into Point Hope, but I was so close to the ground. I finally had to land; I radioed Bill and told him my situation. I estimated I was still fifteen miles south of Point Hope and couldn't see a thing. Bill was able to round up a couple guys with snow mobiles. They came down the trail along the coast and found us. We were then able to follow them back to town. We had to taxi the entire fifteen miles, but we were safe and not piled up on the tundra like many others I have seen.

The next morning, we were up before daylight. The fog had disappeared over the night, the skies were clear, and the weather forecast was for more fog in the afternoon and evening. We lifted off the runway just as the sun started to peek over the eastern horizon. The temperature at the airport was forty-three below zero. We headed due west and had a slight headwind. We anticipated an hour and fifteen minutes, and we would be in good bear country. We had taken several good bears from this area already this year but knew there were many more on this vast expanse of ice.

Just as the doctor had ordered, I spotted our first big bear tracks about an hour and twenty minutes into our flight. The bear was headed southwest following one of the green rivers. When we eventually caught up to him, he was in some very inhospitable territory—chunks of ice strewn everywhere absolutely no safe place to land the airplane, but he was moving rather briskly. At this pace, I estimated he would come into a rather open area in approximately another mile and a half. He had a number of different options and directions he could go, but we decided to take a gamble, flipped a coin, chose our spot, and landed.

Bill Simms was still in the air keeping an eye on the bear. We could tell where the bear was basically by the position of Bill's plane. The bear had changed directions and was getting further away, then he changes again. The bear is now coming directly at us, but he is still approximately a mile away, and evidently he had slowed up considerably. It took almost forty-five minutes before he finally came into sight; on his present course, he was going to be a good three hundred yards at his closest point. Carlsberg and I decided we should change positions. We moved further to our left staying behind a string of broken ice blocks that provided good cover.

By the time we got repositioned, the bear was no more than 1,000 feet from our new location and headed right toward us. Art got into position behind a five-foot chunk of ice. The bear was approximately one-hundred yards when Art shot. The only indication the bear had been hit was the fact that he changed directions, turned directly to his right, and disappeared behind a couple chunks of ice, then disappeared into some fog and a minute later reappeared again still getting farther away by the minute. I thought I could see blood on the snow with my binoculars, but to be sure, we walked out to the point where the bear had made the turn. Sure enough, there was a considerable amount of blood on the snow, but the fog was so thick at time. We couldn't see fifty feet. Very cautiously, we followed the bear tracks and blood trail for at least a half a mile, into the maze of ice and fog. Before we came across, no more than twenty feet in front of us, the bear sprawled out on the ice. Approximately an hour and a half later, we were stuffing the bear hide and the skull in the back of the airplane and were making ready for our departure.

"Art, you need to have this bear checked out when you get home." I believe it will make the record books. And sure enough it did; in fact, it came in the top ten.

And to this date, I believe it's still at number thirteen.

By this time, Bill Sims and Dick had spotted another nice bear about ten miles north of our location. Now it was Bill's turn. I stayed airborne and kept an eye on their bear—he was easy, and he walked up to within about fifty yards. After two shots, Dick had himself a very nice polar bear. By the time they got airborne, it was getting pretty late in the afternoon; not very much light left, and we still had at least an hour and a half of flying before we reached the coast. The fog kept getting thicker. By the time we reached the coast, I don't think I was more than ten feet off the ice; the fog was getting thicker by the minute. The first indication I had that we had reached land was some bush that grows along the coastline about one hundred feet back from the edge of the water.

I immediately turned south staying just to the right of the bush. We traveled like that for about ten miles until I was afraid I would lose sight of the brush, which was my only reference as to where I was. I landed and I decided it would be a lot safer to taxi than to try to fly in these conditions. I knew there were two villages somewhere along this coastline, but I had no idea whether we were north of it or south of it, and I had no idea how far it was to that village. I taxied for perhaps another ten miles with Bill and Dick only twenty or thirty feet behind me. The fog just kept getting thicker. I finally realized there were black rocks or something that seemed to be going the same way we were going. I shut the plane down and got out to see what I was following. Much to my surprise, it was dog turd. I was on a dogsled trail that runs along the coast, and every few feet was a pile of dog turd. We went like that for at least an hour. It was very nerve-racking. There were times when I could not see the dog turds at all; then they would reappear. During one of those times, when I lost sight of the trail, I ran into something with the left wing and cut the engine immediately. I couldn't imagine what I could've run into. There wasn't a tree for one hundred miles; I climbed out of the airplane, and much to my astonishment, it was a radio antenna.

"Denny! It appears we are parked on top of some kind of a building."

"We could both then smell smoke." I shined the light around under the airplane; sure enough right under the fuselage, there was a small chimney spewing smoke.

"Art, this has to be one of the natives houses. They call them Kivalina. Wait till you see how big they are inside."

"Let's slide the plane back off the top of the house, then go see if we can find somebody." By this time, Bill Sims and Dick Carlsberg had parked their airplane and came up to see what was going on. The wind is still blowing at least twenty knots.

Just as we were making our way down around the end of the little house, the occupant of the dwelling was coming out of the door to check and see what all the racket was about. Of course, every dog in the village was yanking at their chains and barking as loud and fast as they knew how, and, of course, his radio went out when we knocked over his antenna.

He wondered where in the world we had all come from. We took him back to the airplanes; he stared in disbelief and thought for sure that we were some kind of mystical creatures that just appeared out of the fog. I grabbed a bottle of vodka out of the backseat and a handful of cigars—both were always very popular with the natives.

He invited us into his house; at this point, I should probably tell you a little bit about this house. It's approximately ten feet wide and twelve to sixteen feet long. It's primarily sod; it is dug into the side of the bank. If no bank exists, then they piled dirt all the way around it except by the entrance. It has no windows and only one door. For the roof, they may use whalebones or wood that washes up on the beach during the summer. The houses are dug down into the ground approximately three feet lower than the surrounding terrain. The inside of the house is usually no more than six feet high; these people are very short. Most of them is no more than five feet tall. Once we all got inside, there wasn't much room. He had just enough glasses, so we could all have a drink.

I gave him a cigar but decided the rest of us had better not. In about ten minutes, the smoke in that hut was so thick you could hardly see across the room.

The wife was fixing fish stew, which consisted of Arctic char and God only knows what else. I was afraid to ask. The stew consisted of the whole fish, heads and eyeballs, tail and fins. Thankfully, they had been cleaned; I can still remember looking in the pot of stew and seeing all those eyeballs floating around on the top;

I can see that as vividly as if it happened yesterday. That's what we ate morning, noon, and dinner for the next three days.

One very interesting tidbit: the couple only had four magazines in their little house, and one of those had a big article about the Carlsberg company and had pictures of both brothers. Needless to say, the natives were more than a little impressed.

Midmorning on the third day, the fog cleared, and we were able to fly. We had a hell of a time getting the engines warmed up to where we could turn them over in this cold weather, but with the help of some whale and seal blubber, we were able to get enough heat in the engine compartment that we finally got them started. A short sixty-minute flight and we were back in Kotzebue. The Carlsberg brothers had a very memorable experience and took home with them two very beautiful Polar Bear hides, and they hunted with use several more times in the future including Africa.

The next year, I had two more men make it into the record books for bear. One was William D. Backman. He got a very nice brown bear. He was also a Weatherby trophy winner.

Then there was Dr. Ben Robson. He got an exceptionally nice grizzly bear near Mount Hayes. This is a hunt I think worth mentioning.

If I remember right, we had just finished getting a very respectable moose about thirty miles northeast of the Lodge in the foothills of Mount Hayes. With approximately six hundred pounds of meat, and the hide in the back of the plane, and the antlers tied to the strut, we were returning to the lodge. Once we were on the ground, the doctor asked if I thought I could get him a nice grizzly bear.

I don't know if that was meant to be a challenge for my ability or just a dumb question. Of course, I could get him a grizzly bear; that is what I do,

Just so happened that about a week earlier, I had spotted a grizzly on a moose kill not more than twenty miles due north of the Lodge. I doubted that he would still be in that exact same spot but felt it was worth checking out. I still had 300 to 400 pounds of moose meat to pick up for the doctor; on my way back, I would just swing by and check out the grizzly, if I could see him, it could be a short hunt. I flew over the site where I had seen the bear a week earlier—no bear. I decided to gain a little elevation and make a couple circles in that general area to see if I could pick up that bear or perhaps another. This was generally a good area for grizzly.

I made my second pass a mile wider than the first; I was about two miles west of where I had seen the grizzly last week, when I spotted what I believe to be the same bear. It appears he had found a Caribou carcass and was wasting no time. He was in the process of dragging the carcass into the edge of the bush. There were several good areas to land within a quarter of a mile. I turned east and headed back to the Lodge.

After we got the meat unloaded boxed up and in the freezer, doctor and I sat down and had a cup of coffee; I never mentioned to him that I had spotted the grizzly. I only told him I didn't think I'd have any trouble finding him a trophy. If he was inclined, we negotiated a price. I wanted a thousand dollars, after a little haggling I agreed to $950.

It was 4:00 in the afternoon, and I suggested we go that afternoon. If it got too late, at least we might know where not to hunt tomorrow. Within twenty minutes, we had spotted the grizzly. He was at the edge of the brush, in a little ravine. The doctor was all excited; I hadn't looked at the bear that close before, but the more I looked, the better he looked. I landed about a quarter mile away. I could've taxied right up to the ravine but didn't want to take a chance on spooking him into the brush. Once we were on the ground, we worked our way up the hill then snuck from one patch of brush to the next. When we reached the ravine, we were about 150 yards uphill from where the carcass of the

Caribou was. In the twenty to thirty minutes, it took us to land and walked the quarter mile; the bear had disappeared.

"Denny, what do you think? Has he left the area?"

"I don't think so. He probably has a belly full and has decided to sleep it off."

"Should we take a look to see if we can spot him?"

"Not on your life, Doctor." That's about the quickest way I can think of to be killed. When a bear has staked out a kill like this, there's nothing more dangerous than a bear that has claimed the carcass. "We're just going to sit down and make ourselves comfortable."

We moved down the gully about thirty yards closer to the carcass to an area about one hundred feet from the closest brush. Not knowing exactly where the bear was made me a bit uncomfortable, but now, at least, if he came out of the brush in a fit of rage, we had a bit of open area, so we can hopefully get a couple of shots off.

A couple of magpies quietly glided into the carcass and then a third and a fourth.

"Doc, you better be ready. It won't be long, and those birds will start to squabble. And when they do, they're goanna wake up the grizzly bear. You'll then see why I told you we don't get anywhere close to that carcass with a live grizzly bear in the neighborhood."

We sat there just a couple more minutes, and as predicted, a couple more birds came to the banquet. These guys must've been strangers from out of town and were definitely not welcome. A racket ensued that would wake the dead. It wasn't but a couple of seconds, and the host arrived. In a flash, he busted out of the brush about thirty feet from the caribou carcass and was on the carcass in the blink of an eye. One of the magpies got tangled up in the brush, just for a second, while making his escape, and it almost cost him his life.

"Doc, are you ready?" I whispered.

"Yes, sir!"

The bear had his butt to us, and his front was slightly higher than his rear end.

"Doc, try to hit him right in the middle of the back." He fired the bullet just grazed the left side of the bear. He spun around on a dime like a cutting horse on a calf and headed our direction with no sign of disabilities created by the bullet.

The doctor swore at himself as he took his second shot. This one struck the bear head-on in the chest. He took a somersault, struggled to his feet, and took a couple of steps trying to regroup his thoughts, which gave the doctor time to deliver the final blow. It appeared the drama had ended as I reset the safety on my rifle.

I lit up a cigar, and we sat there for about ten minutes watching closely to see if there was any type of movement. Seeing none, we decided it was safe to approach the trophy, and it truly was a trophy. It was a beautiful old grizzly, and at that time, I believe it went in the record books somewhere in the top ten.

"Denny, I see what you are talking about." It's unbelievable how fast that bear came out of that brush; if we had been within thirty yards, he would've been all over us before we even had a chance.

We skinned out the bear and were back at the lodge in about two hours; as we were unloading the plane, the doctor asks.

"Denny, you know that only took us about two hours. Don't you think $950 is a little steep?"

"Doc, do you give your patients a discount when the operation goes easier than you expected?"

"You know, Mr. Thompson, you have a good point. Let's get some salt on this hide, and I will buy you a drink. I may even bum one of those stinking cigars off you."

Chapter Thirty-Eight

There were several others who made it in the record books in the latter part of the '60s. Dick Davis got a nice polar bear, and Dick Devereaux, a major in the Air Force, also got a very fine polar bear that to this day I believe is still in the top twenty-five.

In 1969, I had three Japanese hunters who came for polar bear; they were sharpshooters, in the Japanese Army. This hunt took three airplanes and pilots. They brought with them two cameramen and all their gear besides the three hunters.

They each got a polar bear with one shot; they filmed the entire hunt right from the time they got out of the airplane at Kotzebue, and got into their hotel room. The next morning, they took pictures of all of us getting in the super cubs and then each hunter as he killed his bear, the whole skinning operation, and loading the hide's in the airplane, every thing was filmed. and the three hunters were extremely happy. And the next year, they sent twelve hunters for moose and caribou. It was the same ordeal they filmed everything; all twelve hunters got their moose and caribou. The next year, they had a group of thirty that wanted to go hunting, but I could not accommodate them because they all wanted to come at one time.

In 1970, Denny and Marge were invited by the Japanese hunters to be there guest at Expo 70 in Osaka, Japan. They stayed in Japan for thirty days as guest of the Japanese; every day, they were picked up at their hotel and were accompanied by one of the hunters and an interpreter. While they were there, they were invited to the Japanese Safari Club meeting.

They were the honored guest. There were over 600 members who attended the meeting. One of the major events of the meeting was the showing of the movie, of all the hunts of bear, moose, and caribou. The movie was approximately an hour and a half long. When the movie was over, Denny's interpreter ask him to please stand. Denny was told they wanted to pay him a big honor. As he stood up, they all clapped, and then he was saluted with three bonsai cheers, where they thrust their arm into the air and yelled "**Bonsai**."

Denny was told that is only rarely done and for only the most honored guests. He and Marge were treated like royalty.

Denny said he felt totally humble by the whole experience. The only other time he felt like that was when he returned from England in 1944, and they were honored with the parade. Denny said the only downside of the whole trip was the food; at that time, the Japanese had no idea what Americans like to eat, so basically, every day it was rice, seaweed, and fish–most of it raw.

After we had been there about two weeks, we went to the expo, and right inside the front gate was a huge McDonald's. I remember we walked through the entrance, Marge spotted the McDonald's, let out a squeal of delight, and actually ran to get in line to get a hamburger and French fries. After a month of seeing every possible site, there was to see in and around Osaka; it was great to get home and tie into some moose steaks and fried potatoes.

I got home just in time to take several hunters for polar bear; I don't recall any special hunts we had that year, but I do remember one evening at the restaurant and bar. We had a special guest, Roy Rogers. He was on a polar bear hunt with one of the other hunters out of Kotzebue. If I remember right, he had gotten a bear and they were doing a little celebrating. I think someone had spiked Roy's sarsaparilla, but before I get into some of Roy's shenanigans, I should tell you a little bit about the establishment.

We called it "Maggies" I don't think that was the real name, but the lady who worked there was "Maggie"—a no-bullshit type of gal. She was as tough as the country she lived in, and everybody loved her.

The restaurant was a shack like a lot of the other buildings in Kotzebue, at that time, built out of army-surplus material, abandon pallets, and whatever was left lying around whatever they could find. At that time, the restaurant couldn't serve liquor; you had to bring your own, which everybody did in abundance. The beer drinkers, in most cases, were out of luck because the beer would freeze, so almost all the booze was hard liquor. The little restaurant probably had a legal capacity of thirty or forty people. I'm sure there were times when it was double that it had a wood plank floor, and with everybody walking in and out with snow on their boots, it sometimes became extremely slippery.

It was one of those times when Roy Rogers happened to be at Maggie's; the temperature outside was in excess of forty below zero with about a twenty-five-knot wind. I never took a reading on the inside, but it had to be close to freezing because there were actually patches of ice on the floor next to the front door, but, of course, it felt like the tropics after coming in from outside.

Most everybody who came in had a steaming hot cup of coffee, which they spiked with a couple of shots of their favorite sweetener; now, you have to remember most of us left Kotzebue at daylight that morning with very little to eat or drink. So by the time we got to Maggie's, it didn't take much alcohol to get the jaw muscles lubricated and the brain totally disengaged. The decibels in that place, I'm sure, far exceeded EPA standards. Some of the guys would get so involved in their drinking, that they would forget to eat. After a couple hours, they would keep falling out of their chairs. Their buddies would eventually have to take them back to their hotel or, in some cases, drag him over to the corner and set him up again the wall until they were ready to go back to their room. And the stories that were told; after the first couple hours of drinking, seldom resembled the facts, of course, I never partook in any of those exaggerated tales!

Roy, of course, was a celebrity and attracted a lot of attention; he was very gracious, and as the evening went on, very friendly and talkative.

After some dinner and a half a dozen sarsaparillas, somebody produced a guitar. By this time, there was at least a half inch of slush and water all over the floor. As Roy played the guitar and sang, he walked from table to table much to everyone's delight even the overzealous storytellers; "liars" (paused for a moment). But Mr. Rogers had trouble finding stable footing and fell in the slush, at least a couple of times as I remember. Maggie, of course, was present with the towel and wiped him down from head to toe. After several encounters on the floor, Roy decided he needed a stage to perform on and commandeered the most "stable table" he could find and, from there, completed his performance. It was, in fact, a very memorable evening; we were quite used of celebrities, but not many of them were as friendly, gracious, and entertaining as Roy Rogers.

Late that summer, Bert Kleinberger brought the Prince of Indonesia. We scoured the countryside looking for the best brown bear, moose, and caribou. He shot a record book brown bear, a record book moose, and a caribou that possibly could have made it in the record books also, but the Prince never had them measured. I presume they just went into his trophy room along with his tigers, elephants, and, from what I hear, dozens of other animals. At the time, he invited me to hunt tiger in Indonesia, which I took him up on but not until the early 80s, and by that time, the animals had become quite scarce, and I was unsuccessful.

Later that summer of that year, I was contacted by a group of Japanese mountain climbers. they wanted someone to fly them to about 12,000 foot elevation on Mount Hayes from there they would climb to the summit; once they returned to their initial point of departure they would notify me. I would fly in and pick them up. I actually did this several times over the next ten years.

I had lots of military people from Fairbanks who came to the lodge, some to hunt caribou or moose, but most of them wanted to go fishing. The mountain lakes were brimming with trout, Grayling, and walleye Pike; it was a fisherman's paradise back in those days. On one such trip, one of the young man capsized his boat, couldn't swim, and drowned. We retrieved his body from the lake and brought it back to the lodge. The military sent a helicopter from Fairbanks. After they had picked up the body and were on their return trip to the base, the chopper crashed and burned, killing all on board with a total of four including the young man who had drowned. That really got to me. For some reason, I felt responsible. I just couldn't get it off my mind. I couldn't sleep. I just couldn't quit thinking about it. I almost hung it up right then and there, considered closing the lodge, and get into something where I didn't feel responsible for virtually every person I worked with. Every time I put someone in my airplane, they were blindly trusting their life to me. I guess I just felt especially bad for the young men in the military. For them to lose their life for no apparent reason, just a mercy mission to pick up one of their fallen comrades, and for it to end so tragically, just shook me to the bottom of my soul.

But we had lots of hunts booked that fall, and I had to keep up with them; by the time the year had ended, I had worked through my problems and came to the conclusion that this really was what I wanted to do, at least for as long as I was capable. But I did decide that I would sell the lodge and, for the time being, just work out of my house.

Chapter Thirty-Nine

It was the early…'70s Denny purchased the New Hallin Lodge in the Lake Clark area. This was a little different operation, and there were no roads, so everyone had to be flown in.

The early…'70s also saw Denny joined partners with Art Fields of Eskimo and Scandinavian descent in Kotzebue. In a 50 percent venture into the liquor business, Art had acquired the license to supply alcohol in that general area, including several liquor stores in outlying communities. Denny called his friend "Red Dodge" who owned a C-130 cargo plane in Anchorage and normally flew cargo to the North Slope for the oil companies, but if he wasn't flying for the oil company, he would fly just about anything any place for a price.

Denny then ordered thirty-ton of booze and had it flown to Kotzebue. Red said that was probably the happiest load he ever hauled. Denny and Art then fixed up six different establishments, in six different villages, a pool table and a jukebox. These were in addition to Art's restaurant and liquor store in Kotzebue.

This was a very lucrative business, but about the only time it was convenient for Denny to be present and keep an eye on what was going on was during the polar bear season—the rest of the time it was just too far away. With the urging of Denny's attorney, who felt the liability far outweighed the benefits, Denny sold his share of the business to Art—another closed chapter in the adventures of Mr. Thompson.

The Department of Fish and Game, at that time, decided to divvy up the state in different areas for different guides. It was at their annual fish and game meeting that they made the announcement.

Denny Thompson, Ron Hayes, and the majority of all the guides in the state were in attendance. The meeting opened with the normal agenda discussing hunting conditions throughout the state new regulations, tougher enforcement of old regulations, etc., plus the introduction of some new officers that would be enforcing these regulations. Then they got to the interesting part of the meeting where they announced the decision to divide the state up into different hunting areas to be awarded exclusively to individual guides.

The reason behind this decision "they said" was to stop the conflict between the guides over who had the right to hunt a given area, when two hunters showed up in the same general area at the same time. This way, the only time another hunter could hunt on someone else's territory was to get permission from that guide. After a short intermission, where everyone was discussing what areas they thought they might get, the meeting was called back to order, and the announcement was made.

"Mr. Denny Thompson, you are, without a doubt, the top guide in Alaska at this time. You have registered more hunts with the Game Department than anyone else. You appear to have, by far, the largest clientele, and you turn in more hunting reports than anyone else in the state. For that reason, we're giving you first choice of what areas you want. You can choose three different areas."

The areas Denny chose firstly was from King Salmon, east to the Katmai National Forest and north almost to Lake Iliamna. Number two was from the village of Non-Dolton, north, including Lake Clark pass—the southern part of the Alaska mountain range. The third area was the Dillingham area, north to the Kuskokwim Mountains. Each area consisted of approximately 1000 square meters, which is approximately two million acres. If it was flat, at any rate, it was a huge amount of real estate, and over the next few years produced many record trophies, an unimaginable amount of hunting experiences, and memories for thousands of hunters.

Chapter Forty

The '70s saw Denny continue to provide his hunters with the exceptional hunting experiences they had come to expect. During the '70s, Denny would see over thirty of his hunter's trophies make it into the record books, plus an exceptional amount of hunters that took very nice trophies home but weren't quite good enough to make it in the record books but still, to this day, hang proudly in their trophy room.

Who knows what Denny's hunters could have continued to do during the '80s? Had the federal government not decided to go after the top guides in Alaska? I think it was a carryover from the '60s with all the antiestablishment that was ginned up during that time. Any individual or company who appeared to be more successful than the average became a target.

Without a doubt, Denny Thompson, at that time, was probably the top guide in the United States not just Alaska. The state and federal government had been writing and imposing new regulations almost daily. There was the expansion of the park service and areas that couldn't be hunted. The Fish and Game Department, being a typical governmental agency, felt they had the ultimate wisdom to open and close areas for different species whenever they felt like it, which frustrated the guides and made it very difficult to keep up with the paperwork.

The biggest change of course was the elimination of hunting and flying the same day. This had been the acceptable practice ever since hunting started in Alaska, and now, all at once, it was illegal. The state started out with its typical harassment of the hunters as well as the guides. Denny was charged with different violations of the fish and game laws in the late '70s. Three times, it went to the grand jury, and three times, it was thrown out of court for lack of evidence. After failing and being embarrassed three consecutive times, the state Fish and Game Dept in desperation to save face ask the Federal Government for help, By the way, it was found out later that Denny Thompson was number one on the list but not the only one on the list. The state had actually targeted twenty different guides. The state requested the Federal Government with their power to harass and virtually do anything they wanted. The state wanted the feds to take whatever measures necessary to catch or entrap the hunters into doing something illegal. Their way of thinking this group of hunters had just gotten too big, and the state decided it was their duty to take away from one group and give to another—sounds familiar.

We will discuss this later in more detail, but for now, I'd like to tell about some of the good things that happened in the '70s.

In 1971, Denny sold the Susitna Lodge to three men from Anchorage. Denny felt the Lodge had served its purpose. He had established himself as one of the top guides in the entire state of Alaska and had a clientele second to no one else. But changes were in the wind. There was a new highway being built that went from Palmer, directly north to the park then skirted along the east boundary of the park, and terminated in Fairbanks.

This route would totally bypass the Susitna area, almost totally eliminating any drive in traffic to the lodge. All these factors entered into Denny's decision, but first, emotionally, Denny just felt it was time to make a move. He wasn't sure if he would try to build a new lodge somewhere else or if he would just operate out of his house. He just wasn't sure, but knew, given a little time, everything would work out.

The first year for the three men who bought the lodge turned out to be a disaster. In all, they crashed three airplanes that first year, and one of the partners was killed in one of the crashes. By the end of the year, they decided to turn the property back over to Denny; he in turn resold the property to one of the state senators, who would later become the head of the senate of Alaska. He operated the lodge primarily to lodge engineers and geologists who were working in the many gold mines in that area at the time.

During the time all this was happening, Denny's banker called one day, and said he had a building that they were foreclosing on in the Non-Dalton area at Lake Clark and felt Denny should take a look at it.

Denny and Bill Sims flew down to Non-Dalton to take a look at the facility. It had been built primarily as a hardware store. Denny felt that it was in a very good location and definitely large enough. It needed some maintenance work. About a year earlier, it had flooded, and Denny felt he would have to jack the building up about a foot that was going to be the most difficult, and there was a lot of interior work—all things Denny knew he was capable of doing.

They worked out the purchase with the bank, and work started immediately. Raising the building proved to be an all summer job. He installed a kitchen, a dining room area, and, of course, a bar, then built ten rooms on the second story of the building.

By the season of '72, everything was completed, and the lodge is open for business. Most of Denny's clientele flew into the Iliamna airport, which was served by Alaskan Air. Denny would pick them up and fly them to Non-Dalton. Denny named the new facility "The New Halen Lodge" and operated out of there for the next eight years.

Chapter Forty-One

The early '70s was an exciting time for Mr. Thompson—the new lodge, his first trip to Africa, walrus hunting on St. Lawrence Island, the new hunting regulations, the discovery of a new area to hunt sheep were just to mention a few. Where do I start?

The walrus adventure is a little out of the ordinary, so I think that's where I'll start. It didn't take place all at one time but rather than try to break it up into different time frames. I'll present it all in this one segment.

We met our client Ned Payne at the Anchorage International Airport. He had just arrived from Chicago. His claim to fame, he was a world champion weightlifter. His mission was to capture thirty young walruses, put them on board a cargo plane, and deliver them to some place on the East Coast. I don't believe I ever did hear just where that was. We flew directly by commercial airline Alaska Air Lines from Anchorage to the St. Lawrence Island where there are a couple small villages. It may seem out of the ordinary to the people in the lower forty-eight that a commercial airline would fly to small villages with only a couple hundred residents, but that's the way it is in Alaska, primarily because there's no other way for people to travel.

We arrived on St. Lawrence Island about 10:00 a.m. I had made arrangements with one of the local fisherman or walrus hunter to provide us with the boat and a crew, so we could get to the area where there were walruses.

This was primarily an ice flow just off the north coast of the island. Our boat was a native seal skin boat that the natives used for fishing, walrus and seal hunting, and sometimes whale hunting. It was quite a large boat.

I would guess about twenty-four feet long maybe eight feet wide. It held a crew of twelve, plus Ned and I. This operation took place in late spring when the ice was breaking up. The walruses were usually camped on the largest ice flows, so every day we never knew for sure where we were going to find our quarry. I remember one day, in particular, we had to travel almost fifty miles to find the walruses. The boat was equipped with an outboard motor, but many times, we had to pull and push the boat across patches of ice that were blocking our route. It was an extremely strenuous adventure.

When we would finally get to a chunk of floating ice with walrus, there may be one hundred or only be several on that particular ice flow. Our game plan was to scare the adult mother walrus away from their young, and into the ocean, we would then catch and load the young cubs into the boat. We may only be successful in getting one or two of the cubs loaded in the boat, then we would have to move on to the next ice flow. If I remember right, the babies weighed about eighty pounds each. They were like picking up a pig. There wasn't much to hang on to, and they continued to wiggle and squirm all the way back to the boat.

Most days, we were only able to pick up four or five cubs, and then we had to head back to the village; most of the day was spent working our way through the ice flows to the walruses and then our return trip back to the village. Each day, when we returned with the baby walruses, there was a crew that stayed at the airport where we delivered the young walruses. As soon as the babies were in their cages, they would start the process of feeding them some type of a formula, which from what I understood it was very rich—almost like straight cream. They would feed them every couple hours with a bottle and nipple, day and night supposedly, until they were delivered back east. This operation took a total of six days, and we caught thirty young walruses.

When the cargo plane came in to pick up the babies, I couldn't believe it was a B-17 bomber just like the one I had flown over Germany some twenty-seven years earlier. Of course, all the armament had been removed, but it still brought back many old memories.

Mission accomplished—Ned and I caught the next plane for Anchorage; Ned had hunted with me several times earlier and would again in the future.

My next adventure on St. Lawrence Island is a couple years later; I have a hunter who is determined to add some walrus tusk to his collection of trophies. I contacted the same native who had helped us with the baby walruses. They called him Mukluk. He was a little short guy maybe four foot ten, and his boots almost came up to his crotch. I guess that's how he got his nick name. Anyway, Muk-luk put his crew together and waited for us at the airport when we arrived. It was a little later in the year; the ice was not nearly as thick, which made it much easier to get around with the boat and a lot less pushing and shoving to get through the ice flow. We stayed with the natives that night since the wind was blowing very strong and the open water was quite rough. The next morning, the weather was much improved, and Muk-luk felt that day would be about as good as it's going to get.

We shoved off about 9 o'clock, and by 10:30, we had spotted our quarry a huge old bull with tusk that measured in excess of twenty-four inches. The bull probably weighed close to two ton. The tricky part of taking a walrus was to have an instant kill, otherwise, if the animal got to the water before it died, it would sink to the bottom and be lost, so the only shot that was practical was a head shot. Doing that from a boat is tricky at best. As we approached the walrus, everyone in the boat tried not to move. The hunter used the bow as a rest as we drifted closer and closer. The key was to get as close as we could without exciting the walrus. That day, we were in luck. We were probably no more than seventy-five to eighty feet when the hunter fired; the shot was perfect. The walrus collapsed immediately. The excitement in the boat was far beyond what I expected. At first, I felt it must be because it was such a nice big walrus, but I had seen a number of other walrus that were actually bigger. They pulled the boat up alongside the ice a couple of the natives, grabbed the bow and the stern line, climbed out on the ice drove a spike into the ice, and tied off the line. Everybody on board had their knives out and their gloves off as we approached the walrus.

If you have a weak stomach, you may not prefer to read this paragraph. The first order of business was to cut open the stomach of this walrus. They then split open the intestine, reached into this gooey mess, extracted handfuls of undigested clams, and popped them in their mouth like you would eat popcorn. I couldn't believe what I was seeing. They sat there on the snow and ice for at least a half an hour. I had never seen anything like this in my life. Once they had eaten their fill, they tied the gut closed and loaded it in the boat. They removed the head and tusk in their entirety, then commenced to take all the parts that they could use and the delicacies that they could eat.

Once that was completed, we headed back to the village. All the time, I'm watching this 300-pound blob of guts, laying in the front of the boat, wondering what they're going to do with it. Once we get back to the village and get the boat pulled up on the beach, the first thing that's unloaded is this glob of guts, and here they come, at least a dozen of the natives including two old-timers who could just barely walk. The intestines were opened up and spread out on the ground, and everybody dug in and had a good feed. I suspect whatever was left, if there was anything left, was taken home by the Mrs. and went into their famous fish stew. I didn't wait around to see, and I sure had no intention of staying for dinner that night.

A year or two later, I had another couple of gentlemen who had their heart set on walrus tusk. The hunt was basically the same as the first, except one of the hunters wounded a big walrus. He made it to the water and disappeared, but Muk-luk felt we still had a chance. One of the bigger men grabbed his harpoon and stood ready on the bow of the boat. Muk-luk felt the walrus was not mortally wounded and would resurface for air. Sure enough, it took almost ten minutes, but he slowly emerged about fifteen feet in front of the boat. The harpoon hit its mark and plunged deep into the walrus, which quickly submerged once again. But this time, we had a line securing the walrus to the boat. A few minutes later, the walrus reemerged for the last time.

He now had a dilemma. The first walrus was dead on the ice. The routine was the same; first order of business was cut open the belly and dig in. Clam chowder was being served and that had to be cut up and put in the boat. We had another 4,000-pound walrus in the water. There's no possible way to get the walrus back up on the ice pack. That left two options—cut the head and tusk from the rest of the body and let it sink to the bottom or drag it back to the village behind the boat with the little twenty-horse motor. Muk-luk decided, since we were only a couple miles from the village, it would be worth the effort. Once we got to the village, they could round up enough help to pull the walrus up on the beach.

The two hunters, of course, had never seen anything like the scene that was taking place around the walrus gut pile. They couldn't believe what they were seeing. one of the hunters was trying to get some close-up pictures and got downwind from the gas coming from the gut pile and lost his breakfast. The three of us decided to climb aboard the boat and wait for the Eskimos to complete their lunch. After they decided to get back to work, it didn't take them very long to cut up the existing walrus and load it in the boat.

Once we arrived at the village, there were at least fifty people waiting for us; they had ropes, knives, pans, and buckets. I was actually surprised with the ease they hoisted this huge walrus up on the beach; obviously, they had done this many times before. The first walrus's intestine, which the natives had cut into and had feasted on the partially digested clams, had been secured so nothing could be spilled. It was then loaded in the boat. I'm only guessing, but I'll bet there was more than 200 pounds of clams left in that section of the stomach that was carried up on the beach, opened up, and just made available to anyone who wanted to help himself. There were several old-timers who didn't appear to have many. If any teeth, they sat there and ate clam as long as we were there. Once we got the skull and tusk, we headed for the airstrip. Several times, we had been invited to stay for dinner; with a mischievous smile, we were informed they were having clam chowder. Clam chowder used to be one of my favorite dishes, but after watching that operation, it is no longer on my menu.

Hunting the walrus was interesting; I'm glad I had the experience, but it's not really my idea of hunting. I had several opportunities to take hunters walrus hunting after that, but I always turned them down. I never failed to mention that they should be sure to have some of Muk-luks clam chowder. I just couldn't see much sport in pulling your boat up to the edge of the ice and shooting one of those unsuspecting monsters no more than fifty or a hundred feet away—just not my cup of tea.

Chapter Forty-Two

In 1971, we were in the very midst of improving the New Halen Lodge. Adalina Perez, one of my hunters, world traveler, and citizen of Mozambique, had made arrangements to take myself, Bill Sims, and our attorney Bert Biss to Mozambique Africa on a two-week safari. The dream of any hunter, even in the '70s Africa had not yet become within the grasp of most American hunters. We all read the many stories but believed it was only for the very elite. The danger of snakes, charging lions and Buffalo, the chances of getting malaria, or hepatitis, or the possibility of being eaten alive by insects almost outweighed the pleasure of the hunt.

Bill Sims Bert and I flew out of Anchorage, Alaska directly to Copenhagen, Denmark where I remember we had a sixteen-hour layover; from there, we flew to Madrid, Spain. We stayed with a couple of my hunters while we were in Spain. While we were there, we took in a bullfight and what most tourists do just looked at the sites. We were in Spain for a little over two days before we caught the next leg of our flight to Johannesburg, South Africa.

From there, we caught a small commuter flight to Beira in Mozambique on the shores of the Indian Ocean. Adelino Perez met us there. He took us to the Department of Wildlife office where we were to pick up our permits and license. It costs us $150 each, and if I remember right, we were allowed to each take thirty different animals including buffalo, sable, elephant, and lion—an unbelievable deal that you knew couldn't last. Within two years, the entire country was closed to outside hunters.

After we picked up our permits, we stopped at a little outdoor restaurant that was serving all kinds of seafood. They had some of the largest shrimp I had ever seen in my life, and that's what we had, all three of us. I don't recall what Mr. Perez had, but it was not the shrimp; we then caught a small private plane and flew to Laeerdoia about 200 miles north on the Zambezi River. At that point, we were picked up by a couple of professional hunters with a couple almost new Toyota pickups. If I remember right, we drove for about three hours a little bit southwest across the savannah that reached from about ten miles inland all the way to the ocean. It was primarily grassland, numerous little streams, and creeks making their way to the ocean. There was an occasional tree scattered willy-nilly. If there hadn't been an animal on the savannah, it would've been a beautiful sight to behold, but there were animals, hundreds of animals—no, thousands of animals in every size and shape you could imagine. There were giraffe, hippopotamus, cape buffalo not many, but some elephant, and every kind of an antelope you could imagine.

About the time we arrived at the lodge, Bert and I were not feeling very well. By the time we got our bags unloaded and in the bungalow, we were both sick as a dog. I was so sick I had to crawl around on my hands and knees, when I could even move. This went on for the rest of the afternoon and into the night.

I was so sick I never doubted for a moment that I was going to die; right there on the African savannah, I had never been that sick before and never since. Bert and I both felt that it was probably the shrimp, but we could never figure out why Bill Sims didn't get sick. He ate just as many or more shrimp than either of us did.

By morning, I was no longer sick. I did believe there was a chance I might make it, but I was so weak I had to be helped to the pickup. My constitution would not allow them to go hunting without me. The desire was there, but my inability to move was more than a little distracting. By nightfall, Bill Sims and Bert had each shot an animal. That first day, I passed. From what I could see, I was not at all afraid that a day or two was going to deprive me of any animals. I wanted to shoot. The next morning, I was better, still weak but able to eat a decent breakfast, and make it to the pickup unassisted.

To get our animals was not quite as easy as it appeared it would be when you looked over the savannah and saw all those animals and the grass, in most places, four to five feet tall. Most of the time, we drove around trying to find high ground. Most of the time, there were no roads or trails. We just made those as we went along. Several times, I used a termite mound to gain the advantage.

There were three different camps. Every three or four days, we would move to a new camp. Each one, forty or fifty miles south of the last camp, we were slowly working our way back to Beira.

It was the second or third night in our second camp. We had just finished dinner, which were water buck steaks that one of us had killed that day. It was as good as any meat I have ever eaten. We were camped at the edge of the woods overlooking the savannah. The sun was just about to disappear behind us. We were watching a flock of bee catchers, little birds that flew in formation and did all kinds of crazy maneuvers. We were having a drink, and I was having a cigar. The sounds were like nothing you could imagine—lions roaring, some of them very close, and hyena that make a sound like there laughing and makes the hair on the back of your neck bristle. Several times, we heard leopard make their coughing sound so close that I expected to see them come strolling through the camp. We could hear what sounded like a pack of dogs in hot pursuit of something. We could tell they were getting closer.

All at once, the waterbuck exploded out of the high grass, ran right through camp, hit the corner of the table where we were seated, and almost knocked it over. The pack of wild dogs were not more than fifty feet behind the water buck. There were at least a dozen to twenty dogs in the pack; they also came charging right through camp. This all happened probably in less than six to eight seconds. They were gaining on the waterbuck and eventually caught him in a little creek perhaps a quarter mile from the camp. That night, we all slept with our rifles right beside our bed. A couple days later, we were headed back to camp after I had successfully killed a nice buffalo with one shot. We had cut up the bull and loaded him in the pickups and were driving through the tall grass. We ran over something that made a quite a bump. The driver stopped to take a look. It was a huge snake—a python. We couldn't see either end. It took two of us to lift the middle of the snake off the ground. He then commenced to wrap his tail around our legs, and he started to squeeze. I thought, for sure, he was going to break my leg, and we couldn't get free our guide finely, found his head and shot him. It still took me a couple minutes to get free of his grip, then we still had a hell of a time getting him loaded in the truck. Once we got back to camp, we measured him, eighteen feet in length. When it was skinned out, the skin was thirty inches wide. When we got home, I had it tanned, and I still have it to this day.

I believe we were in our third camp the first or second night. We had like army cots, and we slept outside no tent. We still had a fire burning, but we had all turned in it was maybe 10 o'clock. I remember there was just a slight bit of moon and a slight breeze coming off the ocean with a few scattered clouds floating aimlessly past the moon. I was trying not to fall asleep. I just loved to listen to the night sounds on the savanna. All at once, I could feel the ground shaking. I sat up, and between me and the campfire, there was this huge hippopotamus. He was making his way right through the middle of camp. I never realized how big they were until you see one six to eight feet away.

We were in the last day of our hunt. Bill was still trying to get a nice sable, and to date, nobody had gotten a zebra. We all agreed that morning if any one of us got an opportunity to shoot a zebra, shoot three of them if possible. I was in one truck. Bill and Bert were in the other truck pursuing Bills sable. My guide and I spotted some zebra a couple miles away and decided to give them a try. We drove within about a quarter mile. parked the truck under one of the few trees in the area and took off on foot. We knew approximately were the zebra were, but in this tall grass, we couldn't see them. We had spotted a couple of termite mounds not very far from the zebra. Our plan was to get to the termite mounds hoping that would give us enough height to be able to see over the top of the grass.

As we got closer, we could actually hear the herd. just from the sound, I estimated we were less than one hundred yards. Right on schedule, we almost ran into one of the termite mounds. We sat there for couple of minutes to catch our breath. I checked the rifle to make sure everything was ready. I crawled to the top of the mound, about 50 yards. Slightly to my right was a mare and a colt, ten to fifteen yards beyond them were a couple of stallions, and off to their left is another fifteen or twenty head. I zeroed in on the biggest stallion. I shot. and he fell and disappeared in the grass. The other one took a couple of jumps then stopped. I dropped him also with one shot. The rest of the herd milled around but didn't really stampede out of the area as I had expected. I picked one more nice stallion and shot him. None of the three zebra were visible. The guide, who was still down in the grass and couldn't see, was not convinced that I had even gotten one—let alone three as I was claiming. We made our way slowly through the grass. Much to his surprise, the first one I had shot was right where he had dropped. He was elated took his machete out and started clearing the grass from around the zebra.

I asked him, "Don't you want to check on the other two zebra?"

"You really think you got one of them?" he asked.

"Hell, yes," I said, "I got them both." He looked at me as if to say, "Sure you did!"

We went about twenty yards, and there was the second zebra. He looked in disbelief. I took him by the arm, and we made our way through the grass approximately another thirty-five to forty yards, and there was number three. He stood there for about a minute then stuck out his hand and said, "Damn good shooting, Thompson!" Between the three of us, we shot twenty-eight animals with twenty-eight shells, and no cripples that got away. The guides said that was the best shooting they had ever seen.

The skinning crew got right to work. then Bill and Bert and their crew arrived. Bill had gotten a nice sable. I'm not sure, but I believe we had to make two trips back to camp. With all this meat, someone had to stay right with the animals until you got what you wanted; otherwise, the vultures would actually strip an entire carcass in a couple hours.

We shot a waterbuck and didn't go get it immediately. Within an hour, there was nothing left but the bones and the horns.

When I shot my buffalo, he went for about 200 yards before he finally died. Before my guide and I could get there, which was less than ten minutes, there was probably fifty to eighty vultures on the carcass and around it. The guides and professional hunters distributed the meat to several small villages in the area every evening after we finished hunting.

The last leg of our trip back to Beira was quite interesting. The road in that area was better and more traveled than any we've seen to date. The last fifty to sixty miles, we saw at least eight or ten vehicles with bullet holes in the doors, and sides of the vehicles, and then they had been burned. We didn't see anything that appeared to be less than a couple days old, but I don't believe they had been there long. It was a relief when we pulled into the airport. Bill Sims suggested we had enough time to go into town and have another feast on those big shrimp. I didn't even think that was funny. We had much better connections going home. Two days, we were back in Anchorage. That trip to Africa opened my eyes; I could see all kinds of opportunities to fly people to remote areas that were not accessible by vehicle. I knew for sure that someday I wanted to come back to Africa, at minimum, on another Safari.

Headquarters at Bangui Republic of South Africa

Denny working on he Seneca II in the Republic of South Africa

Chapter Forty-Three

After our return from Africa, Bill and I had to make a trip to Anchorage for some reason or another. Lake Clark pass was socked in with fog and low clouds. A layer of fog about 2,000 feet deep covered the entire area. I normally didn't fly more than a couple hundred feet above the ground, but in this situation, I decided to get up above most of the peaks and climbed to 5,000 feet where it was nice and sunny and clear as a bell. We decided to take a shortcut and fly directly to Anchorage on the east side of Lake Clark. I had never flown at this elevation over this area. I guess primarily because I had never had a reason. In this area, 5000 feet did not get you above all the peaks, so we had to wind our way through some of the high passes. We had not traveled more than twenty miles, and we spotted a group of sheep off to our right. I had no idea there were even sheep at this elevation in this particular area. The map that the fish and game department put out that shows the location of different game animals had nothing on it that would indicate there were sheep in this area, but here they were, I decided to take a closer look. Much to our surprise, this was a herd in excess of twenty head, all rams, and several of them were monsters. I already had several sheep in the record books, but I was quite sure there were rams in this herd that were bigger than anything I had taken to date. This was an area with lots of glaciers made to order for Bill and I. We continued to scout out the area, finding another half a dozen pockets of sheep consisting of twenty to thirty head each, and we didn't cover 20 percent of the area. This entire area was less than an hour's flight from our new lodge—a virtual gold mine. We could probably take twenty to thirty head a year out of this area and never even phase the population; Bill and I made a pact right then and there, not to tell a soul what we had found. This discovery probably contributed greatly to me being referred to as the sheep man. Between Bill Sims, Cappy, and I, we put over two dozen sheep hunters in the record books. This, of course, was one of the areas I chose, when the Department of Fish and Game allowed us to choose our exclusive areas. This is the southern end of the Alaska mountain range. I already knew it was great for moose and brown bear, but now sheep. This just about guaranteed the success of the new lodge.

When we made our move to the New Halen Lodge, Cappy decided to go out on his own. He liked hunting up around Denali and the Wrangell Mountains.

You asked me if there was anything specific that I could remember. It happened during the first years at the new Halen Lodge.

One of the first things that come to mind, I had two brown bear hunters from Southern California. We were just loading all the gear in the airplane. We were going to go down by the McNeil River that was a little lower in elevation and usually had a better selection of early bear. One of the pilots out of Anchorage that hauls freight and supplies to all these little towns had just landed. As soon as he got out of the airplane, he came walking over to where we were working. As I saw him approach, I thought, *well, he must have something on that load for me at the new lodge.* I was just thinking what it was I could've ordered.

"Hey, Denny, have you heard what happened to Cappy?" he asked.

"No, what happened? Did he crash?"

"No, he was killed by a grizzly bear."

"Where a bouts? Do you know?"

"Not specifically. All I know it was somewhere south of the park supposedly not too far from your old lodge."

"Any specifics about how he was killed?"

"Not really, but I did hear when the rescue party got there. They only found half of his body, and the bear had eaten the rest."

"What about the hunter? Or was there a hunter?"

"I'm not sure, Denny. There must've been somebody called on the radio from the airplane."

"Thanks for the information. You know, Cappy and I hunted together for over ten years. Cappy was always the impatient one. I suspect that might be what happened"

My two hunters and I got our brown bear; I honestly can't remember one thing about that hunt. I guess my mind was elsewhere. Next morning, I flew up to Anchorage. I was hoping to talk to the hunter, but he had left last night as soon as the sheriff and Department of Fish and Game had finished with him.

This is the story as told by the hunter and then told to me by the sheriff.

Cappy and the hunter had spotted this grizzly bear on the moose carcass. Cappy landed on the other side of the hill almost a half a mile away. He and the hunter walked to the top of the hill, which was only about a hundred yards from the carcass. They crawled over the crest of the hill where they could see the remains of the moose but no bear. The bear was nowhere to be seen. Cappy told the hunter to make himself comfortable. They would sit here and wait for the bear to come out of the brush. It wasn't long, and the bear appears. The hunter said he was a little nervous and only wounded the bear. The bear then went back into the brush. Cappy was quite disturbed with the hunter and told him that if the next time they see the bear, make sure he kills it. Cappy evidently even explained to the hunter how dangerous it would be to go near that carcass unless you are absolutely sure the bear was nowhere in that vicinity.

Evidently, they sat there for about three hours. Cappy started to get impatient and speculated about the bear; maybe the bear had been hit harder than he thought or just decided to leave the area. Evidently, he finally convinced himself that the bear had left the area or was dead at any rate. He finally decided to go down, if not to the carcass at least close enough to see if he could detect if the bear was still in the area. Cappy gave the hunter instructions. If the bear came out of the brush start shooting, don't wait just shoot.

The hunter said that Cappy was very cautious, would take a couple of steps, then he would stop for a minute, look and listen to see if he could detect any sign of the bear. The hunter explained that Cappy was approximately thirty to forty feet from the carcass when the bear came out of the brush. He came from Cappy's right side, so Cappy's rifle would normally be pointing toward the left. Before Cappy could turn, the bear was on top of him, knocked the rifle out of Cappy's hands, and started biting him about the head and shoulders.

Cappy was shouting for the hunter to shoot. The bear finally left Cappy and went back to the moose carcass, then returned to Cappy. The hunter claimed he was afraid to shoot at the bear and was afraid he would hit Cappy. At that point, I suspect it would've been a blessing. The hunter left and went to the airplane to call for help and was so scared that he never returned to check on Cappy. It only took about an hour and a half before a rescue party arrived. By the time they got to the carcass and shot the bear, it was much too late for Cappy. The bear had finished him off and had already eaten part of him. The hunter could have stopped this tragedy from happening. First of all, be a better shot, second, shot the bear when it was attacking Cappy, and last but not least, come back after he called for help. There might have been something he could have done. It's probably a good thing I never had a chance to talk to the hunter in person. I'm not sure I would have been civil.

Cappy was a great pilot and a very good hunter. He loved hunting sheep and goats. He always was a little impatient; unfortunately, this time, it cost him his life.

Chapter Forty-Four

One other interesting situation was when I had the opportunity to hunt with Fritz Carl Flick who was reportedly the richest man in the world at that time. He owned 200 and some corporations including Mercedes-Benz. I believe during the war, I bombed several of his factories. I never brought that up during our conversations. Fritz hunted with me three different times; he got a caribou, a moose, and a brown bear.

He would fly into Anchorage in his 707 passenger jet; he would have with him anywhere from seven to nine people not counting the crew on the 707. He would then rent a twin engine plane in Anchorage, load all his gear and crew, and fly to the New Halen Lodge. His crew would completely take over the Lodge. They would take all our dishes cups glasses silverware and pack them in boxes and replace them with his own stuff.

They would bring with them six large trunks loaded with the dishes and the silverware etc. and all the food they intended to eat while on this trip. He would bring with him his own chef, his accountant and secretary, and a big guy, who I always referred to as his henchmen (mean-looking dude), a couple of servants, and at least two bodyguards.

They would arrive one day before Fritz to get the lodge all set up; Fritz would stay at the hotel in Anchorage, while they got everything ready. While he was there, he would send his airplane to Fairbanks to pick up fresh flowers for the hotel. He did that every day he was there. Once he got his animal, we would return to the lodge. He would usually have something to eat then he would depart and go back to

Anchorage while his crew repacked all their dishes, cups, glasses, and whatever it was that they had brought with them. Then they would unpack all our dishes and put them back where we had them, and they would leave. This would usually not take them more than a couple hours. The private plane would be waiting for them. Once they all reassembled in Anchorage, they would head back to Germany or in one case, I remember, they flew directly from Anchorage to Argentina for another hunt.

I remember the bear hunt. It was late in the season. We had spotted over one hundred bear; we were hunting southwest of Lake Iliamna. We finely spotted the old bore Fritz wanted. We landed approximately a mile from the bear. There wasn't much snow left on the ground, but what was had a crust on it that if you stepped on it sounded like breaking glass, so we had to avoid all snow it took us at least an hour to sneak on this bear. We were able to sneak to within about one hundred yards of the bear. Fritz took his time and made a very good shot. The bear was right on the edge of a little frozen lake that had about six inches of snow on top of whatever ice existed. This late in the season, the ice gets pretty rotten that was about the closest spot to land for almost a half a mile. After we got the bear skinned, I left Fritz with the bear, and I went back and got the airplane. I landed the airplane on the snow and taxied right up to within twenty feet of the Fritz and the bear.

We then loaded the bear hide in the plane. Fritz and I both got in, and I started to taxi for takeoff snow was a little mushy. All at once, my right ski broke through the ice.

I cut the engine immediately. The right side of the plane sunk to where the tip of the wing was resting on the ice. I jumped out of my side of the airplane and started to make my way to shore before the rest of the ice decided to give way. I was about halfway to shore and turned to see how Fritz was doing. He was just setting there still in the plane; I guess waiting for somebody to come give him an invitation or perhaps carry him to shore.

I yelled. "Fritz, get your ass out of that airplane! If that other ski breaks through the ice, it will trap you inside the airplane, and all the damn money in the world won't be able to save you." Fritz climbed out my side of the airplane, which was still above water, and made his way over to where I was standing.

"Denny, do you think this will delay us getting back to the lodge?" he asked. Dumb question!

I would say there's a very good possibility that could happen. I was able to call Bill Sims before I left the airplane. He should be here within a half an hour to an hour.

When Bill arrived, I put him to work making preparations to extract our airplane from the ice. I then took Bill's plane, Fritz, and his bear's hide and flew them back to the lodge. I remember Fritz just had a sandwich, then caught his flight from the New Halen Lodge back to Anchorage, and that's the last we saw of him until he came to get a moose that fall.

I then returned to the crippled airplane. While I was at the lodge, I picked up some rope and pulleys and a saw. We cut three little fir trees and made a tripod over the downed wing. We then used the blocks and the rope to lift that side of the airplane out of the water. We were then able to move the airplane forward, enough to get that ski on solid ice. We then were able to pull it forward enough to get both skis on good solid ice. Without Fritz and the bear's hide and head, I then was able to get in the airplane and fly it back to the lodge, where we had to do a little bodywork, patch a couple dings in the wing, and we were back in business.

Fritz Carl Flick was on his way back to Germany with his brown bear trophy and a little out of the ordinary story to tell about how he almost bought the farm at the bottom of the lake in Alaska.

Carl returned two more times later that fall. He came back with his entourage. They were there for just a couple days. He got himself a nice moose, and they were gone. Next fall, he returned one more time to get a caribou.

A year after the caribou, Fritz called me from his yacht in the middle of the Mediterranean and wanted me to take him sheep hunting. I had to decline. We were in the middle of the problem with the fishing game department, and they had restricted my activities to flying fisherman into the mountain lakes.

This was about when Bert Kleinberger, Rusty Gibbons, the astronaut Stu Roosa, Carl Shelby, and several others started talking to me about going to Africa. Bert Kleinberger and Stew Roosa both had good connections with the leaders of several African countries. The plan was to set up different camps in the bush where there was little or no access by vehicle. We would have the hunters fly into one central location, pick them up in our airplanes, and fly them to whatever camp was appropriate depending on the game they wanted to hunt. I would then, in some cases take, the super cub fly the area and locate whatever I felt would be a good area for them to hunt to save them days sometimes weeks.

These discussions were taking place just about the time the federal government was in the process of closing down as many of the big guiding outfits as possible in Alaska. I guess it's about time you hear my side of that story.

Chapter Forty-Five

I'm not sure, but it wasn't very long after the state had failed for the third time to make the charges stick, where they claimed we were flying the same day we were hunting or that we were hunting inside the park boundaries etc. I had a hunter arrived who wanted to kill a brown bear, but he only had a couple of days. There was something about him that was different. He didn't seem to be as excited about the hunt as most hunters were. It was more like a business trip. I'm here. I want to get a bear, and let's get it over with. I almost turned him down. I had other people who would be much more pleasant to take on a hunting trip than him. When I told him I was reconsidering, he gave me some sad story about why he had to get this bear. At that point, I don't even remember what it was, but I finally conceded. We loaded all the gear in the plane. It was shortly after lunch, he was dillydallying around wasting time. I told him I was ready to leave with him or without him and that I had to get him to camp before 3 o'clock. I explained to him that the rules where I had to have him in camp by 3 o'clock the day before we intended to hunt. He finally boarded the plane, and we took off for the McNeil River area. I had a camp set up down there. Every year, I probably took a dozen or so hunters to that same camp. It was a major route between their hibernation area in the mountains to the McNeil River, where they could feast on dead salmon from last year's spawning run. When we were flying in, I remember we saw well over a dozen brown bear, not very far from the camp. The hunter asked me why we couldn't go shoot a bear this afternoon since we had so much daylight. I explained to him that the rules were we couldn't fly and shoot the same day. Then he argued that it seem to be kind of a dumb rule. I had to agree with him but explained that it was the rule. I don't remember for sure, but I suspect that night we had my favorite fried spam, couple pieces of bread, and some ketchup—just doesn't get any better than that. Next morning, we were up bright and early, and had some breakfast, you guessed it—fried spam sandwich. In case you haven't guessed it, I'm not a very good cook. From the camp, we spotted three or four bear. He picked one he wanted to try, for we spent about an hour sneaking from one brushy patch to another all the time getting a little closer to the bear. We were just a little over one hundred yards away. He looked the bear over with his binoculars and decided that wasn't the bear he wanted.

We got on top of the little knoll and started glassing the area and finally choosing a bear that did appear to be a little better than the last one. It was at least a good half a mile away, but we had lots of time. It was only midmorning same routine—stay behind some type of cover, either a hill or brush. We finally were within range again, probably a little over a hundred yards. He stood to shoot. I told him he could use my jacket and to lay on the ground where he would have a rest. He said no at this distance, this was fine and he shot. The dust and dirt flew up almost right under the bear who took off for parts unknown like a racehorse.

I proceeded to give him a lecture and threatened to load him in the airplane and return to camp with no bear. It was after lunch, and we have succeeded in scaring most of the bear into the brush, and they are now well aware of our presence. This guy is starting to get on my nerves. We now climb up on a little hill so we can see better. There are three or four bears within our view, but they're all in the brush. The afternoon is wearing on into evening. The hunter asked me what we should do. I told him we have to wait until one of these bears comes out of the brush, hopefully that will be before dark, or wait until tomorrow morning by that time the bears will have forgotten all about his bad shot, and things will be back to normal. He said he couldn't wait another day. He had to catch a flight first thing in the morning and started this sob story about how much his son was counting on him getting a bear etc. He asked me if I could take the airplane and buzzed the bear, if that would scare him out of the brush. I agreed. Yes, it will scare them out of the brush. He asked me if I would do that for him I told him, no because it was, again, the law. He kept pleading and telling the sad tale about his son. I knew there was something phony about this guy, but I didn't listen to my subconscious. I finally caved in and agreed since it was getting very late in the day, and he had to leave first thing in the morning. I made him promise he would not mention this to a soul. He swore he would never say anything to anybody. I put him in a position where I felt the bear would come out of the brush. I walked back to the airplane several times. I told myself, *the hell with it! Why should you care if this guy gets his bear or not? He's already had two opportunities that's all you can promise a hunter.* But I didn't listen; I climbed in the airplane stayed about fifty feet off the ground, made a loop around the other side the bear, and buzzed him at about fifteen feet. I had to do this twice before he finally came out of the brush. I heard the blast from the gun tipped the airplane to my side so I could see. The bear was lying dead in the tundra. I then landed the plane as close to the bears I could get,

I walked up to the hunter, stuck my arm out to shake his hand, and he informed me "Mr. Thompson, you are in a bit of trouble" as he flashed his credentials. He was the top agent in the Federal Department of Fish and Game. I commenced to call him every kind of unsavory name I could think of at the time since I was in the Air Force and not the Navy. I felt very inadequate when it came to the use of abusive language, but I did the best I could. It was not a good afternoon. Within a few minutes, a federal helicopter arrived to haul the carcass of the bear back to Anchorage for evidence.

Bill and I continued to hunt for about the next month. We never heard a word except for a couple of our hunters who said they had been approached by the Department of Fish and Game and wanted to know all about their hunting experience with Bill and I. They wanted to know if they flew and hunted on the same day. Some of them hadn't and some of them had. I'm not going to deny that, on occasion, we didn't fly and hunt on the same day, not that it makes it right, but that's what everybody did. I would venture to say the only hunters who didn't fly and hunt on the same day occasionally were the hunters who used horses, and they didn't fly at all.

We never heard another word for a little over a month; it was the last bear hunting party I had for the spring bear hunt. We had successfully killed two bear, and Bill and I were returning to the airport at Anchorage. We landed, and before we could taxi to the tie-down area, we were surrounded by about four federal vehicles. We all exited the airplane with our hands in the air. They put my two hunters under arrest and confiscated our airplanes, the two super cubs. We had another airplane, a Cessna 206 in the hangar. Our attorney met us at the airport. He handed Bill a couple thousand dollars and told him to fly that airplane to Canada as quick as he knew how. The way he understood it, the feds were trying to get a court order to confiscate that plane also,

Bill didn't fly up to Canada, but he did stash it someplace where they couldn't find it. What they didn't understand was we had friends all over the state, people who disliked, and didn't trust the Fish and Game Department, especially the feds. I went down to the sheriff's department and bailed out the two hunters. I then got on the telephone and found a super cub for sale in Utah. I bought the plane over the telephone on one condition that he would deliver it to Anchorage, and I would pay for his trip home. Two days later, I located another super cub for a reasonable price in Orlando, Florida.

I flew commercial air to Orlando, picked up the super cub, and flew it back to Alaska within one week. We had two new super cubs and were able to hunt for the next two seasons. In the meantime, the feds were busy harassing all my hunters. They had gotten a list from the Alaska Fish and Game Department, which showed every hunter we hunted that season, trying to find out where they had killed their bears. The Federal Department of Fish and Game contacted each of those hunters; first offered them immunity if they would testify against me. If that didn't work, they intimidated them and threatened them with all kinds of legal action. Some of the hunters had taken their bears legally and had nothing to testify about, but the feds didn't believe that, but then there were a few hunters where we had flown and shot our bear on the same day. those hunters were scared to death, and most of them, with the promise of immunity, sang like a bird.

It was almost two years from the time the feds confiscated the two airplanes until the grand jury hearings. There were actually three grand jury hearings scheduled. The first two were canceled on the courthouse steps just moments before the proceedings were to get underway. At a cost of hundreds of thousands of dollars to the Federal Government in the first two cases, they had flown in dozens of expert witnesses. The mayor told Denny later that it was great for the economy of the city and wondered if he had anything like that planned for the near future. Several months later, there was a third grand jury hearing. This time, they brought in most of Denny's hunters from that one year and the 1,000-pound bear carcass, which they brought into the court room to show the grand jury. After the testimony was concluded, but before the grand jury made a ruling, the feds offered Denny and Bill a plea bargain, which consisted of the following. Denny would lose his airplanes—the ones that they had confiscated. He would have to give up guiding and his hunting territories. Bill and Denny would each pay $25,000 fine. They wanted Denny to serve two years in prison and Bill one year. Denny and Bill agreed to everything but the time in prison and told the attorney they felt the jury would be much more lenient and decided to go to trial. The feds thought about that for a while, then came back with another proposal. Denny would serve ninety days in jail and Bill thirty. They both agreed to that, and the fact that this would remain a misdemeanor and not a felony, everyone agreed and the whole mess had finally come to a conclusion for Denny and Bill. The government had just spent in excess of two million dollars of taxpayers' money.

Denny was put in a minimum security prison in Palmer where he served thirty-three days. On the thirty-third day, he got a call from Ron Lavachic who was the head of the prison system in Alaska.

"Denny, this is Ron. I'm coming up to pick you up. It seems a couple of congressmen have intervened, and you are being set free. It appears they don't want a fine, upstanding citizen like you locked up with all those bad guys, and I'm afraid you are a bad influence on the prisoners."

"Well, thank you, Ron. I appreciate that, but can it wait till tomorrow? I'm showing hunting movies to the prisoners."

"Thompson, the hell with the prisoners! Get your stuff together. I'll be there in forty-five minutes, and if you're not ready, I'll leave you there for the next sixty days."

Needless to say, I was ready; other than one or two visits to the probation office over the following year, that was the end of my experience with the feds.

Over the next couple years between the state of Alaska and the Federal Government, they were successful in shutting down at least a half a dozen hunters that were on that list, several of them served two years or better in prison.

This was all over with by the latter part of 1979. I had been working with Bert Kleinberger, Rusty Gibbons, Stu Russo, Sam Pancotto, and several others, getting the African hunting consortium put together and operating,

INTO AFRICA

Chapter Forty-Six

This adventure I guess really started back in the early '70s when Denny took his first trip to Africa with Bill Sims, Bert Biss, and Adelino Perez.

As Denny would say, "Once you have hunted Africa, you have to come back." There's something about that country and the abundance of game animals and the fact that it is so diverse; it's like a magnet for anyone who likes it a little on the wild side.

Bert Kleinberger and Stu Russo (Apollo 14 Astronaut) were probably the two that really got it going. Bert had hunted in all those countries, and Stu, being an astronaut, was world-famous, and the dignitaries and leaders in Africa were even more impressed than the remainder of the world. We were getting this African hunting adventure off the ground while we were finishing up the final stages of my battle with the Federal Fish and Game Department in late 1979.

Stu Russo and Bert Kleinberger had negotiated the hunting rights in three different countries—Chad, the Republic of Central Africa, and Zaire. Bert and I first went to Chad in '78. They had virtually negotiated the hunting rights for the entire country. There was one small French hunting operation, but it only had a very small area. The rest was all ours. Bert and I spent six weeks surveying and checking out the areas where we felt would be the best place to set up camps. It was a hunter's paradise. There was game everywhere; we had concluded our investigation of the area. We made a stop in the Republic of Central Africa. Bert wanted to show me a building he was thinking about buying for our future hunting operation in that country. We were there about a week, then I headed back to Alaska. When I arrived home, the news all over the TV was the president of Chad had been killed, and the country was in turmoil.

I received a call the next day from Bert who informed me to forget about Chad and concentrate on the Republic of Central Africa. They were buying the building, and all the equipment that went with it, which consisted of ten Toyota hunting trucks, several bigger trucks for hauling fuel and supplies to the different camps, boats, and motors. and other miscellaneous equipment. Bert asked me if I could come over and help get the camps set up etc. I informed him I had the grand jury hearing coming up in just a couple weeks, and depending what happened with that, I'd have to let him know.

I called Bert as soon as we had made our settlement with the feds and informed him that it looked like I would be at least three months before I could get back to Africa; he was very disappointed.

In our group, he and I were about the only two that were able to get anything done. He said, "I'm going to make a couple phone calls," and mentioned the fact that Carol Shelby knew a lot of important people as did Stu Roosa. I never did know if that's what happened. But in thirty-three days, I was a free man again. I had to get permission to leave the country, which I did. The judge just asked me to check in when I got back.

First order of business was to get our airplanes lined out. I found and bought a twin engine Piper Seneca II, seven passenger plane in Wichita Kansas and then Shelby's Cessna 206" in Florida. I purchased those for the company and made arrangements with a company on the east coast to fly them to Africa. Then I made arrangements to have one of my super cubs also flown to Africa. I flew it back to Lock Haven Pennsylvania. He informed me that I would need to put about $5,000 to $6,000 worth of radio gear in the plane before he would attempt the flight across the Atlantic Ocean in that super cub. I informed him there was no way I was putting that much radio gear in that airplane. I moved the airplane to New York, then I took the plane apart, crated it up, and put it on a ship (destination Douala Cameroon Africa) where I picked it up a couple weeks later. Jeannie came with me on this trip; we picked the crates up, had them transported to the closest airport, put the plane back together. It only took us eleven hours. I had installed a belly tank for the trip across the Atlantic Ocean, so I had plenty of fuel to make the 600 mile trip to Bangui Central African Republic. Bangui is situated right on the Congo River on the border between the Central African Republic and Zaire.

That is where Bert had purchased the building with all the equipment. It backed right up to the Congo River. It was a madhouse around there for the next couple of months. We had three camps to set up. Two of them, almost 600 miles from our headquarters one of those, was near Obo on the border of the Sudan. We had another camp in the very northern part of the country Ndele in the DarRounga area close to the Chad border.

Then we had the camp at Bombari about 400 miles east of Bangui on the Congo River. We had to get a good spot to set up camp, moved several of the vehicles out to those campsites, and the guides had to scout out the area and find out where they could go with the vehicles and where it looked like the largest concentration of animals was located. Most of this area was a large savannah mostly grassland with some brush and trees in scattered areas.

We had eleven white hunters. All but one of those came from Mozambique in southeastern Africa. Several of them, in fact, we hunted with in the early '70s, when Bill Sims, Bert Biss, and I hunted with Adelino Perez in Mozambique. Mozambique had completely stopped outside hunting since we were there. That was a big advantage for us because these hunters all had years of experience in the bush.

We had just about every type of animal you could imagine. In the North, that area was primarily on the edge of the desert we had Lord Derby eland and lots of lions, plus a good assortment of other planes game such as sable, warthogs, leopards, cheetah, and we had lion everywhere in all three areas and a lot of them. The area to the east along the borders of Sudan didn't have any Gemsbok or Oryx but had everything else including a massive amount of cape buffalo, elephant, rhino, and hippos everywhere.

Our prime elephant hunting area was in the jungles. In that area, we had an abundant supply of elephants and bongo. We hunted there for three years. We took forty-one elephants, and that was a drop in the bucket compared to what the poachers were taking. We had great bongo hunting—probably some of the best on the continent. They only exist in jungle type environment and they're almost always nocturnal, which means if you're going to hunt them during the day, you have to go in the jungle and find them. They're not out on the savannah eating grass during the day; that also holds true for the elephants. They're not necessarily nocturnal. They just don't come out into the open very often in that area.

Denny with French officials Paris

President Bokassa Republic of South Africa and Denny

Chapter Forty-Seven

Bocossa was the president of the Central African Republic. There were lots of negotiations that went on between Stu Russo, Bert Kleinberger, and Rusty Gibbons. Some of the territory we had hunting rights to was also very good grazing land. Rusty Gibbons could visualize a mammoth cattle operation in this area. He considered bringing in some cattle from the US and Argentina that had been bred especially for the tropics; however, Bocossa convinced Rusty. They should stick with native raised cattle because they were already immune to most of the diseases and insects that plagued these areas. Rusty felt that made sense, and he didn't want to make the President mad. Bocossa agreed that he would get the cattle if Rusty would pay for them Rusty used $90,000 of company funds gave that to Bocossa and never got a cow or not even a calf, just a lot of bull from Bokassa.

We were told by some of his inside people that he was a cannibal, not totally unheard of in that part of the country. Some of the old hunters that hunted those countries before and just after the second world war found cannibalism in that area to be quite common. We were told he had a couple of people in the freezer just for special occasions.

Bert and I were always sure to be very busy when we got an invitation to dine with the president.

Adelino Perez was the president of our company. Due to his vast knowledge of the African culture, Bokassa put his brother as the second in command. He virtually contributed nothing except take up space in the office and was intoxicated the majority of the time. He really didn't bother us or cause us any problems until the very end. Our deal with the Bokassa regime was they got half of the profits, and as time went on and we started to make money, they got greedier and felt they deserved more. We complained to Bokassa several times about the poachers and told him that was going to eventually cut into our profits. As they eliminated more and more elephants, he agreed and sent some of his people out to track down and capture the poachers. A couple weeks later, we got a report that his people had captured twenty-five or thirty suspected poachers, but we never saw a soul, not one prisoner. We suspected perhaps they killed them on the site and fed them to the crocodiles. We really didn't care what they did with them as long as they would stop the poaching.

It was about a year later Bert Kleinberger and I were checking out one of our airplanes; after we finished, we got a couple chairs out of the hangar, fixed ourselves a good stiff drink, and lit up a good cigar. It was after dark, but there was a fair amount of moonlight; there was a 707 parked at the end of the runway just on the outer fringe of the runway lights. I felt what a weird place to park that airplane. It was right in the way of any incoming flights.

Next thing we know, a couple of army trucks pull up to the airplane. They were loaded with elephant tusks. We sat there in disbelief as they unloaded a total of three trucks of ivory into that airplane; we watched this operation for about two hours. The trucks finally pulled away; they closed the doors on the airplane.

Bokassa showed up in his Mercedes with the flight crew. They climbed aboard the airplane and took off for parts unknown. Now it was quite clear, why nothing was being done about the poachers, and we suspected the cock and bull story about capturing the poachers was just that—a story. We were slowly starting to get an uneasy feeling about the longevity of our operation, but it was going so good and was so successful. I guess we just didn't want to think about what might go wrong.

We hunted from about February to July then it just got too wet; storms would start coming in and it would rain every day. The rivers and the creeks would flood, and some parts of the savannah would just turn into huge lakes. It was beautiful to fly over in the wet season because everything was an emerald green, and the creeks and rivers ran every direction, and there were animals for as far you could see.

I would leave Africa in May, so I had time to get home and get prepared for salmon fishing. I had sold my lodge at New Halen to Bill Sims. I took that money and used it to buy a couple of permits on Bristol Bay and a fishing boat. And then in the late summer, I would set up camps in about six to eight different places, where I would ferry hunters out to those camps for what I call the nonguided hunt. They were on their own. They could only hunt caribou and moose and black bear and goats, nothing that required a guide. I actually made more money doing that than I did guiding individuals because I could have ten to twenty hunters in the field at all times. Usually in two to three days, they would have what they were after I'd pick them up and put a new group of hunters in that same camp. I actually wish I'd thought of that earlier, even when I had my guiding license it was a natural.

We didn't usually start hunting in Africa until February, but as a rule, I would get there two or three weeks in advance. We always had a ton of maintenance that had to be taken care of before we could start hunting.

Chapter Forty-Eight

I remember the first year we had to get fuel out to all those different camps. The closest one was Bombari that was about 400 miles east, right on the Congo River. It was a very good area for elephants and rhinoceros and thousands of cape buffalo, leopards, and lions. The camp up north at Ndele was also about 400 miles maybe a little bit farther. It was primarily on the edge of the desert. That area had an abundance of Lord Derby Eland as well as all kinds of other antelope springbok just about anything you can imagine. Of all the areas, this probably had the highest population of lion. Of any of the other camps, this was the driest of the three main camps.

The third main camp was in Obo on the far eastern border of the Republic of Central Africa right on the Sudan border; this camp was probably our best elephant hunting area, and the only area that had a healthy population of bongo. It also had rhino but not as many as at Bombari.

The professional hunters took care of getting the hunting vehicles from Bangui to the other camps. At one time, when the French were running the country, they had roads to these different areas, but after they left, the local government could never see the importance of maintaining the bridges and road beds, took the money for that, and stuck it in their pocket or a Swiss bank. After a few years in a climate where it rains almost half of the year, it doesn't take long for Mother Nature to wipe out whatever progress man has made. We had to haul gas to these different camps in the two six by six heavy duty

German-made trucks. The roads were so bad, and they had to forge creeks where the bridges had been washed out. It took two full weeks to get from Bangui to Obo.

We would load the trucks with about thirty fifty-gallon drums of gasoline, but by the time they got to Obo, half of the gas in the outside drums was siphoned out by the natives. They were worse than locus; they would steal anything that wasn't nailed down, and if they could get it loose, they'd steal it.

There were many times when our hunters would notify us that they were running out of gas; I would have to load the twin up with six or eight drums a gasoline and fly them to the camps. As time went on, my primary responsibility was flying our hunters to and from their camps and hauling gasoline and supplies. Once in a while, when I had time, I would take the super cub and do some scouting, usually looking for elephants or bongo.

The second year, when I came over, I brought my twelve-year-old son Mark with me, and we went on our own Safari. The first camp we went to was Ndele, about 100 miles south of the Chad border. This was the only area that we had the giant Lord Derby Eland; these bulls could easily weigh over 2000 pounds. On one rather short afternoon, Mark and I both shot an eland. These animals looked big when they were in the bush, but once they were on the ground, they even looked much bigger, 500 to 800 pounds heavier than our moose. We would cut a dozen or two steaks from one of the hindquarters and take a back straps, which was at least three feet long. Then we would turn the rest of the meat over to the natives, who would be just a short distance away patiently waiting; I would have liked to been able to understand what they were talking about. It sounded as if every one of them was talking at the same time. The workforce was primarily women. They had baskets and buckets—every imaginable container that they could put the meat in to get it back to their village. I'd say that at least a third of them were also carrying babies. It reminded me of ants. They would fill their container or perhaps it would be just the blanket that they would wrap the meat in, gracefully swing it up on top of their head, and the way they go, depending on how far away the village was. Within an hour or two, they would return until virtually every scrap of an animal was gone including the tail, which they use to make a flyswatter.

We shot several other animals while we were in that area, then we flew down to Obo where I shot a huge warthog and several other antelope. When we were flying into camp, we spotted a nice herd of elephant just about fifteen miles out of camp. I asked the white hunter (Federico, Fred for short) if he thought that was a good place to hunt. His comment was that if there's elephants there, that's a good place.

So the next day at sunrise, that's where we headed, hoping the herd would be in the same general area. We were a mile or two short of our destination when we ran across a number of elephant tracks that had crossed the road sometime during the night. The tracker felt someplace between midnight and 6 o'clock this morning. Our guide felt he knew where they were headed perhaps another couple miles to our south into some heavier timber.

We made a detour around the area, where the professional hunter felt the elephants would be; we left one of the blacks with the truck, the PH, two trackers, and a couple skinners. Mark and I made our way into the heavier timber. We were coming in downwind, the pH felt if we worked our way into the timber. We could probably hear the elephants up ahead of us eating evidently they tore limbs off the trees and made a quite a racket.

There were a few thunderstorms in the area, but we were still in the sunshine, reminded me of the Midwest where it will be sunny and bright on one hillside, and just a half a mile away, you'll have a rip snorting thunderstorm. When we first entered the heavy timber, it was almost like night the trees were probably eighty to one hundred feet tall with a very heavy canopy. Only occasionally would you see a spear of sunlight that somehow found its way through the leaves, but as our eyes got more accustomed, we could see quite well. We had probably worked our way into the timber at least a half a mile. We would pause for several minutes at a time and listen, but there was so much racket from the monkeys and the birds and the chimpanzees that I couldn't see how in the world Fred could possibly detect an elephant sound from all the other racket. There was a lightning strike not too far away, and then it got dark. big thunderheads had just covered up the sun, and when I say dark, I mean dark. It was almost like night with a little bit of moon light. We stopped dead in our tracks, nobody moved a muscle, then came the wind and the rain. The wind came in from our back swirling around in every direction. Fred whispered to me, "This isn't good."

Now when I say it rained, I'm not talking about a drizzle, it was a cloudburst. It made so much racket hitting the trees and the leaves that it drowned it out all other sounds; we were all huddled as close as we could get to the trees that gave us some protection from the rain. The tree tops were whipping back and forth in the wind. The rain only lasted about five minutes, but everyone was thoroughly soaked.

The next thing I realized, the ground was shaking; Fred yelled at the natives to take Mark and go. They grabbed Mark by the arm and took off on the dead run. Evidently, we had walked right into the middle of the elephant heard. The swirling wind brought them our scent, but they couldn't tell for sure where we were, so they just charged. Thirty head of elephants crashing through the timber and screaming at the top of their lungs is pretty damn frightening. Fred and I stayed put, looking for a big bull to shoot. There were elephants all around us. One old female with a calf passed within six to eight feet of where we were standing behind the tree. In probably thirty seconds, the commotion was all over with right in our immediate area though we could continue to hear the elephants crashing through the brush and trees and making their blood curdling screams, for at least a couple more minutes.

The rain had passed and so had the elephants. Fred said it was evidently a herd of females with some young but no bulls. The natives with Mark returned. They were all looking for their thongs; they evidently kicked them off when they started running. Mark had 1,000 questions as you might imagine being only twelve years old. I showed him where we were standing and where the elephant tracks were. He was quite impressed; actually, I was quite impressed, especially when I stop to think about how big that elephant looked when it went charging past our tree. The babies' tracks were even closer. They were only about four feet away. We made our way back to the truck and decided that had been enough excitement for one day. Fred was quite sure there had to be some bulls in this area. We just had to find them. That night at camp, we had eland steaks and re-lived the day's adventure several times. Mark said they were running so fast through the timber that his feet weren't even touching the ground half the time.

That Night, about 3 a.m., I woke up to the chatter of a native and Fred exchanging information in a language I couldn't understand, sounded like a mixture of French and native. Fred made his way over to my tent. I was setting on the edge of my bunk in anticipation that something exciting was about to happen. Fred informed me that the native was a runner from a village about eight miles away. The runner told Fred there were three big bull elephants in one of the corn fields at the village. They wanted Fred to come and shoot the elephants before they ate all his corn, which sounded like a plan to me. We grabbed a few things to make a sandwich some water, guns, and ammo, piled in the truck and we were off to the village. By the time we got there, it was somewhere between 4:00 and 4:30 in the morning. We went out into the cornfield. It was not hard to find where the elephants had been. They had probably wiped out about a quarter of his corn crop. We had flashlights, but the elephants were gone; we waited about an hour until it started to get daylight. Everyone filled their water jugs, grabbed a couple candy bars and whatever else we thought we might need, left one of the natives with the truck, and started what turned out to be an all-day tracking adventure.

Most of the time, the tracking was quite easy. There were times when we got into the brush where the ground was so dry and hard. They never even left a track, but the trackers were good. They would find a broken twig or a clump of grass that had been stepped on. Several times, we came across elephant dung that was still warm, so we knew we were close. It was about 11 o'clock in the morning when we came across a burn area. It was at least a couple miles wide tracking in that area was very easy, about halfway through the burn area our animals mixed with another herd of elephants. Fred estimated may-be twenty or thirty could've been the same herd we saw yesterday. They mingled together for a quite a ways, but the trackers did a good job. They stayed right on the three bulls; eventually, they separated the bulls, went to the left, and the rest of the herd went to the right. Once they got all those tracks sorted out, we again could make good time.

It's about 2 o'clock, and I'd estimate we had traveled at least twelve to fourteen miles. We were just about through the burn area and back into the grass and brush. Fred took me by the arm and said, "Look at this." A pride of lions had crossed the elephant tracks because there were several lion tracks inside the elephant tracks. Fred estimated the pride to be six or eight adults and a half a dozen cubs. Now we're back into the grass and brush—ideal cover for a pride of lion. There was other game everywhere just about everywhere you wanted to look. You could see some kind of antelope, warthogs, etc. We traveled at least another three to four miles; the trackers felt we were getting very close. I looked at my watch, it's almost 5 o'clock; we had been on the trail of these elephants for at least ten hours, and I would estimate we traveled twenty to twenty-five miles.

We were entering an area where the grass was perhaps eight feet tall and the brush another three to four feet above that now we could pick up the sound of the elephants foraging. As we got closer, occasionally, we could see one of their trunks reach up into the trees and pull a limb down. We had the breeze in our face, so we felt quite comfortable getting closer. We continued to pick our way slowly through the brush and grass being guided by watching their trunks reach up into the trees. Most of the time, we couldn't see the elephants. We spent perhaps forty-five minutes moving ever so slowly. We finally were in position to get a look at all three animals primarily. When they reached up into the trees, we could see their trunk and their tusk. I finally picked what I thought was the best of the three. We spent another ten minutes slowly moving around a couple of thorny acacia trees, so I would have a clear shot. The next time, he reached for a limb, I had a good, clear head shot. We were so close I was shooting up on about a forty-five-degree angle. We were not quite fifteen yards away. The 375 rocked me back on my heels. The old bull collapsed and sounded like a huge tree when it comes crashing to the ground. The other two bulls made a hasty retreat into the thicker brush. I have to say I never worked harder for a trophy.

Eleven hours of tracking perhaps twenty-five miles, and we had at least fifteen miles to walk to get back to our truck.

It was way too late in the day to even think about starting to retrieve the tusk and whatever else we wanted. Everyone was nearing exhaustion. Poor Mark, I think could've went to sleep in a thorn bush. He was really tired. Fred felt there was a small village about six to eight miles to our north. He felt the best thing to do would be to walk to that village and see if someone there would go get the truck. Two hours later, we're stumbling through the tall grass. It's now dark. There are a couple prides of lion roaring at each other across the savanna; one of them doesn't sound very far away. Fred tells us to keep talking. That way, we won't surprise something, but we were so tired we couldn't even talk.

Eventually, we find the village and a native that has a bicycle. We negotiate with him; he agrees to ride up to where our truck is for a pack of cigarettes. I forgot to mention that before we left the elephant, we cut about three feet of his trunk off. This showed that someone laid claim to the elephant and would be back to get the tusk later. I wanted the tusk, at least a couple of the feet, and one of the ears. It's about 10:30 when our truck arrives. We got back to camp about 11:30. The cook fixed a bite to eat for us, and while we were waiting for dinner, we decided to have a couple glasses of wine to celebrate. I had a couple of glasses of wine and could barely make it to the table to eat my dinner. I had to wake Mark up, so he could have something to eat. He fell asleep at least twice setting at the table while he was eating. Once I had completed what I could eat, I wasn't feeling very good. I staggered to my bunk and succeeded to pass out.

I never stirred until the next morning when I smelled breakfast cooking, a couple cups of coffee, and about a half a gallon the water, and I finally started to feel like a human being again. It's just turning daylight. The sky off to our east is a crimson red. The lion and the hyenas appear to be in a pitched battle over somebody's carcass about a half a mile off to our south. At times, it sounded like they were right on the edge of the camp.

I was having my first cup of coffee, when I noticed Fred had this mischievous grin on his face. I could tell it was directed at me.

"Hey, Thompson, you don't remember what happened last night do you?"

"I remember those two glasses of wine. What did we have for dinner?" I ask.

Buzzard was his reply.

That about made me gag. "No, what did we have?" I ask.

Ginny fowl, but that's not what I'm laughing about. You remember that cute little black girl who was flitting around when we were waiting at the village for our truck to arrive?

"Yeah, about fourteen or fifteen years old? Was giving Mark the eye!"

"Yes, that's the one. Well, they arrived just before midnight last night. She was all dressed up in a little white dress. She was supposed to be a gift to you since you were the big shot who killed the elephant, and perhaps saved their corn crop, and hopefully you will give them the meat from the elephant. The first one they've had in, perhaps, six to eight years, and you slept right through the whole thing. And they swore on their spirit that she is still a virgin. They left here very disappointed and hoped that was not a bad omen."

Needless to say I, didn't live that down for a while. After we had taken care of the elephant and got everything back to camp, we drove to the closest community that had a store or two; I bought a nice little dress for about $5 and gave it to her in appreciation for her great offer. Everyone seemed to be appreciative of the gesture.

Now to get back to the retrieval of my elephant tusk, breakfast was complete, and Fred made sure he had a couple of axes some extra rope, a chainsaw loaded in the truck, and we were ready for our next adventure. We spent about two to three hours cutting our way through the bush, so we could get to the elephant with the truck or at least close. Once we were within about a half a mile, Fred felt that it would be quicker and easier to just walk the rest of the way; as we got within a couple hundred yards of the elephant, there were natives coming in and out like locusts, most of them covered with blood. There were at least a half a dozen small fires; they were cooking smoking and drying meat as fast as they could get it off the elephant carcass.

There were bees everywhere once you got close to the elephant where the fires were, and there was a lot of smoke. They didn't bother you too much. Evidently, one of the natives had found a honeybee nest, and they were in the process of stealing all the bees' honey as well as all our elephant meat.

We retrieved our ivory. I took two—the front feet, and I wanted to take one of the ears, but they had cut it up so bad it was not salvageable. By noon, that elephant was nothing but a pile of bones. They even took some of those. I presume to make soup or something. One of the natives was telling Fred that when they arrived that morning before daylight, there were half a dozen lions on the carcass. They had to start little fires and throw burning sticks and rocks at the lions to scare them off.

After we had retrieved everything we wanted and headed back to the truck, Mark pointed up into the sky. I looked up. There had to be one hundred plus vultures lazily circling waiting for the last of the natives to leave the area.

As I reflect back on this hunt, it, nowhere, compares too many of the old elephant hunting stories that I've read about over the years, but in my lifetime of hunting experiences, it's one I cherish and remember in great detail.

Denny with elephant and natives Republic of South Africa

Chapter Forty-Nine

While we were in Obo, I decided this would be a great place for Mark to get a buffalo (these buffalo looked just like the cape buffalo in South Africa, but they were referred to as the Nile River Buffalo—a sub specie of the cape buffalo considerably smaller. I would guess by 400 to 600 pounds, and their horns also were proportionately smaller), but there were thousands of them. There were buffalo everywhere. They also didn't appear to be as aggressive as the cape buffalo, and we could set in camp and pick which heard we wanted to hunt.

We gave Mark a set of binoculars and told him to pick out the bull he wanted while we were having breakfast. From our vantage point, I'm not exaggerating when I say we could easily count a thousand head of buffalo. He finally settled on a small group, looked like all bulls that were only about a mile from camp. They were on a little knoll that was covered with small trees and brush. From camp, it looks like we could come in from the north side through a couple little patches of timber, get within one hundred yards, and then wait for one of them to come out into the open at least that was our plan. I counted about thirty heads but felt there were probably more that I couldn't see because of the brush. After breakfast, we drove across the savannah down to the north side of where we intended to enter the patch of woods, parked the truck, and entered the wooded area. We had traveled about one hundred yards into the trees and brush. When Fred grabbed me by the arm and motioned all of us to kneel down and be quiet, after a couple of seconds, I could hear what Fred had heard—the sound of a lion eating and—that slight gurgling rumble that comes from deep in their throat. Fred very slowly raised, then knelt down again, and motioned for us to slowly retreat back to the pickup. He backed out never taking his eyes off the area where the lions were. Once we got clear of the woods and in the pickup, he told us what he could see; there were at least three or four lions or maybe more. They evidently had killed a zebra during the night or late yesterday afternoon. He said it looked like all, but one had eaten their fill and were sleeping it off, except for the one. Thank goodness, he was eating or we probably would have walked right in on them, and who knows what would've happened in that situation.

We had to change our plans, so we decided to go around the upper edge of the wooded area, which would easily keep us a couple hundred yards from the lions. We made our way around the edge of the woods and then dropped back into the woods once we were well past the lions and once we came to the edge of the woods. It looked like there were several little patches of brush and trees that we could stay behind to get even closer to the buffalo.

Fred had the natives, tracker and skinners, stay at the edge of the woods. As Fred, Mark, and I worked our way up the hill, Fred picked the spot behind a couple of small thorn bushes. We could see the outline of the bulls through the brush; as they milled around, Fred whispered to Mark precisely where he wanted him to shoot the bull when one came into the clear. We sat there for probably an hour, and I know Mark was getting anxious. Several times, a bull would come almost to the edge of the brush but would then turn and go back into the brush and disappear. Fred said and I know he was right, "We just had to be patient." The same speech I've given many a bear hunters.

Then from down in the woods came in unexpected blessing. Two of the lions evidently got into an argument about whose turn it was to eat. Fred put his hand on Mark's shoulder and said get ready. Sure enough, in about ten to fifteen seconds, one of the old bulls walked out to the edge of the brush to see what all the ruckus was about. Mark was ready. He fired, and the old bull lurched forward, then turned and went back into the brush. Another bull took his place. Mark shot again. This time, the bull collapsed on the spot. Mark had shot him in the neck about a foot behind his head. Mark was ready to charge right up the hill to see his new trophy. Fred told him to stay put, then he asked Mark if he thought he hit the first bull.

"I shot him right where you told me to."

"Okay, we will look for him as soon as I'm sure this guy isn't playing possum."

Fred slowly made his way up the hill, looked the bull over closely, then motion for all of us to come including the skinners and the trackers. As soon as the trackers got there, he told them about the other bull and showed him about where it was standing when Mark shot. In less than a minute, they had picked up some traces of blood that were spattered on the brush where the bullet had exited the other side of the bull. With Fred about two steps behind them, they made their way through the brush, which was maybe a couple hundred feet wide. There was plenty of blood. They exited the brush on the other side of the knoll and laying about fifty feet into the grass was the first bull. Mark had shot him through the heart.

We hadn't even finished capping the first animal, when we saw an entourage of natives coming across the savannah with buckets and pans. There would be feasting in the village tonight. Fred left the skinners there to start cutting up the animals. If we didn't leave someone with the animals, the vultures would have them half devoured by the time the natives arrived. The village was about six miles away, and when we saw them, they were about two miles, so they evidently started immediately when they heard the first shot or maybe when they spotted us up on the hill with the truck. I asked Fred if he was going to save any of the meat for the camp. He said, "No, it was too tough." He said we had a good supply of more edible antelope. That pretty well concluded our Safari. Mark had taken nine or ten animals. I think I shot eight including my elephant.

Seneca II after crash, all surved. Republic of Africa

Denny taking Polaroid pictures of Native kids.

Chapter Fifty

The sequence of events is not necessarily in the order that they happened. I remember them with great detail but not necessarily which one occurred before the other.

The Safari with Mark took place the year before I actively became involved in the management and the flying responsibilities of the company. My primary responsibility was to get the hunters to and from there camps and make sure the camps were supplied with whatever they needed, such as food or gasoline.

I had only been there for a couple of weeks. We had a French pilot that was flying our hunters to and from the camps. I remember one afternoon when we had a very important guest show up at Bangui. He was our first customer who had specifically requested an elephant with hundred-pound tusk. He was the president of Pizza Hut—one of the major pizza stores in the US, and we of course were eager to help him achieve his goal. The French pilot complained that it was too late in the afternoon. He didn't think he could get to Obo and back before dark. I assured him the boys at Obo would put him up for the evening and supplied them with food and drink adequate to getting through the night. His comment was:

"I'm not going to stay in that godforsaken country overnight. There are savages out there that still eat people. If you want him out there tonight, Mr. Thompson, why don't you take him?" I took that as a challenge. I was quite sure he didn't think I was capable; in less than a half an hour, I had the plane fueled, had collected all the maps and charts that I needed, and we were taxiing down the runway.

I had never flown in this country before, so I had absolutely no landmarks that I was familiar with, but I did have the Congo River basin just off my right wingtip, and I had more than a little experience, flying over Germany looking for places I'd never been to before. Once I got to where our camp was, I had to search the area for several minutes before I spotted the camp. I buzzed the camp to let them know we were arriving with one of their hunters. Federico was at the landing strip shortly after I touched down. After talking to Fred for a couple of minutes, I decided to stay overnight even though I was sure I could get back to Bangui. Fred felt that if I could take an hour in the morning to fly the hunter and one of the trackers northeast out of camp and spot some big elephants, it would save him a lot of time. That night, we sat around camp and listened to Fred tell stories about his experiences over the last thirty years from being gored by a buffalo to being bitter by deadly cobra and somehow survived. It was two o-clock am before we let him go to bed

The next morning after breakfast, we loaded everybody in the airplane, including Fred who had decided at the last minute to go with us. We spotted hundreds of elephants. There were elephant herds everywhere. About twenty miles northeast of camp, toward the Sudan border, we spotted several big bulls. Fred looked the area over very thoroughly, in hopes that he could find his way back to these specific elephants, then we returned to camp. I dropped everybody off and headed back to the headquarters at Bangui. About a week later, I picked up the hunter at Obo. We had a whole planeload of hides and horns and two elephant tusk that were both over one hundred pounds. He also had taken a very nice lion with a nice fluffy reddish brown mane—one of the best ones I saw all the time I was over there. The French pilot never challenged me again, especially once he heard of all the missions I had flown over France, within several weeks his arrogant attitude got him fired.

Chapter Fifty-One

A couple of German hunters arrived a week or two later. They were a day early, and the PH up in the Ndele wasn't ready for them yet, so it became my responsibility to entertain them. They both decided they would like to go fishing on the Congo River. They were both a couple of hunters I had hunted polar bear with in Alaska, several years earlier. They had heard stories about the tiger fish that prowled the black waters of the Congo River and some of the giant river perch that also inhabited the same area. They asked me if I would take them fishing since that was something I had wanted to do ever since I'd arrived. That sounded like a plan to me.

I asked around to find out what kind of lures and bait they normally use. Bright and early the next morning, we put the boat in the water and headed upstream to an area we were told was exceptionally good for the Goliath tiger fish. From what I'm told, there are tiger fish all over the world from Africa to the Amazon, but the Goliath tiger fish is only found in the Congo River basin and some of its tributaries. This species grows to well over 150 pounds and is supposedly one of the most ferocious fighter in the game fishing world. The fishing lures we were advised to buy were about the size of a Velveeta cheese box with four sets of treble hooks that were at least four inches long and three inches wide. I'm convinced that if you had hooked one of those to the front bumper of a Volkswagen, you could've lifted it off the ground quite easily.

We bought a half a dozen of those and some lures for the river perch, some new line and some steel leader. As we made our way up the river the boys got all rigged up for what they hoped was going to be a very special day of fishing. We were told to fish right at the base of a little rapids off to the side of the main channel. Due to the current, I had to run the boat and let them do the fishing. They threw the lures up into the rapids and then let it drift downstream. It was the second or maybe third cast, and a tiger fish hit the lure and jerked the rod and reel right out of the guy's hand, and we never saw it again. Lure rod and reel—everything was gone. The guy sat there with a stunned look on his face looked at his hands and then at his buddy, who paused for but a moment, and said, "Ufda." For those of you who aren't from Minnesota, South Dakota, and some parts and Wisconsin, that's a rather uncomplimentary statement used by the "Norwegians" to express their opinion of your level of intelligence or lack of. We all laughed until our sides hurt. The other hunter started casting in the same area. He probably threw the lure up into the rapids a half a dozen times before he got a strike. He was hanging onto that rod so tight his knuckles were white. I let the boat drift down the river as he fought the fish for about five minutes. The fish tore back and forth across the river then all at once, the line went slack he reeled it in. The steel leader had been cut.

We repeated this scenario three more times. One time, the line broke, but the other two times, the leader was broke. We decided we had to go back to town and get some stronger leader and another half a dozen lures. I was going to buy them some lunch, but no way they wanted to get back on the river and catch one of those tiger fish. We lost a couple more lures that afternoon but did manage to catch three nice tiger fish—one about twenty pounds and the other two forty pounds or better. We also caught four or five river perch. One of those over sixty pound. I understand they get up as big as 200 pounds. We had been advised that if we got any perch, take them to the restaurant, and they would cook you up a fish dinner to die for, so that's exactly what we did, and it was an excellent dinner. The next day, I flew them up to Ndele where I believe they also had a very good hunt, but I don't really remember any of the details. I did go fishing several more times with very good luck; I caught several tiger fish that were right at eighty pounds. But I lost one that I think would have went over one hundred pounds. I fought him for an hour and a half. He pulled me all over the river. Eventually, he got into an old snag along the riverbank and broke the line. I never even got him close enough to the boat to see what he looked like.

Once I got the super cub to Africa, I had many more opportunities to fly about the country. One time, I had the super cub in Obo. We had an elephant hunter that wanted me to take him out to see if we could locate some elephant. I always enjoyed that type of flying. We were probably fifty to sixty miles northeast of Obo, when we spotted what looked like oil spots on the savannah. After about ten of these, I dropped down to about fifty feet off the ground, then it became obvious what they were. They were elephant carcasses that had been left there to rot. The poachers took the tusk and left everything else out there on the savannah. We climbed back up to about 300 feet, in about fifteen or twenty minutes of flying. We counted over one hundred carcasses; once we got closer to the Sudan border, we actually spotted some poachers. They had donkeys and what looked like several cattle or oxen with elephant tusk strapped to their back. There were at least a dozen animals loaded down with ivory, headed to the east to the Sudan border. We circled about for several minutes and then turned back to the west to see if we could find any live animals for our hunter. Once we returned to camp, I told Fred about the situation. He was aware that the poachers had been working in that area but had no idea they had killed that many elephants in that small area. The hunter and I were talking as I was putting fuel in the airplane. When he spotted a hole in the wing, he asked me how this happened. I had no idea what he was talking about until I looked at it. It was a bullet hole out near the end of the wing, once I finished fueling. I looked the plane over real close and found two more bullet holes, both in the tail section. We never heard any rifle shots or saw any flashes, but it had to be those poachers. It was about three weeks later, when I was asked by the French government to pick up the President of France at the Bangui airport and fly him out to their special reserve not too far from Obo, and very close to the area where I had spotted all the dead elephant.

On the flight over, I, of course, had the opportunity to talk to the president quite candidly, and I explained what I had seen just three weeks earlier. He asked if I would mind flying him over that area, so he could see it for himself, which I did even though he didn't say much. I could tell he was very angry. The French still had a couple of army bases in the country, which I didn't know until later. He evidently authorized troops to round up the poachers and kill the ones that resisted and capture the rest, which I understand they did. That put a halt to the poaching in that particular area basically for the rest of the time I was there, but I suspect as time went on it was back to business as usual.

During the four years of our African adventure, I purchased two twin-engine Piper Seneca airplanes for the company and had Carroll Shelby's Cessna 206 ferried over to Africa plus my super cub. Of those four aircrafts, only one survived. The 206 only made about a half a dozen flights. One of our French pilots was taking a hunter and some supplies out to Bambari. He was only about twenty miles from the airport when the fuel line plugged up, and he had to crash-land. No one was hurt, but the plane was totaled.

Next was the Seneca II. It lasted for a couple years. Again, one of our hired pilots crashed it about fifteen miles out of Bangui. We were able to salvage some of the gear, but the plane would never fly again. In the meantime, I had brought one of my super cubs from Alaska to Africa. We used it for the light work, but that wasn't sufficient to fly 500 to 600 miles to the camps. I was in the states when Shelby called me about the loss of the first Seneca II. I found another one in Atlanta Georgia, flew it to Oakland, California, and turned it over to a company that makes a business of ferrying aircraft across the ocean. When it arrived, the pilot who flew the plane across the ocean, gave the French pilot, who was working for us a couple of hours, instructions on flying and landing the aircraft. The first time, he took the plane up to do some practice landings. He wasn't familiar with a plane that had retractable gear. He failed to put the gear down and did a belly landing, bent both of the props beyond repair. Shelby happened to be at the camp when this happened He immediately called me to locate a couple new props and have them shipped immediately to Bangui, which I promptly did, then made arrangements to be there when they arrived. Other than the bent props, the plane was in real good shape, a few scratches on the belly but nothing of any significant. I remember we got the props on but had a terrible time getting the government official to certify that the plane was flyable. Shelby suggested perhaps he needed a little money to send his kids to college; $500 donation seemed to do the job quite well. We were certified and back in the air.

Chapter Fifty-Two

We were in our third year. Things were going very well. We were making good money, and, of course, so was the government, but they got to the point where they felt like they needed to make even more. We would negotiate for several months, and then usually we would agree to some kind of a compromise. We should've suspected something was going wrong, when Adelino Perez deposited some company funds in a Spanish bank, left Africa, and then reported his resignation. He was our general manager and, of course, knew and understood the natives much better than we did. He had always lived in Africa and could speak their language plus French, Portuguese, and Spanish—a big advantage. This put us in a real dilemma because the man second in command was the kings brother, which meant he control the purse strings. We operated like this for a couple of weeks until Shelby talked to an old friend of his, Wally Johnson, into coming in and managing the company at least on a temporary basis. Wally was an old-time elephant hunter, who I think had been in Africa all his life. Like Perez, he could speak all the languages and knew the way of the natives which, believe me, is a valuable asset in that country.

We were right in the middle of my third season. I'm in the office late one afternoon had just returned with a couple of hunters, and had put them on the airplane for home.

"Wally, said you like what you're doing, don't you?"

"Yes, I guess I do. I guess anything to do with hunting I like."

"I'm going to tell you something you're not going to like."

I poured us both a drink, some excellent Scotch one of the German hunters had left.

"What is it you have to tell me? I'm already working for nothing."

"Nothing like that. What I'm about to tell you is you need to pay attention to. This government is about to be overthrown. Things are in the works to kill or remove Bokassa, and I've heard rumors they plan to confiscate all your equipment, including your airplanes. This is going to happen within the next couple days. You will probably be arrested as an enemy of the state because of your partnership with the Bokassa. I don't think you have a moment to waste.

"Do you think I will have until tomorrow?" I ask.

"I would plan to be out of here before tomorrow night—at the latest."

That afternoon and evening, Jeannie and I put together everything that we wanted to take with us. I had two airplanes the Seneca and my super cub that I wanted to get out of here. We spent the remainder of that afternoon and evening loading stuff such as radio gear out of one of the wrecked airplanes, anything we thought of value. Our guns and what other personal possessions weren't easily replaced. After we had loaded everything, we felt we could get in the airplane. I had to find the ambassador and get a permit to fly to Douala. It took me about an hour, but I finally tracked him down at 10:00 p.m. in one of the local nightclubs. I talked to the ambassador and told him I needed a letter allowing one of the French pilots to fly the twin out of the country. I confided in him what I had heard. He did not confirm or deny. I took that as a confirmation that the information I had was probably correct. He had me follow him back to the embassy where he wrote out the necessary permits and wished us good luck.

Next morning, we were at the airport bright an early 3: 30 a.m. Then we realized we had forgotten something back at the apartment—personal papers that we didn't feel we should leave behind, so we drove back to the apartment only about a mile and a half from the airport, picked up those couple of items, and returned to the airport. I remembered seeing a security guard in that area; both times, we left the apartment. Something we did must've made him suspicious—probably the fact that we were going to the airport at that time of the morning. The twin took off first, and we were right behind him. As we cleared the end of the runway and banked to the right heading due west, we could see two pick up loads of military personnel coming onto the far end of the runway, waving their arms and flashing the headlights on the pickups. We were only airborne about five minutes when the control tower informed us that we must return to the airport. The French pilot idled back to let me catch up. When we got alongside, I pointed due west. He nodded okay, and we never saw him again until we got to Duala on the west coast of Cameroon, about a 600 mile flight. The twin made it a little under four hours, and it took Jeannie and I all of six hours to fly it in the super cub.

When we landed at Duala, we were met by a truck load of security guards just as we pulled off the runway. They wouldn't even let us taxi over to the tie-down area; we, of course, had not filed a flight plan when we left Bangui. We really didn't want those folks to know where we were going. After they checked our passports and confirmed the fact that we had the letter from the embassy, we were released to go to our hotel. We were in the bar having a drink with the French pilot when one of the attendants from the hotel delivered a telegram to me.

It was from Wally. "You escaped just in time. Bokassa left about two hours later. We now have new personnel in the president's mansion." Anybody's guess what will happen next?

Chapter Fifty-Three

The next day, Jeannie and I checked out Duala, a beautiful city at least 500 to 600 years old with a lot of European influence primarily French. Everything seemed very normal no one came to talk to us, but the TVs and the radios were talking about the overthrow of the Bokassa government and that he was "seeking asylum" in one of the little countries on the gold coast.

I had been negotiating with the Benin government to do a game survey in their country. It's a small narrow country just on the west side of Nigeria. They were willing to pay me $250 an hour for my super cub and myself. I was to fly with one of their wildlife management people, a crisscross grid system from one end of the country to the other, and he was to count all the different species of animals that we saw, so I decided the next day we would head for Benin.

The next morning, Jeannie and I were out at the airport about 8:00 a.m. We got the super cub all loaded up with everything I felt we would need, contacted the people in Benin, and told them we were on our way. We taxied out to the end of the runway, filed our flight plan with the tower, and waited for the clearance to take off, when the tower informed us that we were to return to the tie-down area immediately. I told Jeannie, "This doesn't sound good." We taxied back to the tie-down area and were met with about four official looking vehicles full of security police, all carrying rifles or side arm. we got out of the airplane. They wouldn't even let me get the plane entirely off the runway until a big jet landed and almost blew the plane over. They then let me move the planes to the tie-down area.

I have, of course, ask what seemed to be the problem. They said the new government in Bangui had called the Douala airport and said that we had stolen two of their planes. I tried to explain but then realized talking to these people was a futile waste of time. We were transported back to the headquarters; I was ushered into a room. Jeannie was left setting out in the reception area.

For the next eight hours, I was questioned repeatedly about the airplanes. I explained the twin-engine airplane belonged to Shelby and I, and we were a part of the company, and the super cub was my personal plane. After eight hours, I told them I wanted to check with my wife and see if she wanted to go back to the hotel. They agreed to give me about five minutes. I told Jeannie to go to the American Embassy and tell them what was going on, and we needed help. It is now about 10 o'clock at night they have not offered us anything to eat, however they have eaten at least three times. The ambassador arrived within an hour. He convinced the officials that if we turned in our passports and agreed to stay in town until they could get it sorted out, they should just put us under house arrest and let us go back to the hotel—and that's what they did. For the next ten days, we sat around the hotel swimming pool and told hunting stories to the guest and drank a little cognac. We met some very interesting people, not necessarily people you would want to get to know too well but very interesting. Several, I'm almost sure were smugglers, when they realized I was a pilot and had my own plane. They wanted to know how well I knew the bush. I have no way of knowing, but I suspect they were taking diamonds out of the area. They wanted me to fly. We never heard a word from anybody not the embassy not the officials—nobody for ten days. Finally, the tenth day, someone from the embassy came to our room handed us our passports and gave us a couple other official looking documents that said we were cleared of all charges and that we were free to leave. By this time, I had lost my contract in Benin, and it was getting close to fishing season back in Alaska. So I decided to store the planes in a hangar and go home for the summer fishing season.

During that summer, Ron Hayes and I got together several times and talked about setting up a hunting operation in Southwest Africa now known as Namibia. The South African government was very stable. Ron had talked to the government about leasing property etc. On the surface, everything seemed quite favorable virtually no money upfront, but you just had to pay a fee for every animal you took. With the airplanes, we could cover a vast amount of area and offer our hunters a much more attractive package than they were now getting anywhere in South Africa.

Chapter Fifty-Four

After fishing season, I guess probably the middle to end of August. I was ready to head back to the Douala. My dilemma was I had two airplanes there. Donnie McGinski, one of the young guys that fished with me, was a pilot and, in fact, owned a super cub. He had heard me talk about our experiences in Africa and what I was thinking about doing with Ron Hayes. He asked if he could go over with me and help me move the airplanes down to South Africa. I, of course, was delighted and volunteered to pay all his expenses to get there and back.

It was about the first of September when we arrived in Douala; it was the rainy season, and it rained a lot, especially every afternoon. That's the area where most of our hurricane originate. They come out of equatorial Africa hit the warm waters of the South Atlantic; if all conditions are favorable, the US gets a hurricane.

We had a long flight to South Africa. First, we would fly to Pointe Norie, which is on the Atlantic coast in the African country of Congo just north of where the Congo River empties into the Atlantic Ocean. Douala is an old, old city. Many a vessel, carrying slaves, left the ports several hundred years ago on their way to the southern United States. We stayed in Pointe Norie for two days while we rigged the airplanes with extra fuel tanks. The next leg of our flight was 1,400 miles to Windhoek, Namibia, with nowhere to stop, approximately a ten-hour flight for the twin Seneca and fourteen to fifteen hours for the super cub.

We were finally ready to go. We went to the airport to file our flight plan. I knew there were problems with Angola but wasn't sure what kind of restrictions there were. We were told there was no way we could get permission to fry across Angola.

We would either have to fly across Zaire and Zambia to Botswana and then to Windhoek, which added almost another thousand mile.

Or fly out over the ocean and that wasn't even recommended for small aircraft. Donnie and I talked it over and decided we would go down the coast, stay low enough to stay out of their radar, and we should be okay, so that was our plan.

We left at first daylight so Donnie could get to Windhoek while there was still daylight. First hour of the flight, we had scattered clouds; then as we flew further south, cloudy skies turned to clear that you could see for miles,

I hate flying over the ocean. It's so monotonous and hard to maintain your concentration. The blue water and the blue sky all kind of blend together. About four or five hours into the flight, I slowly started drifting closer to the shoreline. Eventually, I was flying right over the beach just 500 above the ground occasionally a small village but mostly just a lot of sand. About six hours into the flight, I knew I was getting close to the southern border of Angola's. I was trying to find something interesting to help me stay awake and give me some indication of just exactly where I was.

When all at once dead ahead, the harbor full of ships, a large landing strip with jet fighters with a big old Russian flag fluttering gently in the breeze. I immediately banked to my right.

I dropped down to about fifty feet off the deck and pushed the throttle to the firewall as best I could tell. By the chart, I was only about fifty to sixty miles not over one hundred from the Namibia border.

After about a half an hour, when I felt comfortable that I had crossed the border, I eased back on the throttle and gained a little altitude. Nothing happened. I never saw another airplane and flew on into Windhoek. I had to have a conversation with the officials at the airport since I had not filed a flight plan to Windhoek after a half hour explanation. The payment of a $60 landing fee I was good to go. The terminal wasn't much just a tin building that was every bit as hot as a Swedish sauna, but it did have a couple coffee pots with black coffee brewed adequately to keep you awake and alert. Now the worrying started.

Like me, Donnie had no idea that Russian base was on the coast any more than I did. And if he did as I did and flew down the beach, probably no more than a couple hundred feet off the ground, he would come on to that base and not even know it was there until he was almost on top of it. Where my twin was fast enough to put some distance between me and the Russians very quickly, especially at full throttle. Donnie was screwed. He couldn't go very far very fast.

There were a couple of outfitters waiting at the airport to pick up their hunters; I got talking to them asking about conditions on the Angola border. They said they both had bullet holes in their airplanes from getting too close to the border. When I told him that I had just flown down the coast and that a friend of mine was bringing a super cub the same route, they both looked at each other and shook their heads. One of the guys said, "I'm surprised you made it, and I'll be amazed if your friend makes it." Those people up there just shoot first and ask questions later. Their hunters arrived. They wished me luck and left me alone to worry.

Ten hours later, it's just me and a couple of security guards at the terminal. It's quite obvious that Donnie had a problem. Even though he had plenty of fuel to make it to Windhoek after twenty hours, he would have been definitely out of fuel. I got what sleep I could on one of the benches in the terminal, waiting for daylight. Shortly after sunrise, activity at the little airport started to increase. Someone made a new pot of coffee, and there was a native lady that was selling some sandwiches and apples. I hadn't had anything to eat since the previous morning other than a peanut butter sandwich on the flight down. I walked out on the tarmac in hopes that somehow Donnie would've landed during the night, while I was sleeping; of course, there was nothing—no Donnie and no super cub. I found the fuel truck got them to fill the twin including the extra tank I had on board. It was a good 500 miles to the Angola border, lots of area were Donnie may have run out of fuel or had engine problems or any amount of other problems and had to do a forced landing. I hoped and prayed that I would fly out into the desert and spot the cub on a sand dune with Donnie setting under the wing in the shade. But deep in my heart, I was quite sure what had happened. I just refused to accept it.

Chapter Fifty-Five

I notified the embassy and the officials of my intentions and reported the missing airplane. As soon as I had permission, I was walking out to the airplane ready to start my search, and a guy came running up behind me with the camera hanging from his neck and a small briefcase. He introduced himself as a reporter from the local newspaper and ask if he could go with me in my search for the missing pilot an airplane. I, of course, said yes. Four eyes are better than two. Later that afternoon, as I got close to the Angola border, the Reporter kept asking me where we were. When I pointed out what I thought to be the border, he got very nervous and kept urging me to stay a little further away.

It became quite obvious that the Seneca with its low wings was not a good search and rescue aircraft. We did not get back to the airport until almost dark that evening. The next morning, I located a Cessna 210 that I could rent quite reasonably. It was much better, when we were getting it out of the hangar. There were a couple other small aircraft that belong to the government that they evidently use occasionally to patrol the borders. Every one of them had bullet holes in them; now, I could understand why the reporter was a little nervous.

The next month, this was the routine. I mapped out a grid flew it back and forth east and west, north and south, all the way to the Angola border not a trace. Our embassy made inquiries with the Angola government. They said they had never seen an airplane or knew anything about a downed pilot etc. but never failed to mention that there was absolutely no flights allowed over their country and any planes caught within their airspace would be shot down.

I can't imagine the number of times I have thought about that decision to fly south along the Angola border. Instead of taking the long way around through Zaire across Zambia and Botswana, all hostile country, but after the fact and now it seems like an easy decision.

I finally had to give up searching and accept the fact that something happened to Donnie; either out in the ocean or perhaps shot down over Angola—questions I guess that will never be answered for sure. Several years later, we even tried to get into Angola to inquire but to no avail. After I had completed my searching, I lost all my desire to try and set up another hunting operation with Ron Hayes in Southwest Africa. I sold the Seneca to a charter operation in South Africa operating out of Johannesburg, and I went back to Alaska. This country seemed pretty tame compared to my experience in Africa.

After returning to Alaska, I got word that Donnie had been shot down by small arms fire when he flew over that base in southern Angola. We applied for permits through the US Embassy to visit that area Angola to see if there was any personal effects or if perhaps his body could be returned to the US, but Angola refused to cooperate even on the most minor request.

Unlikely as it may seem, during Denny's adventures in Africa, he bought a 3,500 -acre cattle ranch in Pendleton, Oregon. They stocked it with 600 head of cattle and operated it for a little over three years, during that time cattle and land prices went up, and Denny had found a niche flying people to and from hunting camps for unguided hunts. This created a real conflict between trying to run the ranch and taking care of his hunting operation. The decision on which way to go "hunt, or raise cows" came quite easy, and Denny sold the ranch.

Salmon Brailer, holds approximately 1,000 pounds of fish

Salmon caught by set-nets from the shore in Bristol Bay, Alaska

AFTER AFRICA

Bryan and Devin at Fish camp, Libbyville on Bristol bay Alaska

Their boss Jeanne Thompson she ran the set-net operation

Chapter Fifty-Six

After returning from Africa, Denny decided Alaska would be adequate to satisfy his thirst for adventure. He sold the new Halen Lodge to Bill Simms. Bill used it primarily to accommodate the growing sports fishing industry, flying sports fishermen to the hundreds of small lakes in the mountains, for trout and grayling, walleye and salmon. Then in late summer during the silver salmon run, there was some great river fishing.

Denny and Marge divorced in 1982; shortly after that, he and Jeannie were married. That marriage lasted until 2007, when Jeannie's life was cut short by cancer.

Denny had picked up two fishing permits in Bristol Bay—the red salmon capital of the world. One permit was out by the cannery, Petterson Point, not far from the headwaters of the Kvichak River. They would anchor the net on the beach and then extended out into the bay 1,000 feet.

The salmon come into Bristol Bay from the Bering Sea. Once they enter the bay, they started and ever expanding spiral, swimming in circles, moving closer and closer to the shoreline looking for their river of origin.

Bristol Bay is a couple hundred miles wide in areas with eight or ten rivers that empty into the bay, where hundreds of millions of young salmon start their journey to the sea. Two to five years later, they return and swim around the bay until they find the river of their origin.

During that process, they become quite vulnerable; there are nets strung up along the beach and then there are thousands of fishing boats that also have nets for entrapping the unsuspecting salmon. But worry not. The Fish and Game Dept. has a system where, periodically, they close the season for a day or two to allow millions of fish to reach their destination. They have fish counters in all the rivers and streams and a quota of how many fish it takes to sustain a healthy salmon population. This has been in play for many years now and seems to be working very well. Some years, there are more fish than others but no matter. The first priority is that all the rivers get their quota of fish.

Denny's other permit was for fishing with the net from the boat. As a rule, Denny's operation caught more fish than they did from the beach but not always. It was a great day when Jeannie's crew on the beach would catch more fish than Denny's. Fishing season usually started around the middle of June, unless Denny decided to get in on the "herring fishing," which was earlier and could only be done from the boat, and usually, he would fish for herring along the north beaches of Bristol Bay. The herring would come in by the billions and lay their eggs on the beach. This would usually only last for ten to twenty days. But during that time, if you were lucky, you could catch $30,000-$50,000 worth of herring, but that meant you had to have your boat in the water at least a month earlier than if you were just fishing for salmon. The sockeye salmon (red) season would last till about the first of August, but in the early '80s, Denny would continue to fish for several other species of salmon. They would not bring the same price as the sockeye, but it was usually worth the effort. He would continue to fish until his hunters started to arrive, which was usually the first week of September. Then things would get very intense for the next couple of months—basically flying from daylight to dark. I remember personally we were coming back from a bear hunt one evening, and we had to land at Naknek in the dark. The runway lights were not working. Thank God, the run way was not asphalt (black). It was white gray limestone, and Denny could see just enough to get us on the ground that was about 10:30 at night.

Denny had a big map hanging on the wall as he came into the house. Every time he took a hunter to a certain area, he would put a pin on the map indicating exactly where that hunter was. This was done for a couple of good reasons; sometimes, he would have fifteen or twenty hunters in eight or ten different camps, sometimes more. He not only had to take the hunters to and from the camps. But each day, he would usually take them fresh water, and he would have to bring whatever game they shot back to Naknek where, in most cases, it was packaged by the local butcher and flash frozen, then packed in insulated boxes ready to be shipped with the hunter back to his home.

Back in those days, you just checked it like your luggage on the plane—no extra charge. I remember coming home several times with four or five, seventy to eighty pound boxes of meat. Keep me in moose meat for the next couple years until my next trip.

In 1982, Fred Bear the famous bow hunter and manufacturer of archery equipment; ask Denny if he could take him and six of his managers hunting. Fred said he wouldn't fly with anyone else. Denny ask the department of fish and game for permission, which they readily granted. Denny set up the camps for the six managers; then he and Fred just flew around the country looking at some beautiful sights including moose, bear, sheep, and caribou.

Fred told Denny that it was one of the most enjoyable times he could remember.

Chapter Fifty-Seven

About 1983 or 1984, Denny bought a house in Sacramento, California where, for the next several years, they would spend the winter, leave Naknek the latter part of October or early November, and not return to Alaska until April or May.

Then in 1986, Denny bought a forty-acre piece of property in the Mother Lode gold country of central California just up the mountain from Sonora and Columbia—two old historic gold-mining towns. In fact, there's at least one and maybe two mine shafts on Denny's property,

I've been waiting for an invitation to the reopening of the mine; since at '93, I believe that's about the only thing I can think of—he hasn't done is mine gold.

I know he used to haul a lot of supplies into different mining operations north and east of his lodge at Susitna, but I don't believe I ever heard him talk about actually mining gold. I do remember him telling me a story about a miner who was running out of food up in the mountains one time, but the snow was too deep for guys to land with wheels, and the ski planes would sink down into the snow and never be able to get airborne again. So Denny decided to try using his pontoons that he sometime used on the glaciers, hoping they would stay on the top of the snow. The area was on a hillside; he had lots of room. He landed up the hill, but while he still had plenty of speed and momentum, he turned the plane, so it was headed downhill. The load he was carrying was quite heavy, everything from gasoline, food, and other miscellaneous equipment that the miner had ordered, at least 800 pounds. Once that was unloaded, the plane was much lighter and glided across the top of the snow with ease and was airborne in a matter of seconds—another mercy mission accomplished.

After Denny moved up in the mountains in California, the first thing he did was build a new house on his forty acres. He built two lakes on the property, a house, barn, and an apartment for his friends when they come to stay with him for a few days. All of these when he was still hunting and fishing in Alaska. When I say he built the house, that's what I mean. Denny didn't hire someone else to build the house for him. He built the apartment first; then over the next couple years, he completed the main house. He did hire a few young people from the neighborhood when he needed help setting rafters or beams, but the majority of it he did by himself.

About the mid-90s Denny quit going to Alaska for the herring season. This allowed him to stay in California for an additional month. Denny continued to take hunting parties until 2005 but kept fishing until 2013. At ninety years old and after sixty-five years of fishing, he decided he would hang up his fishnets one last time.

In 2008, Denny sold his airplane and decided flying just wasn't as much fun as it used to be. He was still qualified and capable but just felt it was time to quit.

To say Denny had an interesting life would probably be the understatement of the century. Mr. Thompson has more lives than the proverbial cat.

From the thirty missions over France and Germany, he returned to England with more holes in the airplane than they could count.

The red hot piece of shrapnel that tore up the back of Denny's jacket hit the ceiling then dropped back at his feet, still too hot to pick up.

Or the eighty-eight shell that went right up behind Denny's seat and out through the top of the plane and never exploded.

Planes on either side, blowing up after being hit with German flak, being wounded twice, limping home on two engines, only clearing the cliffs on the English coast by 300 to 400 feet, but yet making it to the runway and landing with two flat tires because they'd been shot full of holes during the bombing run.

Most of the thirty missions could be considered life-and-death experiences.

He crashed his plane and was stranded overnight in the Arctic Circle in sixty-below-zero weather for twenty-two hours, waiting for daylight and his friend Cappy to come and rescue him. Most people would have perished and many have, but not Lieutenant Thompson.

Getting caught in a crosswind on a little lake in the Kenai Mountains and flipping the airplane on its side.

A polar bear stood over Denny with one foot on his camera and the other one on his gun barrel and yet not a scratch. I would bet he wasn't even scared. His mind was racing thinking about what he should do to correct this situation.

Then there were several times when the polar bear charged Denny and the hunter, as they were firing at will, when the bear finally drops. Denny can touch the bear's nose with the barrel of his empty gun. He's that close. Another time, when the bear finally expired, his nose was laying on Denny's boot.

The ten or twelve seagulls that hit Denny's plane when he was spotting salmon in the Shelikof Straits, and then the nights he spent in the airplane on the beach, with bear all around the airplane.

The time he got caught in the terrible storm in the Shelikof Straits eighty or more mile an hour winds.

Or the flash flood that could have carried the plane and him out to sea and certain death.

Or the times he got caught in the fog and had to land and set in the airplane overnight while he waited for the weather to clear. Or perhaps the times polar bear hunting when the ice fog got so bad; he couldn't even see to taxi along the beach in forty-below-zero weather.

Or the time in the fog when he follows the trail of dog turds along the beach finally stopping the plane on the roof of one of the native huts.

The time the shotgun went off in the airplane, when he was wolf hunting and blew the side of his mukluk off but never hit his foot.

Or the time he was getting out of the airplane in about two-feet of snow and a big black wolf he had shot that came to life. Denny had one foot in the snow and one foot hung up in the airplane. The wolf is charging, and Denny is falling and has to shoot from the hip. When it's all over with, Denny's laying in the snow with the dead wolf less than four feet away.

Or the time in Africa, there in the woods—there hiding behind a tree—in the middle of thirty head of charging elephants, several of them no more than six to eight feet away.

Or of course the time he was flying down the coast of Angola. If the Russians had scrambled their fighters, they could've easily caught and shot him down before he reached the Namibia border.

More than once, Denny and his sheep hunter were stranded on a glacier high in the mountains when the snow and ice got so mushy. Denny couldn't take off, and they had to stay the night in the airplane and hope the ice froze hard enough by the next morning that they could take off again.

Several times, Denny rescued mountain climbers at a much higher elevation than his super cub would normally be able to operate at. He did that by riding oxygen-rich thermals on the windward side of the mountain to elevations of 10,000 feet and above, making the rescue then taxiing off the edge of the glacier in freefall until he picked up enough airspeed to regain control of the airplane.

The hundreds of trips he made over the tundra and through the mountains no more than fifty feet above the ground just under the overcast and still able to find his way back.

Denny Thompson and author Neil Burckart 2007 at Namibia, Africa

Denny Thompson And his Kudu and Neil Burckart, Namibia South Africa

Chapter Fifty-Eight

You might argue that he was exceptionally lucky, and I don't know that I'd argue that fact, but you know that you can't fly 25,000 hours in those kind of conditions and depend on luck. I agree a little luck probably helped once in a while, but I contribute his success primarily to his exceptional ability as a pilot, but more than that, his exceptional ability to make the correct choices when he was confronted with life-threatening situations.

Denny is now ninety-four years old and still stays busy every day. If there is a veterans' celebration or event any place in central California, you can bet Denny will be one of the guest, and he will show up. If humanly possible, he still likes the hunts. About three weeks ago, he made a trip to Oregon to go deer hunting with his old attorney friend.

I don't know this to be a fact. I've never ask him but of all his achievements and glory days as one of the biggest and best guides in Alaska.

The hundreds of hunters who gained notoriety hunting with Denny by winning the Weatherby Award or getting their names in the record book and recognition by the ultimate sportsman's club in the world, The Safari Club International. By the way, Denny was one of the original founders and charter members of the Safari Club with all of these achievements.

With all my conversations over the last couple years, I can hear it in his voice, and see it in his eyes when we talk about the war. I firmly believe Denny's proudest moments occur when he dons his seventy-one-year old uniform—the same one he wore when he returned from England in 1944—and he proudly represents his country.

At this time, he is making arrangement for another trip to Normandy next June 2016 to participate in some type of "D-day celebration." This will be his sixth trip to Normandy in the last twenty-two years, doesn't include the trips he made in 1944.

I believe most of us would probably be satisfied with just a few eight or ten of those action packed years that would last us a life time, but Denny lived it for seventy years.

There are hundreds of other hunting stories, but we thought these were the most interesting. Believe me, we have only hit the high spots.

Some of these stories are worthy of more than honorable mention. The question is where do you draw the line.

Closing statement by LIEUTENANT THOMPSON!

"In closing I would just like to express my appreciation, I hope you enjoyed the stories".

"What worries me now is the way the country is going. It seems all the things we fought for and so many young men and woman died for are now, somehow, bad. A lot of young people don't know what great people there grandparents were and how hard they worked and struggled to make life better for their kids and grandchildren. There aren't many of us left who lived that life. To say the least, it's very troubling."

"Political correctness should be disposed of like a rotten fish, and anyone who wants to live in this country should love it like I do or be sent back to where they came from."

"Believe me, there is no greater place in this world than the United States of America."

Book Summary

This story is about a young man who joins the army air corps in 1942, becomes a bomber pilot, and flies thirty missions over enemy territory. He was wounded twice and received thirteen medals for his exemplary service.

After the war, he moved his young family to Alaska to find work. He worked as a stevedore in the docks. During his off hours, he started commercial fishing and hunting. He eventually became a guide. As the years passed, he became one of the very best guides in all of Alaska and guided thousands of hunters over the years in some of the most inhospitable country in the whole world—one of the charter members of the prestigious Safari Club International.

Lieutenant Thompson's story goes beyond the imagination, from being attacked by angry bears to surviving more than one bush pilot accident. More than 25,000 hours of flying in the bush, he escaped a revolution in the Republic of Central Africa, where one of his planes was shot down and one of his pilots was killed. This is his story, where he performs numerous life and death rescues including the coast guard. This book is one adventure after another. It is a must read for those who admire war heroes and the adventures between man and beast and the great outdoors.